365 TRUE STORIES OF FAITH AND COURAGE

HEROES, Dreamers, AND SAINTS

WRITTEN BY
AMY KERR

ILLUSTRATED BY
ISABEL MUÑOZ

An Imprint of Thomas Nelson
thomasnelson.com

CONTENTS

Introduction vii

Jan. 1	Wilma Rudolph	1
Jan. 2	Antonio Vivaldi	2
Jan. 3	Saint Geneviève	3
Jan. 4	Michael Faraday	4
Jan. 5	Dietrich Bonhoeffer	5
Jan. 6	Vincent van Gogh	6
Jan. 7	Rusty Staub	8
Jan. 8	Antoine Frédéric Ozanam . . .	9
Jan. 9	Betsey Stockton	10
Jan. 10	Toyohiko Kagawa	11
Jan. 11	Edith Cavell	12
Jan. 12	Jimmy Stewart	13
Jan. 13	Nicholas of Cusa	14
Jan. 14	Hans Christian Andersen . . .	15
Jan. 15	Saint Devasahayam Pillai . . .	16
Jan. 16	Saint Justin Martyr	17
Jan. 17	Mahalia Jackson	18
Jan. 18	Saint Charles of Sezze	19
Jan. 19	Elizabeth Blackwell	20
Jan. 20	Maria Fearing	21
Jan. 21	Anne Bradstreet	22
Jan. 22	John Havlicek	23
Jan. 23	Frederick Douglass	24
Jan. 24	Charles Correa	25
Jan. 25	Lucian Tapiedi	26
Jan. 26	Lena Richard	27
Jan. 27	Dr. Shi Meiyu	28
Jan. 28	Tertullian	29
Jan. 29	Flannery O'Connor	30
Jan. 30	John Newton	31
Jan. 31	Pat Summerall	32
Feb. 1	John Knox	33
Feb. 2	Aretha Franklin	34
Feb. 3	Saint Aelred of Rievaulx . . .	36
Feb. 4	Roberto Clemente	37
Feb. 5	Leonardo da Vinci	39
Feb. 6	Corazon Aquino	40
Feb. 7	J. R. R. Tolkien	41
Feb. 8	Mary Lyon	42
Feb. 9	Phillis Wheatley	43
Feb. 10	Jim Irwin	44
Feb. 11	Saint María Antonia de Paz y Figueroa	45
Feb. 12	Jack Soo	46
Feb. 13	Saint Giles Mary of Saint Joseph	47
Feb. 14	Caedmon	48
Feb. 15	Cimabue	49
Feb. 16	Rosa Parks	50
Feb. 17	Lou Brock	51
Feb. 18	Fra Angelico	52
Feb. 19	Melito of Sardis	53
Feb. 20	Pandita Ramabai	54
Feb. 21	Filippo Brunelleschi	55
Feb. 22	Elizabeth Keckley	56
Feb. 23	Augusta Savage	57
Feb. 24	Rich Mullins	58
Feb. 25	Blessed Sebastian of Aparicio	59
Feb. 26	Dr. Edward Jenner	60
Feb. 27	Don Baylor	61
Feb. 28	Saint Oswald of York	62
Feb. 29	George Williams	63
Mar. 1	Sir Isaac Newton	65
Mar. 2	Giotto	66
Mar. 3	Dr. Wangari Maathai	67
Mar. 4	Desmond Tutu	68
Mar. 5	Jackie Robinson	69
Mar. 6	John Bunyan	70
Mar. 7	Don McClanen	71
Mar. 8	George Fredric Handel	72
Mar. 9	Brother Lawrence	73
Mar. 10	C. S. Lewis	74
Mar. 11	William Tyndale	76
Mar. 12	George Herbert	77
Mar. 13	Carl Bloch	78
Mar. 14	Ira D. Sankey	79
Mar. 15	Babe Ruth	81
Mar. 16	Keith Green	82
Mar. 17	Dr. Harold Moody	83
Mar. 18	Jeanette Li	84
Mar. 19	Thomas Cole	85
Mar. 20	Alessandro Volta	86
Mar. 21	Oswald Chambers	87
Mar. 22	Mev Puleo	88

Mar. 23	Claudio Granzotto	90	**May 7**	Edmonia Lewis	137
Mar. 24	Saint Óscar Romero	91	**May 8**	Dorothy Sayers	138
Mar. 25	Jovita Idar	92	**May 9**	Mincaye Enquedi	139
Mar. 26	Harriet Powers	93	**May 10**	Wang Zhiming	140
Mar. 27	Roger Maris	94	**May 11**	Saint Cyril and Saint Methodius	141
Mar. 28	Blaise Pascal	95	**May 12**	Roger Bannister	142
Mar. 29	Diego Velázquez	96	**May 13**	Leonhard Euler	143
Mar. 30	Saint Peter Regalado	97	**May 14**	Antonín Dvořák	144
Mar. 31	Christina Rosetti	98	**May 15**	Albrecht Dürer	145
Apr. 1	Catherine Marshall	99	**May 16**	Saint John of Nepomuk	146
Apr. 2	Pelé	100	**May 17**	Thomas Merton	147
Apr. 3	René Descartes	101	**May 18**	Payne Stewart	148
Apr. 4	Hannah More	102	**May 19**	Saint Celestine V	149
Apr. 5	Donatello	103	**May 20**	Arthur Holly Compton	150
Apr. 6	Chiune Sugihara	104	**May 21**	Danny Thomas	151
Apr. 7	William Wordsworth	105	**May 22**	Walter Wangerin Jr.	152
Apr. 8	Wolfgang Amadeus Mozart	106	**May 23**	Ralph Houk	153
Apr. 9	Octavia Hill	107	**May 24**	Ludwig von Beethoven	154
Apr. 10	Fred Rogers	108	**May 25**	Saint Bede the Venerable	156
Apr. 11	Antoine Lavoisier	109	**May 26**	Charles Hard Townes	157
Apr. 12	Hank Stram	110	**May 27**	Anthony Trollope	158
Apr. 13	Lewis Carroll	111	**May 28**	John Wycliffe	159
Apr. 14	Blessed Peter Gonzalez	112	**May 29**	Jimmy Carter	161
Apr. 15	Saint César de Bus	113	**May 30**	Bart Starr	162
Apr. 16	Floyd Patterson	114	**May 31**	Mary Jackson	163
Apr. 17	Bernhard Riemann	115	**June 1**	Andrei Tarkovsky	164
Apr. 18	Blessed James Oldo	116	**June 2**	Eusebius of Caesarea	165
Apr. 19	Billy Sunday	117	**June 3**	Bessie Coleman	166
Apr. 20	Michelangelo	119	**June 4**	Mary Kay Ash	168
Apr. 21	William Wilberforce	120	**June 5**	Claudio Monteverdi	169
Apr. 22	Gustavo Gutiérrez	121	**June 6**	Ida Lewis	170
Apr. 23	Brownie Wise	122	**June 7**	Mickey Mantle	171
Apr. 24	Tony Gwynn	123	**June 8**	Johannes Vermeer	172
Apr. 25	Franz Joseph Haydn	124	**June 9**	Walker Percy	173
Apr. 26	Aristides	125	**June 10**	Blessed María del Tránsito de Jesús Sacramentado	174
Apr. 27	Anthony van Dyck	126	**June 11**	Irena Sendler	175
Apr. 28	John Donne	127	**June 12**	Blessed Jolenta of Poland	176
Apr. 29	Gregor Mendel	128	**June 13**	Josephine Butler	177
Apr. 30	Constantine I	129	**June 14**	Saint Albert Chmielowski	178
May 1	Martin Luther King Jr.	131	**June 15**	John Milton	179
May 2	Frances Ridley Havergal	132	**June 16**	Althea Gibson	181
May 3	Dr. Mary McLeod Bethune	133	**June 17**	Masaccio	182
May 4	Johnny Unitas	134	**June 18**	Sigrid Undset	183
May 5	Saint Hilary	135			
May 6	Robert Boyle	136			

Date	Name	Page
June 19	Søren Kierkegaard	184
June 20	Martin Niemöller	185
June 21	Johann Sebastian Bach	186
June 22	Eddie Robinson	187
June 23	Francisco de Zurbarán	188
June 24	Blessed Jutta of Thuringia	189
June 25	George Washington Carver	190
June 26	Bob Hope	192
June 27	John Wooden	193
June 28	Saint Irenaeus	194
June 29	Jesse Bushyhead	195
June 30	Ginger Smock	196
July 1	David Wilkerson	197
July 2	Vince Lombardi	198
July 3	John Lewis	199
July 4	Galileo Galilei	201
July 5	J. B. Phillips	202
July 6	Theophilus of Antioch	203
July 7	Gordie Howe	204
July 8	Hélder Pessoa Câmara	205
July 9	Mary Anning	206
July 10	André Trocmé	207
July 11	Tom Landry	208
July 12	Fanny Crosby	209
July 13	Saint Teresa of the Andes	210
July 14	Louis Zamperini	211
July 15	Katherine Johnson	212
July 16	Georges Rouault	213
July 17	Jesse Owens	214
July 18	J. J. Thomson	215
July 19	Lucy Maud Montgomery	216
July 20	Maggie Lena Walker	217
July 21	Johann Pachelbel	218
July 22	John Napier	219
July 23	Walter Payton	220
July 24	Saint Sharbel Makhlouf	221
July 25	Endō Shūsaku	223
July 26	Tiyo Soga	224
July 27	Saint Titus Brandsma	225
July 28	Mary Prince	226
July 29	Allan Rohan Crite	227
July 30	Saint Peter Chrysologus	228
July 31	Henryk Górecki	229
Aug. 1	Martyn Lloyd-Jones	230
Aug. 2	Olivier Messiaen	231
Aug. 3	Saint Theophilus of Corte	232
Aug. 4	Saint John Vianney	233
Aug. 5	Phil Rizzuto	234
Aug. 6	Hank Aaron	235
Aug. 7	Raphael	236
Aug. 8	Jane Austen	237
Aug. 9	Christy Mathewson	238
Aug. 10	Walter Rauschenbusch	239
Aug. 11	Duke Ellington	240
Aug. 12	George Müller	241
Aug. 13	Saint Dulce of the Poor	243
Aug. 14	Saint Maximilian Kolbe	244
Aug. 15	Yogi Berra	245
Aug. 16	Tycho Brahe	246
Aug. 17	François Mauriac	247
Aug. 18	Saint Helena	248
Aug. 19	Richard Allen	249
Aug. 20	Jesse Boot	250
Aug. 21	Janani Luwum	251
Aug. 22	Frederick Buechner	252
Aug. 23	Henry Purcell	253
Aug. 24	Alvin York	254
Aug. 25	Saint Louis IX of France	255
Aug. 26	Branch Rickey	256
Aug. 27	Henry ʻŌpūkahaʻia	257
Aug. 28	George Gabriel Stokes	258
Aug. 29	Sandro Botticelli	259
Aug. 30	Dorothy Day	260
Aug. 31	Athenagoras	261
Sept. 1	Paul Farmer	262
Sept. 2	Bobby Bowden	263
Sept. 3	John J. Egan	264
Sept. 4	Mother Theresa Maxis Duchemin	265
Sept. 5	Mother Teresa	266
Sept. 6	Wang Ming-Dao	267
Sept. 7	Madam C. J. Walker	268
Sept. 8	Anthony Ashley Cooper, Lord Shaftesbury	269
Sept. 9	Amanda Smith	270
Sept. 10	Madeleine L'Engle	271
Sept. 11	Johannes Kepler	272
Sept. 12	Franz Schubert	273
Sept. 13	Stan Musial	274
Sept. 14	Peter Paul Rubens	275

Sept. 15	Isaac Watts	276	**Oct. 29**	Percy Julian ...324
Sept. 16	Saint Ludmila	277	**Oct. 30**	Rembrandt ...325
Sept. 17	Pope Francis	278	**Oct. 31**	Jim Parker ...326
Sept. 18	William Gladstone	279	**Nov. 1**	Ruby Hirose ...327
Sept. 19	Dr. Louise "Lulu" Fleming	280	**Nov. 2**	Joseph Henry ...328
Sept. 20	Ernest Thomas Sinton Walton	281	**Nov. 3**	Henry Ossawa Tanner ...329
Sept. 21	Connie Mack	282	**Nov. 4**	Dante Alighieri ...330
Sept. 22	Georg Philipp Telemann	283	**Nov. 5**	Franz Jägerstätter ...331
Sept. 23	Phoebe Palmer Knapp	284	**Nov. 6**	Gene Upshaw ...332
Sept. 24	Frederic Edwin Church	285	**Nov. 7**	Sojourner Truth ...333
Sept. 25	Lucy Goode Brooks	286	**Nov. 8**	Angela Burdett-Coutts ...334
Sept. 26	Horace Pippin	287	**Nov. 9**	Sam Mills ...335
Sept. 27	Antoni Gaudí	288	**Nov. 10**	Sister Gertrude Morgan ...337
Sept. 28	Gil Hodges	290	**Nov. 11**	Sir George Gilbert Scott ...338
Sept. 29	Brooks Robinson	291	**Nov. 12**	Saint Didacus ...339
Sept. 30	Sor Juana Inés de la Cruz	293	**Nov. 13**	Thomas Andrew Dorsey ...340
Oct. 1	Jasper Francis Cropsey	294	**Nov. 14**	Petrarch ...341
Oct. 2	Felix Mendelssohn	295	**Nov. 15**	Jim Otto ...342
Oct. 3	Ernie Davis	296	**Nov. 16**	G. K. Chesterton ...343
Oct. 4	Carl Friedrich Gauss	297	**Nov. 17**	Bill Glass ...344
Oct. 5	T. S. Eliot	298	**Nov. 18**	James Clerk Maxwell ...345
Oct. 6	Esther John	299	**Nov. 19**	Tomás Luis de Victoria ...346
Oct. 7	James VanDerZee	300	**Nov. 20**	Dan Reeves ...347
Oct. 8	Alopen	302	**Nov. 21**	Harriet Tubman ...348
Oct. 9	Papias of Hierapolis	303	**Nov. 22**	Magda Trocmé ...349
Oct. 10	Nelson Mandela	305	**Nov. 23**	J. Willard Gibbs ...350
Oct. 11	Saint Gummarus	306	**Nov. 24**	Harper Lee ...351
Oct. 12	César Franck	307	**Nov. 25**	William Edmonson ...352
Oct. 13	Wayman Tisdale	308	**Nov. 26**	Baron William Thomson Kelvin ...353
Oct. 14	Sir William Rowan Hamilton	309	**Nov. 27**	Carter G. Woodson ...354
Oct. 15	John Constable	310	**Nov. 28**	Maria Gaetana Agnesi ...355
Oct. 16	Georges Bernanos	311	**Nov. 29**	Nicolaus Copernicus ...356
Oct. 17	Betty Greene	312	**Nov. 30**	John Blow ...357
Oct. 18	Christopher Wren	313	**Dec. 1**	Saint Charles de Foucauld ...358
Oct. 19	Gale Sayers	314	**Dec. 2**	Blessed Rafal Chylinski ...359
Oct. 20	Marian Anderson	315	**Dec. 3**	Evangeline Cory Booth ...360
Oct. 21	Georges-Eugène Haussmann	316	**Dec. 4**	DeFord Bailey ...361
Oct. 22	El Greco	317	**Dec. 5**	Laura Ingalls Wilder ...362
Oct. 23	Jan Hus	318	**Dec. 6**	Blessed Adolph Kolping ...363
Oct. 24	Lew Wallace	319	**Dec. 7**	George Halas ...364
Oct. 25	Lee Roy Selmon	320	**Dec. 8**	John Michell ...365
Oct. 26	Corrie ten Boom	321	**Dec. 9**	Alexander Pope ...366
Oct. 27	Christine de Pisan	322	**Dec. 10**	Gary Carter ...367
Oct. 28	Ella Fitzgerald	323	**Dec. 11**	George MacDonald ...368

Dec. 12	Frances Perkins 369		**Dec. 23**	John Harper 381
Dec. 13	Grand Duchess Elizabeth. . .370		**Dec. 24**	Romare Bearden. 382
Dec. 14	Jan Karski. 371		**Dec. 25**	Ida B. Wells. 383
Dec. 15	Blessed Mary Frances Schervier 372		**Dec. 26**	Gerard Manley Hopkins . . 384
			Dec. 27	Saint Fabiola 385
Dec. 16	George Whitefield 373		**Dec. 28**	Chico Mendes 386
Dec. 17	Ann Lowe. 374		**Dec. 29**	Sophie G. Lutterlough . . .387
Dec. 18	Don Shula 376		**Dec. 30**	Florence Nightingale 388
Dec. 19	Blessed Urban V. 377		**Dec. 31**	Sadao Watanabe. 390
Dec. 20	Benjamin Banneker 378			
Dec. 21	Jenny Lind 379		*A Note on Sources* 391
Dec. 22	Blessed Jacopone da Todi. . 380			

INTRODUCTION

Heroes, dreamers, and saints are all around us! From literary figures to artists to athletes to scientists to saints and more, this devotional explores the many people who have helped shape Christianity, have showed their devotion to God in helping others, and have made a difference in the world.

This interesting and fact-filled 365-day journey through history highlights notable Christian and Catholic figures who have made a difference in the world such as Martin Luther King Jr., Wilma Rudolph, Florence Nightingale, Saint Dulce of the Poor, Fred Rogers, and so many more!

Each entry explores a new person and includes a scripture, a devotional reading, a fun fact, and a prayer to help you apply what you've learned as you go out into the world.

Each person in this book will inspire you to love Jesus more and to share His love with others. As you read these stories, remember that everyone—including you!—can be a hero for Jesus and change the world for the glory of God.

JANUARY 1

WILMA RUDOLPH

1940–1994 • UNITED STATES

A BIGGER PURPOSE

Let us run with perseverance the race that is set before us,
looking to Jesus, the pioneer and perfecter of our faith.

HEBREWS 12:1–2

When Wilma was four years old, she got a disease called polio. Doctors said she'd never walk again without a leg brace. Her family prayed that God would allow her to walk again. When Wilma was nine, she removed the brace and took her first unaided step. At age eleven, Wilma could walk easily. She joined the school track team and began winning races. At sixteen, she won a bronze medal in track at the Olympics. Four years later, she broke world records and won the Olympic gold! The entire time, she asked God: *What is my purpose? Surely it isn't just to win gold medals.* After retiring, Wilma went overseas to help others. She visited Japan with the preacher Billy Graham to tell people about Jesus. She coached high school track and mentored college and Olympic athletes. Wilma inspired others to reach for a bigger purpose.

> WHEN BASEBALL LEGEND JACKIE ROBINSON SAW WILMA RUN, HE SAID, "ONE DAY YOU'RE GOING TO BE THE WORLD'S FASTEST WOMAN." AND HE WAS RIGHT!

*God, help me to remember the bigger
purpose You have for me.*

JANUARY 2

ANTONIO VIVALDI

1678–1741 • ITALY

A GOOD STOP

Let us not grow weary in doing what is right.

GALATIANS 6:9

A priest as well as a talented composer and violin player, Antonio became a violin master at the Ospedale della Pietà, a home for orphan children in Venice. Antonio taught the girls at the Pietà to participate in the orchestra and choir. It wasn't long before a tourist's visit to Vienna included a must-see concert featuring the girls! Antonio's talent for bringing a group together and coaching them became evident. As more people found out about the Pietà, more people donated to the home, and the children there were provided for. Antonio eventually departed the school for other opportunities, composing more than 600 works in his lifetime. But his stop on the way to musical greatness brought goodness to many children.

ANTONIO'S MOST FAMOUS PIECE IS *THE FOUR SEASONS* WITH FOUR MOVEMENTS—SPRING, SUMMER, AUTUMN, AND WINTER—THAT SOUND JUST LIKE THOSE SEASONS!

God, help me to do good on this big adventure called life!

JANUARY 3

SAINT GENEVIÈVE

C. 422–C. 500 • FRANCE

BLESSING OTHERS

Pray without ceasing.

1 THESSALONIANS 5:17

From the time she was seven years old, Geneviève dedicated her life to God. She faithfully shared her faith with others. At age fifteen, she became a nun. She looked after other young women who had devoted themselves to God. When Paris experienced a famine, Geneviève traveled to another town by boat to bring back corn for the hungry. King Clovis listened to Geneviève and freed certain prisoners at her request. When another army threatened Paris, Geneviève counseled the city to pray for God's protection instead of running. The army suddenly turned away from Paris. Because of Geneviève's great faith in God, many people began to believe in Him too.

> IN PICTURES, SAINT GENEVIÈVE IS OFTEN SEEN CARRYING A LOAF OF BREAD TO REPRESENT HER GENEROSITY.

God, I want my faith to cause others to know You as well.

JANUARY 4

MICHAEL FARADAY

1791–1867 • UNITED STATES

SHOW YOUR SPARK!

"Be strong and bold . . . it is the LORD your God who goes with you."

DEUTERONOMY 31:6

Michael's dad was a blacksmith and was often hurt on the job, so Michael left school at fourteen to work for a bookbinder. One day, Michael started reading a book he was binding about electricity. He was fascinated! He tried experiments using methods in the book. One day, Michael got to hear a scientist talk at a school in London. He listened and took lots of notes. Michael sent a letter to the scientist, hoping he could work as a lab assistant. The scientist didn't have any jobs, but he didn't forget Michael. When one of his lab assistants was dismissed, he invited Michael to work for him! Michael became a pioneer in studying electromagnetism. Almost every electronic appliance we use today, from cars to phones, relies on the principles Michael discovered!

> THE FARADAY INSTITUTE FOR SCIENCE AND RELIGION HONORS MICHAEL'S DEEP FAITH AND REMARKABLE SCIENTIFIC CAREER.

God, give me courage to boldly put myself forward for new roles!

JANUARY 5

DIETRICH BONHOEFFER

1906–1945 • GERMANY

ENDURING FAITH

Whenever you face trials of any kind, consider it nothing but joy, because you know that the testing of your faith produces endurance.

JAMES 1:2-3

Dietrich Bonhoeffer was a brave pastor in 1930s Germany. People were talking about how much they hated Jewish people. Bonhoeffer knew this was wrong! Government leaders, called Nazis, were forcing Jews out of their homes and into small neighborhoods without enough food, water, or space to live. It became unsafe for Jews and for anyone who disagreed with the Nazis. *Should I leave Germany and go somewhere safer?* he wondered. Ultimately, he decided to stay—to resist the Nazis' actions and to help the Jewish people. He got some Jews to safety in Switzerland and spoke out against the unfair treatment of the Jewish people. Dietrich's resistance ultimately cut his life short. Bonhoeffer's selfless efforts show the courage we can have when we follow God to fight against hate.

> THERE IS A STATUE OF BONHOEFFER OUTSIDE WESTMINSTER ABBEY IN LONDON—A GREAT HONOR FOR ANY NON-BRITISH CITIZEN.

God, I want to be brave and to speak out against hate.

JANUARY 6

VINCENT VAN GOGH

1853–1890 • THE NETHERLANDS

GIVE WHAT YOU HAVE

Do not neglect to do good and to share what you
have, for such sacrifices are pleasing to God.

HEBREWS 13:16

Many know Vincent's beautiful paintings but don't realize that he started painting because of his faith in God. In the winter of 1879–1880, Vincent had been doing mission work, living among the poor. He watched families struggle to find food to eat and coal for their fires. So Vincent did what he thought Jesus would do: He gave all his things to his neighbors. Even when he had nothing left, he wanted to give more. Around that time, Vincent started to paint and realized he had a new mission—to bring joy and peace through his art. Vincent's paintings are of beautiful fields of bright, yellow sunflowers, clouds swirling in bright blue skies, and twinkling starry nights. They show the joy and hope he wanted to bring.

> **VINCENT ONLY SOLD ONE PAINTING DURING HIS LIFETIME. IN 1990, ONE OF HIS PAINTINGS SOLD FOR $83 MILLION.**

God, help me give what I have to others who might need it.

JANUARY 7

RUSTY STAUB

1944–2018 • UNITED STATES

MEET THE NEED

Care for orphans and widows in their distress.

JAMES 1:27

"Tell me what you need." Rusty said that phrase often, whether he was talking to an MLB baseball coach or to someone off the field. Rusty was a helper through and through. He used his bat to gather more than 500 base hits for four different teams in the major leagues, becoming the first player to do so. But more importantly, he used his platform as a ball player to help different groups that gave back to people in the community. He created an organization that helped the spouses and children of police and firefighters who died in the line of duty. He also founded the Rusty Staub Foundation, which gave food to children in New York who needed it. No matter where he was, Rusty's faith led him to look for ways to help others.

> WHEN RUSTY PLAYED FOR THE MONTREAL EXPOS, HIS NICKNAME WAS "LE GRAND ORANGE" FOR HIS RED HAIR!

God, help me see who needs my help today.

JANUARY 8

ANTOINE FRÉDÉRIC OZANAM

1813–1853 • FRANCE

GIVE BACK

Speak out for those who can't speak.

PROVERBS 31:8

Antoine loved God very much. But when someone asked how he had shown his faith, Antoine realized his faith needed to include action. He and a friend began visiting poor sections of Paris and tried to help meet people's needs. People noticed what a great help Antoine and his friend were. They were inspired to help too. Soon Antoine and a group of helpers formed the Saint Vincent de Paul to serve the poor, and their mission continues to this day. In 1848, more than 275,000 people in Paris lost their jobs. The government asked Antoine and his group to take charge of giving aid to the poor. Antoine spent the rest of his life seeking justice for the poor. They deserved respect, and their lives mattered—to him and to God.

> ANTOINE'S GROUP, THE VINCENTIANS, STILL DOES CHARITABLE WORK TODAY.

God, I want my faith to be visible in my actions.

JANUARY 9

BETSEY STOCKTON

C. 1798–1865 • HAWAII (FORMERLY THE SANDWICH ISLANDS)

SCHOOL OF THOUGHT

*Let the wise . . . hear and gain in learning
and the discerning acquire skill.*

PROVERBS 1:5

Betsey was born enslaved but learned how to read. In 1822, now a free woman, Betsey joined a voyage to what is now known as Hawaii, where she started a school. At the time, many schools were open only to important people. But Betsey's school was open to everyone. Betsey shared her passion for learning with her students. One day, Betsey's close friend became sick, so she traveled back to the US with her. But before she left, Betsey trained native Hawaiians to keep the school going. Betsey continued teaching in North America. She taught at an "infant school" (like a preschool) for Black children in Philadelphia, started a school for indigenous children in Canada, and taught at a public school in Princeton, New Jersey. Betsey gave her students a strong foundation to help them make wise choices for the rest of their lives.

> **BETSEY WAS THE FIRST BLACK WOMAN TO TRAVEL TO HAWAII.**

God, I love learning about the world You made.

JANUARY 10

TOYOHIKO KAGAWA

1888–1960 · JAPAN

FIGHTING FOR PEACE

Pursue peace with everyone.

HEBREWS 12:14

As a teen, Toyohiko enrolled in a Bible class to learn English. But soon after, he became a Christian! He continued his Christian studies in Japan and then the US. When he returned to Japan, he spent more than ten years living with the poor in Kobe. Toyohiko was a gifted writer and speaker. He began to share about ways people could change their lives for the better. Toyohiko campaigned for voting rights for all Japanese people. Men got the right in 1925, and women in 1945. He helped farmers and laborers organize so they could get fair wages. He even traveled to the US in 1941 to speak out to prevent World War II. Toyohiko was committed to peace and devoted his life to pursuing it.

> KAGAWA WROTE MORE THAN 150 BOOKS! HE WAS NOMINATED FOR THE NOBEL PRIZE FOR LITERATURE TWICE.

God, help me use my talents to bring peace to the world.

JANUARY 11

EDITH CAVELL

1865–1915 • BELGIUM

GREAT CARE

"No one has greater love than this, to lay down one's life for one's friends."

JOHN 15:13

Edith loved caring for others. As a nurse, she traveled from England to Belgium to help in their hospitals. She also established schools to help train new nurses. During Edith's time in Belgium, World War I broke out. England, Belgium, and France were on one side, called the Allies, while Germany was on the other side. Troops from each side of the war were brought to Edith's hospital. Edith and her team treated all the soldiers. But Edith knew the Germans would take any recovering Allied soldiers prisoner. So she disguised the Allied soldiers and helped them escape. More than 200 soldiers escaped before the Germans found out what she was doing. Edith lost her life for her bravery. Before she died, she said she hoped people remembered she was just "a nurse who tried to do her duty."

ONE OF THE MOST MAJESTIC MOUNTAINS IN CANADA IS NAMED MT. EDITH CAVELL, IN EDITH'S HONOR.

God, help me remember nothing is more important than showing Your love to others.

JANUARY 12

JIMMY STEWART

1908–1997 • UNITED STATES

A TRULY WONDERFUL LIFE

Whoever pursues righteousness and
kindness will find life and honor.

PROVERBS 21:21

Westerns, thrillers, holiday classics—Jimmy Stewart could act in any movie and steal the hearts of the audience. Jimmy often played characters who went through hard times but were dedicated to doing the right thing. Jimmy's onscreen characters often reflected his life as a Christian. In 1941, he enlisted in the army to fight in World War II. But when he returned home, Jimmy was sad about the friends he'd lost and the destruction he'd seen. He decided to make a movie called *It's a Wonderful Life*. His character, George, feels hopeless. George prays to God for help and realizes how much his friends and family love him. Jimmy's character showed that living each day with faith in God and serving others makes a truly wonderful life.

> IT'S A WONDERFUL LIFE IS ONE OF THE MOST-LOVED MOVIES OF ALL TIME. MANY FAMILIES WATCH IT EVERY CHRISTMAS.

*God, help me show others that living
for You makes life wonderful.*

JANUARY 13

NICHOLAS OF CUSA

1401–1464 • TRIER (MODERN-DAY GERMANY)

GREAT BIG GOD

Surely God is great, and we do not know him.

JOB 36:26

Nicholas had spent a lifetime going to school and earning fancy degrees. He wrote lots of books with deep thoughts. And his most popular book was called *On Learned Ignorance*, where he made a flabbergasting remark for someone who had the answers to a lot of things. Nicholas said that there's no way humans would ever know all there is to know about the universe—or even about God! Nicholas didn't say this to be a downer. He was trying to reassure people that even when we work hard to learn different things, we won't know all there is to know. That's because God is so great and big, He's way outside of what we humans can understand. And that's okay! And since God is so big, we'll spend our whole lives learning new things about Him. How cool is that?

NICHOLAS ALSO LOVED TO CONDUCT DIFFERENT SCIENCE EXPERIMENTS. HE CONCLUDED PLANTS ABSORB NUTRIENTS FROM THE AIR— THE FIRST MODERN BIOLOGY EXPERIMENT!

God, I'm excited to learn more and more about You!

JANUARY 14

HANS CHRISTIAN ANDERSEN

1805–1875 • DENMARK

UNIQUELY, WONDERFULLY YOU

Your hands have made
and fashioned me.

PSALM 119:73

An ugly duckling who grows into a beautiful swan. A mermaid who dreams of living as a human on land. A young woman no larger than a thumb who wonders if she'll ever meet someone her size. All of these stories were created by Hans! Children and adults alike were fans of his fairy tales. Hans had a knack for telling stories about people and creatures who felt like outsiders—because Hans himself sometimes felt like an outsider. Hans knew what it felt like to be left out and lonely, to feel different from those around you. In his stories, his characters realized that their unique traits didn't make them weird. Their uniqueness made them special— just like God makes each of us special.

> IT IS BELIEVED THAT HANS WAS BORN WITH DYSLEXIA. HIS MANY WRITINGS WERE FULL OF SPELLING ERRORS!

*God, thank You for all the things that
make me special and unique.*

JANUARY 15

SAINT DEVASAHAYAM PILLAI

1712–1752 • INDIA

SHOW HIS LOVE, NO MATTER WHAT

[Love] bears all things, believes all things,
hopes all things, endures all things.

1 CORINTHIANS 13:7

As a young man, Devasahayam went to serve in the royal house of India's Travancore province. In this job, he met the captain of the navy, who was a Christian. Devasahayam was intrigued by the man's faith and soon came to believe in Jesus. He was so excited about his new faith. But his enemies at court convinced the king that Devasahayam was trying to get control by persuading others to follow Jesus. Devasahayam was thrown in prison. His captors were not kind to him. But their bad behavior didn't change Devasahayam's commitment to Jesus. He was always kind to his captors, no matter what they did. Devasahayam wanted to show others the love he had found in Jesus, whether showing that love was easy or hard.

> WHEN DEVASAHAYAM WAS BAPTIZED, HE CHOSE "LAZARUS" FOR HIS NEW NAME—PROBABLY BECAUSE HE FOUND NEW LIFE IN JESUS!

God, please help me show Your love to others, no matter if it's easy or hard.

JANUARY 16

SAINT JUSTIN MARTYR

C. 100 AD–C. 165 AD • ROME (MODERN-DAY ITALY)

SHARING THE TRUTH

"Return to your home and declare how much God has done for you."

LUKE 8:39

Justin grew up in a family that didn't know about Jesus. But when Justin was a young man, he heard about Christianity—and everything began to make sense. He had learned Old Testament history and about a messiah who would come to save the world. *Of course!* he thought. *Jesus is the Messiah the prophets wrote about.* Justin was well educated, and he set out to talk to other educated people about Jesus. Sometimes when we've been taught one thing, it can be hard to consider new ideas. But Justin believed if someone could show people evidence, they might change their minds like he did. Justin traveled far and wide to share the new ideas about Jesus he'd discovered.

JUSTIN WAS THE FIRST KNOWN WRITER TO QUOTE SCRIPTURE FROM THE BOOK OF ACTS.

God, please give me words to show others how real You are.

JANUARY 17

MAHALIA JACKSON

1911–1972 • UNITED STATES

SING FOR HIM

Sing to the Lord, bless his name; tell of his salvation from day to day.

PSALM 96:2

Mahalia Jackson, the "Queen of Gospel Song," was brought up in a family that loved music very much but loved God even more. At sixteen, Mahalia joined the church choir, and her rich singing voice inspired everyone who heard it. Within a few years, she was singing on the radio and on TV. She sang for US presidents, the queen of England, and even the emperor of Japan. People offered Mahalia lots of money to sing songs that weren't gospel, but she said no—God wanted her to sing gospel music. And with her powerful singing voice, she shared God's love with every person around the world who listened to her.

> MAHALIA'S MUSIC WAS POPULAR OUTSIDE THE UNITED STATES TOO. HER RECORDING OF "SILENT NIGHT" IS ONE OF THE ALL-TIME BESTSELLING RECORDS IN DENMARK!

Thank You, God, for giving me gifts. Please help me use them to share Your love with others.

JANUARY 18

SAINT CHARLES OF SEZZE

1613–1670 • ITALY

EYES TO SERVE

Those who are generous are blessed, for they share their bread with the poor.

PROVERBS 22:9

As a boy, Charles thought God would send him somewhere far away, like India, to do big and exciting things for Him. Charles waited and waited, but the call never came. Instead, Charles sensed that God was telling him the opposite—"Give away everything you have." So Charles became a Franciscan friar. He did whatever the brothers needed: cooking, gardening, asking for money for the poor. Charles wanted those in need to be helped. When his superior said to serve food only to traveling friars who came to the door, Charles asked him to reconsider. When the brothers gave to everyone who asked, Charles noticed that they received more donations for the poor. Saint Charles lived a life of service, attentive to others' needs.

> CHARLES WASN'T THE BEST COOK. HE ONCE STARTED A HUGE KITCHEN FIRE AFTER A PAN OF ONIONS BURST INTO FLAMES!

God, help me keep my eyes open to what the people around me need.

JANUARY 19

ELIZABETH BLACKWELL

1821–1910 • ENGLAND AND THE UNITED STATES

CRITICAL CARE

Look not to your own interests but to the interests of others.

PHILIPPIANS 2:4

Elizabeth's friend had died. And her friend believed her situation might have been better if her doctor had been a woman. In the 1800s, few medical colleges accepted women. But Elizabeth wanted to become a doctor anyway. She applied to several different medical colleges. Each school told her no—except for one. Despite obstacles and discrimination, Elizabeth graduated above all 150 male students. She opened a small clinic to treat poor women and provide jobs for female doctors. A decade later, Elizabeth launched her own medical college in New York City so more women could become doctors, and female patients could see doctors who understood their needs.

> ELIZABETH WAS ABLE TO EMPLOY HER SISTER, DR. EMILY BLACKWELL, AT ONE OF HER CLINICS.

God, help me to listen to others and care for their needs.

JANUARY 20

MARIA FEARING

1838–1937 • CONGO

MADE FOR A MISSION

We are ... created in Christ Jesus for good works, which God prepared.

EPHESIANS 2:10

As a little girl, Maria loved listening to stories. Her favorites were about the Bible and missionaries in Africa, where her ancestors were from. She dreamed of a day when she might be free and could travel to Africa too. Though Maria loved stories, she didn't learn to read and write until she was thirty-three. At church one day, fifty-six-year-old Maria heard a missionary ask if anyone would travel with him to Africa to work as a missionary. Maria said yes! She sold all her belongings and boarded a ship to the Congo. While there, Maria opened an orphanage for formerly enslaved girls. Maria taught them the Bible and life skills. She wanted them to have rich lives and to share their faith with others.

> MARIA'S STUDENTS IN THE CONGO NICKNAMED HER *MAMA WA MPUTU*, MEANING "MOTHER FROM FAR AWAY."

God, help me have the courage to follow my dreams and bring glory to Your name.

JANUARY 21

ANNE BRADSTREET

1612–1672 • ENGLAND AND THE UNITED STATES

CLOSER TO GOD

Draw near to God, and he will draw near to you.

JAMES 4:8

"We're *moving?*" Anne Bradstreet asked her new husband, Simon. Traveling three months on a ship crossing the Atlantic Ocean to America would be difficult. But Anne had faith that helping other Christians in the New World was the right thing to do. After Anne and Simon landed in Massachusetts, they had eight children. Anne wrote about her new life. She looked at the hard times—leaving comfort in England to start over in the New World, missing her husband while he traveled for work, suffering from illness—as events that brought her closer to God. Anne's brother-in-law secretly took some of Anne's poems back to England, where they were published and enjoyed by many. Nearly 400 years later, people are still talking about her poems.

> **ENGLAND'S KING GEORGE III HAD A COPY OF ANNE'S POETRY IN HIS LIBRARY.**

Lord, help me remember that even hard times in my life can bring me closer to You.

JANUARY 22

JOHN HAVLICEK

1940–2019 • UNITED STATES

ROLE ON THE TEAM

*As in one body we have many members and not
all the members have the same function.*

ROMANS 12:4

Sometimes what's good for you isn't what's best for the team. When John arrived at Ohio State on a basketball scholarship, he was ready to shatter records for himself. But the coach told the team that whoever scored the most points or grabbed the most rebounds didn't matter—the final score of the game did. Even bad teams might have one or two good players. But on the best teams, all five players are working together. John was a great shooter, and other teams knew it. If they were guarding him, he'd play more aggressive defense so his teammates could get an open shot. It takes humility to give an opportunity to shine to someone else. But John saw that when people work together for a common good, great things can happen!

> JOHN WENT ON TO WIN EIGHT NBA CHAMPIONSHIPS WITH THE BOSTON CELTICS.

God, thank You for making each of us with a unique role!

JANUARY 23

FREDERICK DOUGLASS

1818–1895 • UNITED STATES

FREEDOM FIGHTER

Look not to your own interests but to the interests of others.

PHILIPPIANS 2:4

Frederick had spent the first few decades of his life enslaved and believed if more people knew how hard it was to be enslaved, they would think slavery was wrong. Publishing a book about his life might put him in danger, since he had escaped and was on the run. But he decided sharing his story to persuade others to end slavery was more important than his safety. Frederick's book quickly sold many copies. And many began to agree with Frederick, that the way some Christians in America used the Bible to justify slavery was wrong. Frederick's selfless acts continued in other areas. He tried to help women in the US get the right to vote and helped young activists achieve equal rights and pay for the Black community. Frederick never stopped fighting for the freedom of others.

> FREDERICK WAS THE MOST PHOTOGRAPHED AMERICAN MAN IN THE 1800S.

God, give me courage to speak out for others who need help.

JANUARY 24

CHARLES CORREA

1930–2015 • INDIA

BLUEPRINTS FOR A BETTER WORLD

"Everyone then who hears these words of mine and acts on them will be like a wise man who built his house on rock."

MATTHEW 7:24

As an architect, Charles Correa's goal was to design buildings to make people feel closer to heaven. For Charles, that meant creating places where people could get to know the people around them and make friends. Some architects design high-rise buildings that house many people. These buildings make lots of money for architects. But it's hard to get to know your neighbors in a big building. Instead, Charles designed smaller buildings so people could feel close to their neighbors.

> CHARLES IS CONSIDERED "INDIA'S GREATEST ARCHITECT."

He also used traditional Indian building methods and materials to work better with India's landscape and climate, breaking with Western tradition and honoring Indian architecture. Charles even launched the Urban Design Research Institute so he could improve the quality of life for people without a lot of money living in cities around the world.

God, give me the courage to do things differently, especially if it helps others.

JANUARY 25

LUCIAN TAPIEDI

C. 1921–1942 • PAPUA NEW GUINEA

I WILL STAY

It is required of stewards that they be found trustworthy.

1 CORINTHIANS 4:2

Lucian was born on the island of Papua New Guinea, out in the Pacific Ocean. Lucian's father was a sorcerer, but after he died, Lucian became a Christian while attending an Anglican school. Lucian grew up to become a teacher and was beloved by students for his cheerful attitude and his love of sports and music. During World War II, the Japanese invaded Papua New Guinea. Lucian was determined not to leave the missionaries. "Even if . . . we were all to perish . . . the Church would not perish," Lucian said. Lucian and the missionaries tried to escape to safety, traveling to a village where a rival tribe lived. But the villagers turned them over, and Lucian was killed by a man named Hivijapa. Later, Hivijapa became a Christian and built a church in Lucian's honor!

> LUCIAN IS AMONG THE MODERN MARTYRS CARVED ON THE OUTSIDE OF WESTMINSTER ABBEY.

God, please help me stay loyal to Your people and Your work.

JANUARY 26

LENA RICHARD

1892–1950 • UNITED STATES

BLAZING A TRAIL

"Do to others as you would have them to do to you."

LUKE 6:31

Lights, camera, action! Lena would smile and welcome viewers of her cooking show, *Lena Richard's New Orleans Cook Book*. Lena was known for showing both Black and white TV viewers how to create bubbling pots of New Orleans classics like gumbo and shrimp bisque.

She was one of the first chefs on television—all the way back in 1949! She also wrote down more than 300 of her recipes and published the first Creole cookbook by a Black chef. Lena was also known for her New Orleans cooking school. She helped train Black chefs so they could get higher wages for their work. She had received training like this early in her career, and Lena thought it was important to pass on her knowledge to other chefs. Lena was a trailblazer who worked to make the path easier for those who followed.

> LENA WAS ALSO A FROZEN FOOD ENTREPRENEUR! IN 1946, SHE CREATED DISHES THAT COULD BE SHIPPED ALL OVER THE COUNTRY.

God, help me make the path easier for those walking behind me.

JANUARY 27

DR. SHI MEIYU

1873–1954 • CHINA

HEALING HANDS

He heals the brokenhearted, and binds up their wounds.

PSALM 147:3

Meiyu had two goals: to help heal people's bodies and to heal their hearts. She and her friend Cheng traveled from China to the United States to study medicine, and they became the first Chinese women to receive medical degrees from an American college. Now Dr. Shi, Meiyu later returned to China and opened a clinic. Dr. Shi not only helped thousands of patients heal from illnesses and broken bones; she also talked to people about Jesus. She shared her faith so her patients could know about God and follow Him. Eventually, Dr. Shi opened her own hospital. She trained more than 500 nurses and helped more than 5,000 patients each month!

> DR. SHI WAS AN ACTIVE LEADER IN THE CHURCH. SHE WAS THE FIRST CHINESE CHRISTIAN WOMAN TO BECOME A PASTOR IN CENTRAL CHINA.

God, help me see people with broken hearts so I can tell them about Jesus.

JANUARY 28

TERTULLIAN

C. 155–C. 220 • CARTHAGE (MODERN-DAY TUNISIA)

NOTICE THE DIFFERENCE

Come out from them, and be separate from them, says the Lord.

2 CORINTHIANS 6:17

As he spent time in Rome, Tertullian noticed that the people who called themselves "Christians" were unlike other people. Instead of following several different gods, they believed in one great God. Christians seemed to be dedicated to doing the right thing and to helping others. And they believed so fiercely in God that they were even willing to die for that belief. As he traveled back to his home in Carthage, in North Africa, Tertullian couldn't stop thinking about the Christians he'd met in Rome. He decided to become a Christian himself! Tertullian grew in his faith and became a powerful and passionate teacher. As a writer, he used his pen to instruct new believers about their faith and encouraged long-time believers to stand strong for God.

> TERTULLIAN WROTE ABOUT CHRISTIANITY IN LATIN. HE BECAME A TRENDSETTER FOR WRITING ABOUT THE CHURCH IN LATIN.

God, I want to live in a way that shows others I believe in You!

JANUARY 29

FLANNERY O'CONNOR

1925–1964 • UNITED STATES

DIFFERENT AND SPECIAL

I praise you, for I am fearfully and wonderfully made.

PSALM 139:14

When she was a young woman, Flannery learned that she had lupus, the same disease that had killed her father. Lupus kept her mostly homebound in later years as she needed crutches. But the disease couldn't stop Flannery from writing. She was a gifted storyteller who thought up tales of people who struggled with their faith. Her characters were often outsiders, and the heroes who saved or taught them were usually grumpy or strange. Flannery considered herself an outsider too. Lupus had kept her isolated and even made her hair fall out. She didn't look or feel like everybody else. But she could connect with people through her stories. Lupus and her deep faith made Flannery unafraid to think and write about hard subjects, and her humor and honesty drew people to her books.

FLANNERY KEPT SOME UNUSUAL PETS—SHE RAISED PEACOCKS ON HER FARM!

God, help me remember that what makes me different makes me special.

JANUARY 30

JOHN NEWTON

1725–1807 • ENGLAND

CHANGE OF HEART

"A new heart I will give you, and a new spirit I will put within you."

EZEKIEL 36:26

John was a sailor. As a boy, his mother had taught him about God, but as he grew older, he chose not to follow Him. One night, John was caught in a fierce storm. He was scared his ship would sink. When the storm calmed, John realized God had saved his life. Part of John's job on the ship was to trade enslaved people. He saw nothing wrong with how he made his money. Eventually, John left his job on the ship and became a preacher in England. As he grew deeper in his Christian faith, he realized that buying and selling people was wrong and spent the rest of his life working to end the slave trade in England. Nine months before John died, slavery was abolished in the British Empire.

> JOHN WROTE ONE OF THE MOST-LOVED HYMNS OF ALL TIME, "AMAZING GRACE."

God, help me see when I'm wrong so I can change my ways.

JANUARY 31

PAT SUMMERALL

1930–2013 • UNITED STATES

GETTING HELP

The Lord is near to all who call on him.

PSALM 145:18

Things came easy for Pat. Playing football. Charming viewers on TV alongside the legendary John Madden. But Pat had a problem he didn't tell many people about. Pat would often drink so much alcohol that he'd get sick. His family asked him to stop. *Okay*, Pat thought. *That'll be easy.* But it wasn't. Pat finally got treatment for his drinking. He asked Jesus to help him and was finally able to quit drinking. He started reading the Bible every morning. He prayed and asked God for help with everything he did, even before he went on TV. Before Jesus, Pat thought he had to do everything himself. But when he trusted his life to Jesus, something new came easy to him: peace.

> THE MOST NERVOUS PAT EVER FELT WASN'T PLAYING OR ANNOUNCING FOOTBALL; IT WAS SPEAKING ALONGSIDE THE GREAT PREACHER BILLY GRAHAM. (DON'T WORRY, PAT DID GREAT!)

God, when I need help, please help me turn to You.

FEBRUARY 1

JOHN KNOX

C. 1514–1572 • SCOTLAND

ACCEPT THE CALL

> One thing I do: forgetting what lies behind and
> straining forward to what lies ahead.
>
> **PHILIPPIANS 3:13**

John was a brilliant man who was also a teacher. He enjoyed his quiet life instructing his students and keeping his nose in a book. Others heard John teaching and knew he had a deep love for God too. They thought his talents would be better used to preach to large crowds of people instead of to a few students in a small classroom. John's eyes filled with tears. He didn't want lots of people looking at him and critiquing what he said. But after lots of prayer, he decided that maybe God could use him on a larger stage. That's exactly what God did. John became one of the most famous preachers not only in Scotland but also in history. He helped many people find a relationship with God.

> JOHN SPENT MUCH OF HIS PREACHING LIFE TRAVELING. IT WASN'T THE QUIET CLASSROOM LIFE HE HAD IMAGINED. TO HIM, IT WAS BETTER.

*God, show me how to follow Your call,
no matter where it leads.*

FEBRUARY 2

ARETHA FRANKLIN

1942–2018 • UNITED STATES

SINGING FOR CHANGE

But I will sing of your might; I will sing aloud of your steadfast love in the morning.

PSALM 59:16

Aretha was known as the "Queen of Soul." She used her powerful voice not only to sing incredible songs but also to make a positive change for others. Aretha learned to sing at the church where her father was pastor. As she grew older, others began to recognize Aretha's talent and put her on the radio. Songs like "Respect" and "Think" inspired many people. Aretha also used her voice to speak up for the Black community. She toured with Dr. Martin Luther King Jr., singing at his gatherings. She even paid the salaries for people working on civil rights. Her work has inspired many artists not only to sing but also to use their talent to empower others.

> IN 1987, ARETHA WAS THE FIRST WOMAN TO BE INDUCTED INTO THE ROCK & ROLL HALL OF FAME.

God, help me use my voice to bring positive change to the world.

FEBRUARY 3

SAINT AELRED OF RIEVAULX

C. 1110–1167 • NORTHUMBRIA (MODERN-DAY ENGLAND)

TRUE FRIENDS

"You are my friends if you do what I command you."

JOHN 15:14

What does it mean to be a true friend? For Saint Aelred, the answer pointed to our best Friend of all: Jesus! Saint Aelred realized that friendship was one of life's greatest blessings because friendship ultimately brings each person in the relationship peace and rest. That peace and rest are possible because of love that says to the other person, "I've got you." That's why Jesus is the ultimate Friend—because He loves us so much that He gave His life to save us! Saint Aelred realized that when groups of people love each other like Jesus did, where other people's needs are important, then everyone can grow and thrive since they're all helping each other.

> SAINT AELRED WAS A GIFTED WRITER. HIS WORKS ARE SOME OF THE FINEST IN ENGLAND DURING THE MEDIEVAL PERIOD.

God, thank You for my friends! I want to love them well, the way You love all of us.

FEBRUARY 4

ROBERTO CLEMENTE

1934–1972 • PUERTO RICO

ROBERTO'S BIG HEART

Do not neglect to do good and to share what you have,
for such sacrifices are pleasing to God.

HEBREWS 13:16

While growing up on the island of Puerto Rico, Roberto dreamed of playing baseball in the big leagues. When he was twenty years old, he finally got the chance! Roberto played for the Pittsburgh Pirates, and fans loved watching him run lightning-fast around the bases, throw baseballs from the outfield with his cannon-like arm, and hit home runs. He even helped the Pirates win two World Series titles! But Roberto's good deeds off the field, inspired by his love for God, were even more impressive. He loved helping others, especially back home in Puerto Rico. He took baseballs and gloves to sick fans and ran baseball clinics for kids across the island, teaching how to play the sport and also the importance of being a good citizen. In 1973, he became the first Latin American baseball player inducted into the Baseball Hall of Fame.

> EVERY YEAR, MAJOR LEAGUE BASEBALL HONORS PLAYERS WHO SERVE IN THEIR COMMUNITIES. THE AWARD IS CALLED THE ROBERTO CLEMENTE AWARD.

*God, help me remember the greatest title
I could ever strive for—Your helper.*

FEBRUARY 5

LEONARDO DA VINCI

1452–1519 • ITALY

EXPLORING IT ALL

O Lord, how manifold are your works! In
wisdom you have made them all.

PSALM 104:24

The most well-known painting in the world just might be Leonardo's *Mona Lisa*. But Leonardo was more than a famous artist. He studied many areas of science, sketching some of the most detailed drawings of the human body seen at that time. Because of this, scientific drawings from then on became more detailed. He was also an architect and an engineer (someone who uses science to solve problems or design new structures and systems). For example, nearly 300 years before the Wright brothers,

> LEONARDO WROTE *BACKWARD* IN HIS NOTEBOOKS. THE ONLY WAY YOU CAN READ THEM? HOLDING THEM UP TO A MIRROR!

Leonardo designed plans for an airplane and a helicopter. Leonardo didn't keep himself to one job or talent. He followed his big imagination, which led him to explore many parts of the world God created!

*God, the world You made is so big, with so many
things to discover. I want to explore it all!*

FEBRUARY 6

CORAZON AQUINO

1933–2009 • PHILIPPINES

WILLING TO HELP

[God] . . . will not overlook your work and the love that you showed for his sake in serving the saints.

HEBREWS 6:10

Corazon and her husband, Benigno, loved their country, the Philippines. But it was ruled by a cruel leader named Ferdinand Marcos, who treated the people very badly. Benigno wanted to run for president to change things, but he was suddenly killed. Corazon didn't want to be president, but she knew that was how she could help her people. So Corazon ran for president in 1986. At first the government said Corazon didn't win, but she thought Marcos was cheating. She and Filipino citizens decided to protest. Eventually Marcos stepped away—and Corazon became president! She gathered a group to rewrite the constitution and reinstate the Congress. She let people who had been wrongly imprisoned go free. Her devout faith helped her love her people well and restore democracy to the Philippines.

CORAZON WAS THE FIRST FEMALE PRESIDENT OF THE PHILIPPINES AND IS KNOWN AS "THE MOTHER OF PHILIPPINE DEMOCRACY."

God, I want to be brave when You call me to a big task.

FEBRUARY 7

J. R. R. TOLKIEN

1892–1973 • ENGLAND

HELPING FRIENDS FIND GOD

*Faith is the assurance of things hoped for,
the conviction of things not seen.*

HEBREWS 11:1

When J. R. R. Tolkien was a little boy, his mother taught him to love God. Faith became an important part of Tolkien's life, even after he became a professor at Oxford University. Tolkien made friends with some of his fellow teachers. They called themselves "the Inklings." They met often to talk about books and ideas. One of his friends, a fellow professor named C. S. Lewis, didn't believe in God. He didn't know how Tolkien could believe that God was real. But Tolkien was patient with Lewis. He'd calmly explain why he believed in God. Over time, Lewis began to see that his friend was right. God is real!

> TOLKIEN AND LEWIS WROTE SOME OF THE MOST POPULAR FANTASY BOOKS OF ALL TIME—*THE HOBBIT* AND *THE LORD OF THE RINGS* (TOLKIEN) AND *THE CHRONICLES OF NARNIA* SERIES (LEWIS).

*God, when I meet someone who doesn't know
You, help me show them Your love.*

FEBRUARY 8

MARY LYON

1797–1849 • UNITED STATES

DOGGED DETERMINATION

Let us not grow weary in doing what is right, for we
will reap at harvest time, if we do not give up.

GALATIANS 6:9

Mary loved school so much that after finishing high school, she began to earn money teaching so that she could afford further education. At the time, not many women were able to go to college. Mary thought women should have the same opportunity as men to further their education. She began to raise money to start a school just for women. Mary traveled to her home state of Massachusetts asking for donations. Many people told her no. Even the state legislature was unsure of Mary's idea. For a while, they wouldn't let her open the school—but changed their minds. Mount Holyoke Female Seminary opened in 1837 and is still operating today. Mary's determination paved the way for many women to go to college.

> ONE OF MOUNT HOLYOKE'S MOST FAMOUS STUDENTS WAS THE POET EMILY DICKINSON.

*God, thank You for the people who
worked so hard to help me learn.*

FEBRUARY 9

PHILLIS WHEATLEY

1753–1784 • UNITED STATES

USE YOUR VOICE

Speak out, judge righteously, defend the
rights of the poor and needy.

PROVERBS 31:9

Becoming a famous writer in the 1700s was difficult—especially if you were Black. But Phillis Wheatley's poems were special. Phillis had been brought to the US from Africa as an enslaved person when she was only seven. The family she lived with quickly recognized Phillis's intellect. By age ten, she was translating Latin and Greek into English. She also wrote poems about all kinds of things: her faith in God, her friends, famous figures who

> PHILLIS EXCHANGED LETTERS WITH MANY FAMOUS PEOPLE—INCLUDING PRESIDENT GEORGE WASHINGTON!

had died, and why slavery should be abolished. She was the first Black woman in America to publish a book—even before the Revolutionary War! Phillis's gift brought awareness to many people.

*Lord, I want to use my voice to share
about Your love for everyone.*

FEBRUARY 10

JIM IRWIN

1930–1991 • UNITED STATES

HELP FROM ABOVE

I lift up my eyes to the hills—from where will my help come?
My help comes from the Lord, who made heaven and earth.

PSALM 121:1-2

Jim couldn't believe his eyes. Stretched before him was the dusty, craggy surface of the moon—and he was standing on it! For the next few hours, he explored the terrain, taking photos and setting up scientific experiments. Back in the shuttle, he told the NASA team in Houston that spending time on the moon had reminded him of his favorite Bible verse—our verse today! Jim knew that God had helped him arrive at this moment. He had applied to become an astronaut not once, not twice, but *three times* before NASA said yes. Then he went through rigorous training for his mission. Jim's perseverance paid off. After he returned to earth, Jim spent the rest of his life telling others how he saw God's handiwork in space.

> ON THE APOLLO 15 MISSION, JIM AND HIS FELLOW ASTRONAUT DAVID SCOTT WERE THE SEVENTH AND EIGHTH AMERICANS TO WALK ON THE MOON.

God, thank You for helping me do amazing things to show Your glory.

FEBRUARY 11

SAINT MARÍA ANTONIA DE PAZ Y FIGUEROA

1730–1799 • ARGENTINA

WALKING TO WITNESS

I will walk among you, and will be your God, and you shall be my people.

LEVITICUS 26:12

Born in a wealthy family, María left home at age fifteen to spread the gospel to the poor in her country of Argentina. María often worked alongside the Jesuits. But in 1767, the Jesuits were banished from Argentina. If the priests couldn't do the work, María would! She walked from village to village, talking with people and spreading joy wherever she went. María walked in any weather, making her way across the country no matter how hilly or rocky the journey. Eventually María reached Buenos Aires. There she founded a place where people could learn more about God and get help if they were sick or returning to the community after time in prison. People called her "Mama Antula" for the way she helped them.

> MAMA ANTULA IS CALLED "THE MOTHER OF ARGENTINA" FOR HER WORK TO HELP ARGENTINIANS SPIRITUALLY.

God, I want to spend my life walking with You no matter where the road leads!

FEBRUARY 12

JACK SOO

1917–1979 • UNITED STATES

SPREADING JOY

Rejoice always.

1 THESSALONIANS 5:16

No matter the hardship in front of him, Jack faced it with his not-so-secret weapon: humor! From his earliest days, Jack tried to help others find joy, especially in a difficult situation. Jack's parents were Japanese immigrants who had settled in the US. During World War II, Jack and his family had to move away from their homes and into a camp with other Japanese families. To cheer everyone up, Jack would put on shows where he'd sing and dance. He also loved singing in church. After the war, Jack went into show business! He sang and danced in plays on Broadway, then landed roles in movies and on TV. His most famous role was on the comedy show *Barney Miller*, where Jack played police detective Nick Yemana—who could never make the coffee right!

> JACK WAS THE FIRST JAPANESE AMERICAN TO BE REPRESENTED IN THE SMITHSONIAN MUSEUM'S COLLECTION OF ENTERTAINMENT HISTORY.

God, no matter what happens, help me find joy in each day.

FEBRUARY 13

SAINT GILES MARY OF SAINT JOSEPH

1729–1812 • NAPLES (MODERN-DAY ITALY)

FIRST RESPONDER

"If I am still alive, show me the faithful love of the Lord."

1 SAMUEL 20:14

Francesco wanted to become a priest. But his family couldn't afford the education he would need. So at twenty-five, Francesco became Giles Mary of Saint Joseph and joined a brotherhood of friars instead. For nearly six decades, Giles opened the brothers' door when someone rang the bell looking for help. Some were looking for food or help for a sick loved one or comfort while grieving. When Giles opened the door, he responded with kindness and compassion. He knew that every person was going through a hard time,

> FOR GILES'S KINDNESS AT THE DOOR, PEOPLE CALLED HIM "THE CONSOLER OF NAPLES."

and he wanted them to first experience kindness. Sometimes he'd leave his post to visit lepers outside the city or walk the streets calling out, "Love God, love God," as a reminder that Someone was always there to turn to when they needed help.

*God, please help me respond to someone
in need with kindness first.*

FEBRUARY 14

CAEDMON

?-680 • NORTHUMBRIA (MODERN-DAY ENGLAND)

SHARE YOUR GIFTS

Cast all your anxiety on him, because he cares for you.

1 PETER 5:7

Caedmon tended the cows that grazed outside the monastery. At night, when folks passed around the harp to sing and recite poems, Caedmon always left the table. He didn't want to embarrass himself. He couldn't sing and didn't know any poetry. One night, Caedmon dreamed someone asked him to sing about "the beginning of created things." In the dream, Caedmon began to sing a beautiful, poetic hymn! He woke up amazed. Should he tell someone about his dream? Would they laugh at him? He decided to tell his boss and to recite the poem for her. She thought the poem was beautiful! She encouraged Caedmon to become a monk and learn the Scriptures. For the rest of his days, Caedmon wrote beautiful poetry. He faced his fears and used his gift to inspire others.

> **CAEDMON IS THE FIRST-KNOWN ENGLISH POET.**

God, when I'm nervous to use my gifts, give me courage.

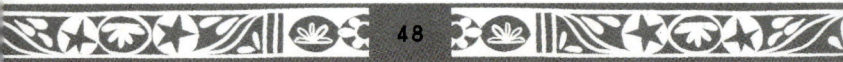

FEBRUARY 15

CIMABUE

C. 1240–1302 • ITALY

TRY AND TRY AGAIN

In all toil there is profit.

PROVERBS 14:23

Cimabue, born Bencivieni di Pepo, was an Italian artist who painted frescoes and mosaics of Bible stories and saints such as Saint Francis of Assisi. He played an important role in the transition to more realistic styles of painting and is often considered the first "modern" painter. Many painters from the Middle Ages were lost to history because they didn't sign their work. But not Cimabue! He took great pride in the artistic gifts God had given him and was determined to do great work. When he was painting, if Cimabue wasn't getting the results he wanted, he'd throw away the piece and start again. He wasn't afraid to start over. He worked hard to create paintings that glorified God using the skills God had given him.

> LEGEND HAS IT THAT CIMABUE SPOTTED A TWELVE-YEAR-OLD SITTING ON A ROCK, SKETCHING A SHEEP. HE WAS SO IMPRESSED THAT HE MADE THE BOY—FUTURE ITALIAN MASTER GIOTTO—HIS PUPIL.

God, sometimes I mess up. Instead of getting frustrated, I want to stay calm and try again. Please show me how.

FEBRUARY 16

ROSA PARKS

1913–2005 • UNITED STATES

SITTING DOWN TO STAND UP

When one's case is subverted—does the Lord not see it?

LAMENTATIONS 3:36

In 1955, a bus driver in Montgomery, Alabama, saw white passengers standing in the aisle. He asked the Black riders to give up their seats. The Black riders stood up—except Rosa. Although the law said that Black riders had to give up seats for white riders when asked, Rosa refused. She knew the law was wrong. Rosa was arrested and fined, but she refused to pay the fine. She knew she was opening herself to danger with this choice. But perhaps people would see what had happened to her and agree that discriminating against Black people on buses and at restaurants, schools, and drinking fountains was wrong. Rosa's choice sparked a civil rights movement that ended with overturning the unfair law and introducing new laws that said each person, no matter their race, has a right to equal treatment.

> WHEN ROSA DIED, HER BODY LAY IN STATE AT THE US CAPITOL. SHE WAS THE FIRST WOMAN TO RECEIVE THAT HONOR.

God, thank You for the example of Rosa's courage and determination.

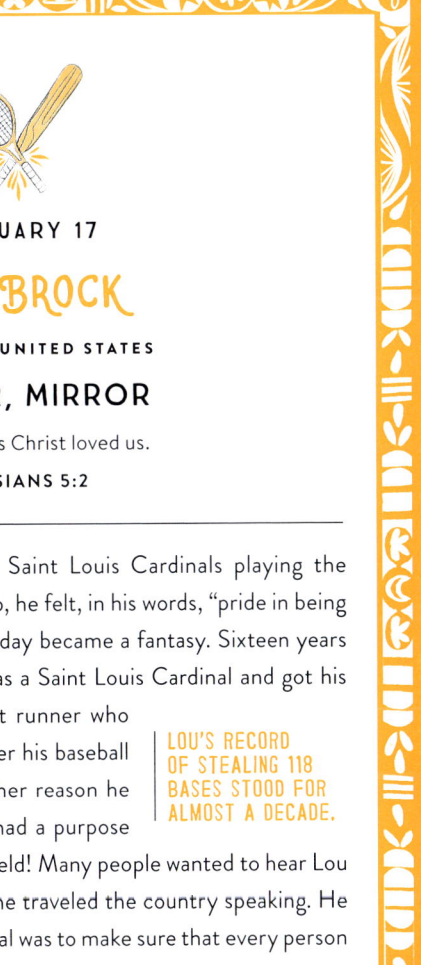

FEBRUARY 17

LOU BROCK

1939–2020 • UNITED STATES

MIRROR, MIRROR

Live in love, as Christ loved us.

EPHESIANS 5:2

As young Lou listened to the Saint Louis Cardinals playing the Brooklyn Dodgers on the radio, he felt, in his words, "pride in being alive." Playing on that field someday became a fantasy. Sixteen years later, Lou jogged onto the field as a Saint Louis Cardinal and got his chance! Lou was a lightning-fast runner who set records in stealing bases. After his baseball career ended, Lou realized another reason he had "pride in being alive." God had a purpose for him far beyond the baseball field! Many people wanted to hear Lou talk about his life and career, so he traveled the country speaking. He also shared about his faith. His goal was to make sure that every person he met could see Jesus reflected in him.

> LOU'S RECORD OF STEALING 118 BASES STOOD FOR ALMOST A DECADE.

*God, I want to remember my real purpose
in life: showing You in all that I do!*

FEBRUARY 18

FRA ANGELICO

C. 1400–1455 • ITALY

ASK FOR GUIDANCE

Those who seek me diligently find me.

PROVERBS 8:17

As a boy, Fra Angelico was known as Guido. And Guido had two great wishes: to follow God and to become the best painter he could be. When Guido grew up, he became a Dominican friar and took a new name: Giovanni. Back then, many people couldn't read, so they learned about the Bible through art that showed different Bible stories. To serve his community, Giovanni painted beautiful art that showed people from the Bible. Every day before he painted, Giovanni asked God to guide his hands so he could create art that would inspire people to follow Him more. People loved Giovanni's art, and his work became so popular that even the pope asked him to paint portraits of saints to put in chapels in Rome. Many of his paintings still survive today.

> AFTER GIOVANNI DIED, PEOPLE STARTED CALLING HIM "FRA ANGELICO," WHICH MEANS "ANGELIC BROTHER." THIS NICKNAME REFERS TO THE GOOD EXAMPLE HE SHOWED OTHERS.

God, help me see the ways I can show others who You are.

FEBRUARY 19

MELITO OF SARDIS

C. 101–C. 200 • SARDIS (MODERN-DAY TÜRKIYE)

A CELEBRATION TO REMEMBER

We know love by this, that he laid down his life for us.

1 JOHN 3:16

To Melito, one of the most special things about being a Christian was that Jesus sacrificed His life on the cross. After all, His heroic act saved all of humanity. Melito thought this needed to be celebrated! So Melito decided to write about it. In his sermon called *The Lord's Passion*, Melito talked about how special Jesus' sacrifice was. He reminded people that no other God had come to earth as a human and then laid down His life for ours. Before Jesus came, people would sacrifice an animal to show God how sorry they were for the wrong things they had done. But Jesus became that sacrifice for us! Melito said we should honor this sacrifice every single year. This celebration came to be known as Easter.

> IT'S BELIEVED THAT MELITO COMPILED ONE OF THE FIRST VERSIONS OF THE OLD TESTAMENT.

God, thank You for Your Son, who sacrificed Himself to save us.

FEBRUARY 20

PANDITA RAMABAI

1858–1922 • INDIA

OUTSIDE THE BOX

*Lead me in your truth, and teach me, for
you are the God of my salvation.*

PSALM 25:5

Rama spent her life "outside the box." For starters, her father homeschooled her at a time when girls in India weren't commonly educated. Before he died when Rama was sixteen, Rama's father told her to "serve God all your life." Rama had been born into a "high caste" family. That meant she had to follow certain rules for people with high social standing, like marrying a man who was also high caste. But Rama chose to marry for love! However, soon after their daughter was born, Rama's husband died. High-caste widows weren't allowed to leave home or remarry, which Rama thought was unfair. Unlike other widows, Rama had an education that equipped her to provide for herself and her daughter. So she opened the "Home of Learning" so other widows could learn skills like carpentry, sewing, and gardening and provide for themselves too. The home is still active today.

> "PANDITA" IS NOT RAMABAI'S FIRST NAME; IT'S A TITLE THAT ACKNOWLEDGES HER HIGH LEVEL OF LEARNING. "BAI" WAS ADDED TO HER NAME AS SHE GREW OLDER AS A SIGN OF RESPECT.

*God, give me the courage to serve You, even
if it means thinking "outside the box."*

FEBRUARY 21

FILIPPO BRUNELLESCHI

1377–1446 • ITALY

A NEW IDEA

He has filled them with skill to do every kind of work.

EXODUS 35:35

Filippo loved designing buildings and believed that architecture could honor God. People in Filippo's town of Florence had been building a huge church for more than a hundred years. Now it was time to build a top for the church, a kind of ceiling called a *vault*. The vault had to be in the shape of an octagon without any buttresses, or outside supports, to hold its weight. But that hadn't been done before! Filippo began to sketch, using mathematical calculations and his imagination to engineer a brand-new dome as the ceiling. He and a few other architects submitted plans—and Filippo's was chosen! People were skeptical. For sixteen slow years, the huge dome took shape. Then finally, in 1436, it was complete. Filippo's imagination and ingenuity made it happen!

> YOU CAN TRAVEL TO FLORENCE AND SEE FILIPPO'S DOME TODAY! IT'S AT THE CATHEDRAL OF SANTA MARIA DEL FIORE.

*God, when I have to go to the drawing board,
help me to be brave—and have fun!*

FEBRUARY 22

ELIZABETH KECKLEY

1818–1907 • UNITED STATES

SEW MANY GIFTS

Do not seek your own advantage, but that of the other.

1 CORINTHIANS 10:24

Elizabeth was a talented seamstress who created clothes and gowns for some of the most important people in Washington, DC—including First Lady Mary Todd Lincoln! Elizabeth had been born enslaved. But through hard work, perseverance, and business savvy, Elizabeth had purchased her freedom through her sewing business. While in Washington, Elizabeth met people who raised money for causes they cared about and had an idea. With her church, Elizabeth started an organization called the Contraband Relief Association, which gathered money and clothes to help enslaved people after gaining their freedom. Elizabeth asked influential people she'd met in the White House to give money to the cause. Both President Lincoln and Frederick Douglass donated. Elizabeth's courage and skills helped many people.

> ELIZABETH WROTE ABOUT HER DAILY LIFE WITH THE LINCOLNS IN HER BOOK *BEHIND THE SCENES.*

God, give me eyes to see how I can use my gifts to help people around me.

FEBRUARY 23

AUGUSTA SAVAGE

1892–1962 • UNITED STATES

JUST KEEP GOING

The one who began a good work among you will bring it to completion by the day of Jesus Christ.

PHILIPPIANS 1:6

Augusta reached down and rubbed the wet clay outside her Florida home. *I can work with this*, she thought. Augusta loved to sculpt—animals, figurines, people. She was so good that her high school principal paid her a dollar a day to teach her classmates. She dreamed of studying in Paris, so she applied to a scholarship program—and she got in! But when the committee learned that Augusta was Black, they said she couldn't come. Augusta was sad but worked to save money. But when a hurricane hit her family's home in Florida, she gave them the money instead. In her spare time, she kept sculpting. A photo of a sculpture she had done of her nephew made the front cover of a magazine. And when a scholarship committee saw it, they decided to help with her dream. They gave her money to study in France!

> AUGUSTA SAVAGE WAS COMMISSIONED IN 1937 TO CREATE A WORK FOR THE NEW YORK WORLD'S FAIR.

God, help me keep working hard for my dreams, no matter the obstacles.

FEBRUARY 24

RICH MULLINS

1955–1997 • UNITED STATES

OPEN UP

> I am content with weaknesses . . . for whenever
> I am weak, then I am strong.
>
> **2 CORINTHIANS 12:10**

Rich wrote beautiful music that connected others to God. He wrote songs like "Awesome God," which people still sing at churches and chapel services today. But what drew people to Rich wasn't just his beautiful songs—people were drawn to his brave honesty. Whenever he performed, Rich would share about something he was struggling with or wrong things he had done. He wanted people to know that if they were wrestling with a certain kind of sin, they weren't alone. Rich's honesty showed people that God is always with them, even in their weakness. Rich's willingness to be authentic encouraged people to know that God never leaves our side.

> RICH MADE LOTS OF MONEY BUT CHOSE TO LIVE SIMPLY. HE TOOK AN AVERAGE AMERICAN SALARY AND DONATED THE REST TO CHARITY.

God, thank You for loving me, even when I make mistakes. And thank You for forgiving me.

FEBRUARY 25

BLESSED SEBASTIAN OF APARICIO

1502–1600 • SPAIN AND MEXICO

WORKING FOR GOD AT ANY AGE

You are my strong refuge.

PSALM 71:7

Sebastian was a bridge builder: physically and spiritually! He was born into a poor family in Spain. As a young adult, he decided to sail across the ocean for a new life in Mexico. As he worked in the fields there, he noticed a lack of roads to transport crops or other resources. So he decided to try building a road from Zacatecas to Mexico City. Zacatecas mined silver. A road to transport the silver to a major city would make selling and trading easier. Sebastian spent ten years building the road and made lots of money in the process. But Sebastian didn't just sit on his wealth. At age seventy-two, he gave away his fortune and became a Franciscan brother. He spent the next twenty-five years standing on street corners collecting money for the poor.

> SEBASTIAN IS KNOWN AS THE PATRON SAINT OF TRAVELERS.

God, I'm glad I can serve You, no matter my age!

FEBRUARY 26

DR. EDWARD JENNER

1749–1823 • ENGLAND

TRY AND SEE

For now we see in a mirror, dimly, but then we will see face to face.

1 CORINTHIANS 13:12

A disease called *smallpox* was common in the late 1700s. When someone got it, they often died. Dr. Edward Jenner was curious about God's creation—whether he was watching birds migrate across England or working as a doctor. One day, he saw a woman who milked cows get cowpox but not smallpox. Cowpox wasn't deadly like smallpox. So Dr. Jenner tried an experiment. He took a sample of cowpox from the woman and placed it into a healthy patient.

> DR. JENNER'S FAVORITE HOBBIES WERE PLAYING THE VIOLIN AND WRITING POETRY.

The patient got a little sick but recovered quickly. Then Dr. Jenner gave the patient a shot filled with smallpox, and the patient didn't get sick! Through his curiosity and willingness to try something new, Dr. Jenner discovered a vaccination for smallpox. He saved millions of lives.

God, open my eyes to what You'd like me to see.

FEBRUARY 27

DON BAYLOR

1949–2017 • UNITED STATES

ROAD TO MVP

The appetite of the diligent is richly supplied.

PROVERBS 13:4

Don sat on the bench next to his coach. "But I don't want to be traded! I want to keep playing for the Orioles!" Don was sad to leave the team where he'd made his MLB debut. His coaches there had taught Don a new respect for baseball. That meant playing every second with passion and attention, whether the first inning or the ninth. Respecting the game also meant dressing a certain way—uniforms worn properly, hair neat and clean. It also meant exercising and treating their bodies with care. "You're going to be an MVP someday," Don's coach said. And since Don had created a strong foundation of discipline and faith, a few years later he proved his coach right. Don was voted American League MVP in 1979.

> DON'S DISCIPLINE LED HIM TO A SUCCESSFUL CAREER AS AN MLB MANAGER.

*God, help me have "respect for my game,"
no matter what I'm doing.*

FEBRUARY 28

SAINT OSWALD OF YORK

C. 925–992 • NORTHUMBRIA (MODERN-DAY ENGLAND)

FAMILY GATHERING

"Where two or three people are gathered in
my name, I am there among them."

MATTHEW 18:20

Some folks are good at organizing items, like toys in a playroom. Some are good at organizing people. Saint Oswald was great at the latter! Oswald grew up with his uncle, the Archbishop of Canterbury. His uncle encouraged him to spend time in a monastery in France. Oswald enjoyed his time and saw the benefit of having Christian brothers to worship with and how the monastery was a place of learning. People could share ideas easily in one place!

DURING LENT, OSWALD WOULD WASH THE FEET OF TWELVE POOR MEN EACH DAY TO FOLLOW JESUS' EXAMPLE.

When Oswald returned to England, he established many monasteries and abbeys. He asked experts in math and astronomy to visit and share their findings. The monasteries and abbeys were also hubs for serving the poor and needy. Oswald showed the importance of gathering God's family together to do good work.

*God, thank You for the family You've given
me, both physical and spiritual!*

FEBRUARY 29

GEORGE WILLIAMS

1821–1905 • ENGLAND

STAYING CLOSE

I am continually with you; you hold my right hand.

PSALM 73:23

Factory smokestacks dotted the London skyline, and new shops were popping up everywhere. By 1844, more than 150,000 young men from surrounding farmlands were filling the streets, looking for work and lodging. Finding a safe place to live, surrounded by good people, was difficult. A young draper named George gathered ten young men, and together they launched the Young Men's Christian Association—also known as the YMCA! It was a safe space where they could escape the dangers of the streets. The Y eventually offered young men affordable lodging, Bible classes, English classes for immigrants, and gyms. George's desire to stay close to God eventually helped millions do the same, as YMCAs opened up in America and around the globe.

> IN 1891, JAMES NAISMITH, A YMCA TEACHER IN SPRINGFIELD, MASSACHUSETTS, INVENTED THE GAME OF BASKETBALL!

God, whenever I'm in a new place, help me to find You and stay close to You.

MARCH 1

SIR ISAAC NEWTON

1642–1727 • ENGLAND

AN OPEN MIND

Be transformed by the renewing of your mind, so
that you may discern what is the will of God.

ROMANS 12:2

Isaac was curious about the world God made. One day when he was home from college, he was sitting by an apple tree. When one of the apples fell to the ground, Isaac noticed it fell *straight* down, not sideways or upward. Later he observed if an object is moving, it tends to stay moving (and if it's resting, it stays resting). He also noticed if he pushed on an object, it pushed back with the same force but in the opposite direction. In 1687, Isaac published these ideas

> NASA SCIENTISTS USED ISAAC'S THREE LAWS OF MOTION TO SEND PEOPLE TO THE MOON!

in a book called *Principia Mathematica*, and science changed forever. In fact, scientists have been building on Isaac's ideas ever since. In Isaac's lifetime, his ideas weren't always popular with other scientists since they were different. But Isaac kept an open mind and courageously shared his brand-new ideas.

God, Your creation reveals so much we can learn.

MARCH 2

GIOTTO

C. 1266–1337 • ITALY

JUST LIKE ME

God created humankind in his image.

GENESIS 1:27

I'm going to do this a little differently, Giotto thought as he looked at the wall in front of him. Eventually known as "the father of European painting," Giotto changed art forever. For the thousand years before him, paintings were two-dimensional. The figures—people, places, plants, animals—looked flat, kind of like cartoons. Giotto had a vision to paint the world as it actually looks, with depth and expression, making it more natural and powerful for the viewer. Bible stories with lifelike three-dimensional characters suddenly came to life. Giotto's work became quite famous in his lifetime. He painted Bible characters and stories inside many churches and chapels, and his work continued to inspire artists a hundred years later during the Renaissance.

> GIOTTO WAS KNOWN TO FEATURE HIS FRIEND, THE WRITER DANTE, AS A BACKGROUND CHARACTER IN HIS PAINTINGS.

God, give me courage to try something new.

MARCH 3

DR. WANGARI MAATHAI

1940-2011 • KENYA

TREES OF LIFE

> "I will send down the showers in their season; they shall be showers of blessing. The trees of the field shall yield their fruit, and the earth shall yield its increase."
>
> **EZEKIEL 34:26-27**

Professor Wangari Maathai studied life on earth—plants, animals, and people. And she realized how important it was to treat God's creation with care, just as He had. Because if the humans and animals God made live in a place without clean air or water, and if the soil cannot grow plants, then God's living creatures cannot grow and thrive. So Dr. Maathai started the Green Belt Movement, which did a small thing to make a big difference for the planet: planting trees. Trees help clean the air, reduce energy costs, and improve people's health. Eventually, the Green Belt Movement planted more than 30 million trees in Kenya and inspired the United Nations to plant more than 11 billion trees around the world! On March 3, people celebrate both Wangari Maathai Day and Africa Environment Day.

> DR. MAATHAI WAS THE FIRST BLACK AFRICAN TO WIN A NOBEL PRIZE.

God, help me take good care of the planet You created.

MARCH 4

DESMOND TUTU

1931–2021 • SOUTH AFRICA

LIVE IN PEACE

If it is possible, so far as it depends on you, live peaceably with all.

ROMANS 12:18

Desmond, a priest and archbishop, believed everyone in South Africa could live together in peace, including the different African tribes and people from European countries or other places around the world. For much of Desmond's life, South Africa had been governed by a rule called *apartheid*. This meant people of different races were segregated, and any nonwhite person did not receive equal treatment. Desmond

> IN 1984, DESMOND WON THE NOBEL PEACE PRIZE.

believed this was against God's will and led peaceful protests against apartheid. He asked other countries to stop doing business with South Africa until apartheid was stopped. In the early 1990s, Desmond's plan worked! Apartheid was stopped, and the people of South Africa began to live in peace—together.

God, help us live in peace with our neighbors, no matter who they are.

MARCH 5

JACKIE ROBINSON

1919–1972 • UNITED STATES

TURN THE OTHER CHEEK

"Do not resist an evildoer. But if anyone strikes you on the right cheek, turn the other also."

MATTHEW 5:39

On April 15, 1947, Jackie made baseball history. As he jogged onto the field wearing a Brooklyn Dodgers uniform, Jackie became the first Black baseball player in a league filled with only white players. Jackie's choice was brave. He knew that many people wouldn't like to see a Black man playing with white players. But he had the full support of the Dodgers' president Branch Rickey, who was a Christian like Jackie. Branch asked Jackie if he'd join the team. He knew Jackie would face anger and hatred but asked if Jackie would be willing to "turn the other cheek," which meant Jackie wouldn't retaliate when others were unkind to him. Jackie said he would, even though it would be hard. Jackie's courage paved the way for talented players, regardless of their skin color, to play in the majors.

> JACKIE WAS AN IMMEDIATE SUCCESS ON THE FIELD! HE WAS VOTED ROOKIE OF THE YEAR AND EVENTUALLY HELPED THE DODGERS WIN A WORLD SERIES.

God, even when it's hard, help me turn the other cheek.

MARCH 6

JOHN BUNYAN

1628–1688 • ENGLAND

MAKING PROGRESS

"The scriptures . . . testify on my behalf."

JOHN 5:39

The Bible is the bestselling book of all time. For a long time, the second bestselling book was *The Pilgrim's Progress* by John Bunyan. John was a preacher who taught the Bible in ways people understood and got excited about. To reach more people than he could by preaching in his church, John decided to write *The Pilgrim's Progress*. It tells the story of a man named Christian who makes his way through the world to reach the Celestial City, a place like heaven. Christian meets people who both hurt and help him as he encounters obstacles on his journey. Readers understood these challenges because they had faced similar problems. Watching Christian navigate these moments helped readers think about ways they could navigate them too.

THE PILGRIM'S PROGRESS HAS BEEN TRANSLATED INTO MORE THAN 200 LANGUAGES!

God, thank You for books that show me how to stay close to You!

MARCH 7

DON MCCLANEN

1925–2016 • UNITED STATES

SLAM-DUNK FAITH

> I pray that the sharing of your faith may become effective when you perceive all the good that we may do for Christ.
>
> **PHILEMON V. 6**

When Don McClanen stood at the free throw line, he knew if he missed the shot, his teammates would have his back. He also knew if he messed up in life, God would have his back. Don grew up and became a basketball coach. He'd often see professional athletes in magazines talking about their favorite type of toothpaste or shaving cream. *Why aren't they talking about how they enjoy a relationship with Jesus?* he wondered. So Don began to look for athletes in magazines who talked about how their faith helped them, and he shared these articles with his team. Don's players were encouraged by the stories, and he knew other athletes would feel the same way. In 1954, Don helped start an organization called the Fellowship of Christian Athletes, where athletes could gather and share about their faith.

> MILLIONS OF ATHLETES HAVE JOINED FCA SINCE ITS FOUNDING.

God, help me share my faith journey with others.

MARCH 8

GEORGE FREDRIC HANDEL

1685–1759 • ENGLAND AND IRELAND

FAITH IN EVERY NOTE

Sing praises to him; tell of all his wonderful works.

PSALM 105:2

George was a gifted music composer who allowed his faith to lead the way. He didn't just want to entertain audiences; he wanted to make them "better people"! So he wrote musical pieces, called *oratorios*, about Bible characters. His most famous oratorio is called *Messiah*, which he wrote in only twenty-four days. People poured into grand concert halls across England and Ireland to hear the story of Jesus' birth. Some thought this music should be played only in churches, not in concert halls. But George thought that since God is everywhere, His music should be everywhere too. "I have read my Bible well and will choose for myself," he said. George's conviction brought the beauty of God's music to everyone.

> THE "HALLELUJAH" CHORUS, FROM *MESSIAH*, IS OFTEN SUNG AT CHRISTMAS, BUT HANDEL ACTUALLY WROTE IT FOR EASTER!

God, help me bring You everywhere so I can show Your light to as many as possible.

MARCH 9

BROTHER LAWRENCE

1614–1691 • FRANCE

LITTLE THINGS FOR GOD

Do everything in the name of the Lord Jesus.

COLOSSIANS 3:17

"We can do little things for God," said Brother Lawrence. For him, that meant keeping God in mind with every task he completed as a cook for his monastery. Every potato he peeled, every pot he scrubbed, he was thinking about God and thanking Him. Why? Because God had given Lawrence many blessings that allowed his work as a cook to happen. God gave sunshine and rain that allowed the potatoes to grow. God gave skill to the blacksmiths who made the iron pots Lawrence used to cook the potatoes in, and then later scrubbed. And God gave friendship to the brothers, who ate the potatoes together with thankful hearts. Lawrence did his humble work in the kitchen with great love for God.

> AFTER THIRTY YEARS AS A COOK, BROTHER LAWRENCE'S FEET GREW TIRED STANDING AT THE STOVE. HE DISCOVERED A NEW TALENT: AS A SANDAL MAKER!

God, help me remember that I don't have to do big things to worship You. Small things count too.

MARCH 10

C. S. Lewis

1898–1963 • ENGLAND

A NEW WAY TO SHARE

"As the heavens are higher than the earth, so are my ways higher than your ways and my thoughts than your thoughts."

ISAIAH 55:9

Clive Lewis's parents knew their son was bright. But they never expected him to learn to read by age three or write stories filled with animals dressed in clothes by age five. Eventually Clive became a college professor and wrote books about history and faith. But he remembered how much he enjoyed writing about animals and dreamed up a new tale. This time, the animals became heroes who helped children fight evil and bring goodness and light to the world. Through Clive's clever stories, he showed readers God's love. They became some of the bestselling books ever. *The Chronicles of Narnia* series has sold more than 100 million copies and helped millions connect with God in a new way.

> ONE OF C. S. LEWIS'S BEST FRIENDS WAS J. R. R. TOLKIEN, THE WRITER OF THE *LORD OF THE RINGS* SERIES!

God, help me remember that I can show others who You are in unexpected ways.

MARCH 11

WILLIAM TYNDALE

C. 1490–1536 • ENGLAND AND GERMANY

WORDS OF COURAGE

God did not give us a spirit of cowardice but rather a spirit of power and of love and of self-discipline.

2 TIMOTHY 1:7

William believed everyone should have the opportunity to read the Bible in their own language. That way, they could understand God's guidance for their lives. William began to translate the New Testament from Greek into English. But some people thought only priests should read and share the Scriptures. Those people tried to stop William, but he traveled from England to Germany so he could finish his translation. Eventually, some printed William's New Testament and sneaked copies into England for others to read. Meanwhile, William began to translate the Old Testament into English. But before he could finish, he was captured. By the time William died, more than 18,000 copies of his New Testament had been printed in English. His courage helped people learn more about God and deepen their faith.

> ONLY TWO COPIES OF WILLIAM'S NEW TESTAMENT CAN BE FOUND TODAY. YOU CAN FIND THEM AT LONDON'S BRITISH LIBRARY.

God, thank You for the example of William's courage. Help me to be brave like him.

MARCH 12

GEORGE HERBERT

1593–1633 • ENGLAND

CHANGE OF HEART

Those of steadfast mind you keep in
peace . . . because they trust in you.

ISAIAH 26:3

George was torn. He wasn't sure what kind of job he wanted to have! As a young man he was the orator, or the spokesperson, of Cambridge University. Many people wanted this job, because lots of orators went on to work at the royal court. And if you worked at court, you were considered important. But George was really good at writing poems that talked about how much he loved God. He thought maybe he'd enjoy working for the church. But he wasn't sure! For a while, he worked at the university and enjoyed how important the work made him feel. But eventually he realized his love for God was stronger than his desire to have a job that other people considered important. So he left his job, became a priest in the Church of England, and found the peace he was looking for. For the rest of his life, he was thankful he changed his mind.

> AFTER GEORGE DIED, HIS FRIEND NICHOLAS FERRAR PUBLISHED MANY OF HIS POEMS. THANKS TO NICHOLAS, GEORGE'S WORK SURVIVES TODAY.

*God, help me remember it's okay to change my mind,
especially when my new choice leads me closer to You.*

MARCH 13

CARL BLOCH

1834–1890 • DENMARK

DREAM CHANGE

May he remember all your offerings.

PSALM 20:3

Carl dreamed of becoming an artist, maybe painting pictures of important people or landscapes. But as he traveled through Italy, far from his home in Denmark, paintings that stretched across large, airy rooms showed Bible scenes he'd only imagined. And Carl's dream changed. He wanted to paint scenes from the Bible that would inspire people. Back at the Danish Royal Academy, he began painting Bible stories with

> CARL CREATED MORE THAN 250 PAINTINGS IN HIS LIFETIME!

a close attention to detail. People all over the country, including the king, loved them. The king asked Carl to create a series of paintings of Jesus' life to be hung in the castle. Carl's decision to change his big dream affected a whole nation—including a king!

God, help me to be unafraid to dream big—
and possibly to change my mind!

MARCH 14

IRA D. SANKEY

1840–1908 • UNITED STATES

YES TO CHANGE

I will sing to the Lord.

PSALM 13:6

Ira worked at his father's bank. But on the weekends, he loved to sing at church! One day, a famous preacher named Dwight Moody heard Ira sing. "Why don't you come sing for me, before I preach?" he asked. Dwight knew that music, and Ira's voice, would help people connect with God. But Ira hesitated—he'd have to leave his job and move his young family from Pennsylvania to Chicago. Were they ready for such a huge change? Ira didn't know what God had planned for him, but he said yes. Ira and Dwight traveled the world together, singing and preaching about God. Ira even became a famous gospel music songwriter. Ira's yes helped many people know God.

> WHILE ATTENDING A CHURCH SERVICE IN LONDON, IRA SANG FOR QUEEN VICTORIA!

God, help me use my gift to help others.

MARCH 15

BABE RUTH

1895–1948 • UNITED STATES

MAKE TIME FOR GOD

Devote yourselves to prayer.

COLOSSIANS 4:2

Babe Ruth changed the entire game of baseball. Before Babe, not many players hit home runs. The most in a season had been twenty-seven. But Babe set a brand-new record of sixty home runs! Thanks to Babe's big hits, his team, the New York Yankees, won many games.

Everyone wanted Babe on their team. After games, Babe would go back to his apartment in New York City and look at the twinkling lights of the skyscrapers around him. And in front of the window, Babe would kneel to pray. He asked God to help him live in a way that would measure up to what God expected of him. This larger-than-life man who dominated the baseball diamond stayed humble before his great big God.

> BABE WON SEVEN WORLD SERIES CHAMPIONSHIPS. ONLY THREE PLAYERS HAVE WON MORE!

God, help me make time to talk to You and remember what a great God You are.

MARCH 16

KEITH GREEN

1953–1982 • UNITED STATES

A BETTER DREAM

I will praise the LORD as long as I live.

PSALM 146:2

When Keith was a boy, his mother discovered he was a gifted singer and piano player. Keith knew from an early age he wanted to be a star. He signed a record deal when he was only eleven but didn't have much success. *What if I don't achieve my dream?* he wondered. Keith decided to quit music for a while. During that time, he discovered a better dream: becoming a Christian. Keith started writing songs again, this time using his music to praise God and help others get to know Him. Onstage, Keith would tell the audience to worship Jesus with both their mouths *and* their lives. He knew how much better life is when you live for God.

> KEITH WANTED EVERYONE TO HAVE HIS MUSIC. HE SENT MORE THAN 200,000 FREE ALBUMS TO PRISONERS AND THE POOR.

God, I want my whole life to reflect You!
Help me to look like You in all I do.

MARCH 17

DR. HAROLD MOODY

1882–1947 • JAMAICA AND ENGLAND

HEALING BODY AND SOUL

In everything do to others as you would have them to do to you.

MATTHEW 7:12

Growing up in Jamaica, Harold committed his life to Jesus and wanted to become a doctor. He traveled to London for medical school and graduated at the top of his class. But no one would hire him because he was Black. So Dr. Moody opened his own practice and treated everyone, even if they couldn't pay. When Dr. Moody heard that other Black professionals were denied jobs because of their race, he talked to the people at those jobs and asked them to reconsider. Dr. Moody also challenged the government for denying his son military service because of his race. As a result, the laws were changed. Dr. Moody even changed the way people of color were talked about in the news. Because of Dr. Moody's deep faith, he committed himself to loving others and helping them flourish physically and socially.

> IN 1931, DR. MOODY FOUNDED A GROUP CALLED THE LEAGUE OF COLORED PEOPLES TO FIGHT FOR EQUALITY IN THE UK AND ABROAD.

God, thank You for Dr. Moody's example of courage and love. Help me model it today.

MARCH 18

JEANETTE LI

1899–1968 • CHINA

STAYING TRUE TO GOD

Do not fret because of the wicked.... Trust in the LORD and do good.

PSALM 37:1, 3

Jeanette Li had a big problem. She had a sick mother and a young son to care for but not much money. Attending college would help her get a good job. But when she applied to a government college in China, they said she needed to give up her Christian faith. But Jeanette refused to do that. This wasn't the last time her faith would be tested. In 1950, the Communist Party began putting Christians in prison, including Jeanette. But even there, she shared about Jesus with guards and other prisoners. Eventually, Jeanette was released. She traveled to Hong Kong and the United States, where she talked about her faith with anyone who would listen.

> JEANETTE'S SON, MIN CHIU LI, BECAME A CANCER RESEARCHER. HE WAS THE FIRST DOCTOR TO USE CHEMOTHERAPY TO CURE A MALIGNANT TUMOR.

*God, I know You'll always take care of
me. Help me stay close to You.*

MARCH 19

THOMAS COLE

1801–1848 • UNITED STATES

WHAT A WONDERFUL WORLD!

In him all things in heaven and on earth were created.

COLOSSIANS 1:16

Seventeen-year-old Thomas paced the ship, excited to disembark. He wasn't in England anymore; he was about to start his new life in America! Thomas's family settled in Philadelphia. And soon, Thomas was off to travel the country, painting signs and portraits in exchange for a place to sleep. In 1826, Thomas went to the Catskill Mountains. There, he began to paint the mountains and valleys, rivers and forests, for the first time. He became the first painter to capture the natural beauty of America! Thomas was awestruck by this beauty, certain that it held a promise from God for a new beginning. Along with painting the land he loved, Thomas also used his canvas to create images of Christians finding hope and comfort in their faith.

THOMAS WAS THE FOUNDER OF THE FAMOUS PAINTING GROUP THE HUDSON RIVER SCHOOL.

God, thank You for the beautiful world You made!

MARCH 20

ALESSANDRO VOLTA

1745–1827 • LOMBARDY (MODERN-DAY ITALY)

FOLLOW THE SPARKS

Open my eyes, so that I may behold wondrous things out of your law.

PSALM 119:18

Something's not adding up, Alessandro thought to himself. From youth, Alessandro had been fascinated by electricity. He wanted to learn all he could about it! By the time he was eighteen, he was writing letters to accomplished scientists asking questions about electricity. In 1780, Alessandro heard of a scientist named Luigi Galvani who said he'd discovered *animal electricity*, something Alessandro had never heard of. Luigi said frogs could produce electricity in their bodies. But the experiment didn't make sense. So Alessandro decided to follow his curiosity and show that he didn't need an animal to produce electricity. Alessandro put together a stack of metal discs of zinc and silver with a piece of soaked cloth between them. And that's how Alessandro created the world's first battery! Alessandro believed his scientific work was evidence of God's intelligence.

> IN 1881, THE UNIT USED TO MEASURE ELECTRIC FORCE WAS NAMED THE *VOLT* IN ALESSANDRO'S HONOR.

God, help me follow the sparks of my curiosity!

MARCH 21

OSWALD CHAMBERS

1874-1917 • SCOTLAND

LEAP OF FAITH

We walk by faith, not by spirit.

2 CORINTHIANS 5:7

What am I supposed to do? thought Oswald. He was a gifted artist and musician, and he was sure God would call him to serve through art. But as a student at the University of Edinburgh, Oswald suddenly wasn't certain of God's path for him. *Maybe*, Oswald thought, *God is calling me to become a minister*. This would mean Oswald needed to change schools—and also his entire life. He wouldn't create art or spend time with artists. He would need to travel to talk to people who were lost. It was scary, but Oswald

> OSWALD WROTE A BOOK CALLED *MY UTMOST FOR HIS HIGHEST,* WHICH MANY PEOPLE STILL READ TODAY.

decided to follow where his faith was leading. He became a minister and traveled around Scotland, Ireland, Japan, and the US. "Faith never knows where it is being led," said Oswald, "but it loves and knows the One who is leading."

God, I trust that You will lead me where You want me to go.

MARCH 22

MEV PULEO

1963–1996 • UNITED STATES

BRIDGE THE GAP

The rich and the poor have this in common:
the Lord is the maker of them all.

PROVERBS 22:2

When Mev was fourteen years old, she was riding a bus with her parents in Rio de Janeiro. She was excited to finally see the famous statue of Jesus called *Christ the Redeemer*. While riding the steep road to look at the statue, Mev noticed that on one side of the hill were large, luxurious homes that stretched down to the beaches below. On the other side were small, rundown shacks, with children begging in the streets. Mev knew God had given her a mission to create a bridge between those two places. She became a talented photographer and took pictures of the poverty she saw. Mev believed she could show the world that others they might ignore are full of hopes, dreams, and dignity.

> IN 1995, MEV RECEIVED THE US CATHOLIC AWARD FOR CHAMPIONING THE CAUSE OF WOMEN IN THE CHURCH.

God, help me show love and dignity to every person, no matter who they are.

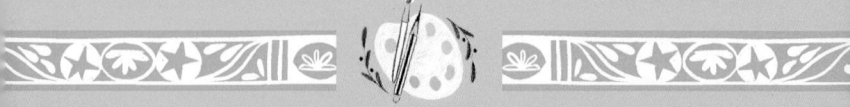

MARCH 23

CLAUDIO GRANZOTTO

1900–1947 • ITALY

MEET THE CHALLENGE

*You need endurance, so that when you have done the
will of God, you may receive what was promised.*

HEBREWS 10:36

Some people meet challenges with courage, working to make the best of the situation. That's how Claudio was. When Claudio was nine, his father died. Claudio began working in the fields with his family to get by. When he was fifteen, he was drafted to fight in World War I. After the war, Claudio eagerly returned to school, where he discovered his gift for sculpting. After school, he made friends with a Franciscan priest and decided to become a Franciscan brother. Claudio focused on serving the poor and creating sculptures that brought people closer to God. Most of his sculptures depict Jesus and the saints, and people still grow closer to God through his work today.

> WHEN CLAUDIO BECAME A FRANCISCAN BROTHER, HIS PARISH PRIEST WROTE, "THE ORDER IS RECEIVING NOT ONLY AN ARTIST BUT A SAINT."

*God, help me make the most of every
situation, no matter how easy or hard.*

MARCH 24

SAINT ÓSCAR ROMERO

1917–1980 • EL SALVADOR

STAND UP SELFLESSLY

"You shall not profit by the blood of your neighbor."

LEVITICUS 19:16

Saint Óscar Romero, the archbishop of San Salvador, was tired of watching the poor, innocent people in his country of El Salvador suffer violence from people who wanted to take power. Many innocent people had been killed as two groups fought for government control. During one of his weekly radio sermons, Óscar was bolder than ever. "You kill your own brothers, but the law of God says, 'Do not kill.' So in the name of God and in the name of this long-suffering people, I beg you: Cease this repression!" Speaking this courageously was dangerous, but Óscar had mourned too many deaths to be silent. The next day, while celebrating Mass, Óscar lost his life. He selflessly spoke up for the people he served, even to the end.

> ÓSCAR WAS NOMINATED FOR A NOBEL PEACE PRIZE IN 1979.

*God, thank You for Saint Óscar's courage
to speak out against violence.*

MARCH 25

JOVITA IDAR

1885–1946 • UNITED STATES

PROBLEM SOLVER

Be strong and courageous . . . for the LORD your
God is with you wherever you go.

JOSHUA 1:9

Jovita knew that big problems could be solved with two things: education and courage. She was a journalist at her father's newspaper. She often shared stories that weren't easy to write about. Jovita wrote about people who weren't being treated fairly or equally. She wrote to encourage women to campaign for the right to vote. Some people didn't like this. Their lives were easier if things stayed just the way they were. They arranged for Jovita's newspaper to be shut down. But Jovita kept writing on behalf of people who weren't getting fair treatment. She also volunteered as an interpreter for Spanish-speaking hospital patients so they could get the care they needed. Later she was an editor for her church's publication. Jovita never backed down from a challenge—especially when she was defending what she believed was right.

> JOVITA WAS KNOWN TO OFTEN SAY, "WHEN YOU EDUCATE A WOMAN, YOU EDUCATE A FAMILY."

*God, give me the knowledge and courage to
solve problems that come my way.*

MARCH 26

HARRIET POWERS

1837–1910 • UNITED STATES

SEW COOL

"Tell [your friends] how much the Lord has done for you."

MARK 5:19

People attending the cotton fair in Athens, Georgia, slowed down when they approached Harriet's quilt. They needed time to take in the eleven Bible stories Harriet had created with different colors and patterns of fabric. Harriet's quilt told the stories of Adam and Eve, the Last Supper, even Jesus' crucifixion and resurrection. Harriet had likely developed her skill as a quilter during her earliest days, when she was an enslaved person on a plantation in Georgia. Using a storytelling technique called *appliqué*, which originated in West Africa, Harriet created a beautiful quilt showing God's story of love. The quilt stopped viewers in their tracks. And it is still causing viewers to stop and think! Today the Bible Quilt hangs at the Smithsonian in Washington, DC.

> THE BIBLE QUILT WASN'T HARRIET'S ONLY QUILT TO TELL BIBLE STORIES. ANOTHER QUILT SHOWS FIFTEEN STORIES, INCLUDING JONAH AND THE BIG FISH AND THE LIFE OF JOB.

God, help me use my unique gifts to show others how awesome You are!

MARCH 27

ROGER MARIS

1934–1985 • UNITED STATES

WHO AM I?

Lord, you have searched me and known me.

PSALM 139:1

I wish those reporters would just leave me alone, Roger thought. He loved playing baseball for the New York Yankees. He and his teammate, the legendary hitter Mickey Mantle, were batting so well that they were both close to breaking the all-time home run record set by Babe Ruth thirty years before. But sometimes Roger wished he *wasn't* doing so great. Reporters would whip up untrue stories to sell more newspapers. They said that Roger, who'd only been with the team for a year, didn't deserve to break the record like Yankees veteran Mickey. They even hounded Roger at church with questions about his "feud" with Mickey. But Roger knew reporters couldn't tell him who he was; only God could do that. He kept playing his hardest. And then, late in the season, he broke Babe's record!

ROGER'S RECORD OF SIXTY-ONE HOME RUNS IN A SINGLE SEASON STOOD FOR THIRTY-SEVEN YEARS.

God, thank You for telling me who I am!

MARCH 28

BLAISE PASCAL

1623–1662 • FRANCE

SHARE YOUR FAITH

"Everyone therefore who acknowledges me before others,
I also will acknowledge before my Father in heaven."

MATTHEW 10:32

Blaise was a *genius*—someone with exceptional intelligence, creativity, or ability in a subject—in math and physics. More importantly, Blaise was a genius in his faith. When Blaise was about thirty, he had an experience that convinced him God was real. After that, he started to think about how to help other people find God. That includes the way believers like you talk to others! First, he said, present your ideas about faith in a way that is well-researched, open-minded, and helpful. Next, show people how your faith has helped

PASCAL AUTHORED "PASCAL'S PRINCIPLE," WHICH MAKES THE SCIENCE OF HYDRAULICS— THINGS LIKE FANS, TURBINES, BRAKES, AND DAMS—POSSIBLE.

you. Talk about the peace it's given you. Talk about the loving relationships you've found, your strength on hard days, your hope for a brighter tomorrow. When people see and hear these things, they'll be excited to learn more about Jesus and will become believers themselves.

God, give me the words to tell others about You.

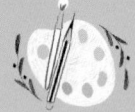

MARCH 29

DIEGO VELÁZQUEZ

1599–1660 • SPAIN

PAY ATTENTION!

Those who are attentive to a matter will prosper.

PROVERBS 16:20

Diego was a noticer. He noticed the way sunlight and shadow fell across folds of fabric. He observed a sleeping dog and saw how the browns, tans, and creamy whites blended together in its downy fur. He was skilled at seeing what many overlooked—and one brushstroke at a time, painting what he saw, often lifelike images or scenes that reflected his faith. No one painted quite like Diego. With a few colors and brushes, he could create stunning realistic images on canvas. To improve his skill, Diego also studied the techniques of artists before him, such as Italian painter Titian. He knew that if he paid attention, he would see small details that reflected the world God made.

> DIEGO PAINTED A PORTRAIT OF YOUNG KING PHILIP IV. PHILIP WAS SO DELIGHTED BY THE PAINTING THAT ONLY DIEGO COULD PAINT HIM FROM THEN ON!

God, help me notice the small blessings that bring joy to my world.

MARCH 30

SAINT PETER REGALADO

1390–1456 • SPAIN

FOCUS!

Looking to Jesus the pioneer and perfecter of faith.

HEBREWS 12:2

Peter's family was wealthy. But at age thirteen, he decided to give up his life of comfort to learn more about God. Peter lived with friars, or a brotherhood of Christians, who spent much of their days in quiet prayer, along with reading spiritual books and doing chores. The men didn't have many possessions and dedicated their time and attention to God. Eventually Peter became the leader of the brothers. He was known for his compassion and generosity for people in need. He brought many people to the convent where the brothers lived, feeding them and caring for them himself. For most of the year, Peter gave up eating meat and dairy, eating mostly bread and drinking water so he could spend more time focusing on God.

> PETER OFTEN WORSHIPPED WITH SO MUCH PASSION THAT HE WAS, UNASHAMEDLY, MOVED TO TEARS.

God, help me keep my focus on You!

MARCH 31

CHRISTINA ROSETTI

1830–1894 • ENGLAND

NEVER-CHANGING GOD

Jesus Christ is the same yesterday and today and forever.

HEBREWS 13:8

Christina was one of the greatest poets of her era. From the time she was a child, she wrote about all kinds of things—princes, nursery rhymes, even goblins at a market. But a huge portion of her poems were about God. Christina suffered many losses in her life. Her father died when she was young. Her family didn't have a lot of money, and everyone had to pitch in to pay for the basics. She broke off her engagement with someone because he changed his mind about his religious beliefs. Her poetry was criticized by reviewers and sometimes even her own siblings. But Christina knew one thing for certain: God was always with her. Many readers enjoyed reading her poems about God, considering them devotionals they could be inspired by.

> BEFORE HER DEATH, CHRISTINA HAD BEEN CONSIDERED AS A POSSIBLE SUCCESSOR TO POET LAUREATE ALFRED, LORD TENNYSON.

God, no matter what happens, help me remember I can always rely on Your love.

APRIL 1

CATHERINE MARSHALL

1914–1983 • UNITED STATES

STORY OF FAITH

[Jesus] told them many things in parables.

MATTHEW 13:3

"Just one more story, Mama," Catherine pleaded. She loved hearing her mother's stories from when she was a young schoolteacher in the Smoky Mountains of Tennessee. Catherine's mother had come from a larger city and was shocked that mountain homes didn't have electricity or running water and didn't see any need for a teacher. Catherine marveled at the way her mother talked about her students and the residents, how strong they were and how their faith gave them hope to get through hard times. When Catherine grew up, she became a writer and told her mother's story in a novel called *Christy*. Catherine was one of the first people to write a novel with faith woven into its pages. Millions of readers were inspired by the story filled with hope and faith.

AN AWARD IS NAMED AFTER ONE OF CATHERINE'S BOOKS! THE CHRISTY AWARD IS GIVEN EVERY YEAR TO HONOR A NOVEL THAT TELLS A CHRISTIAN STORY WITH EXCELLENCE, IMAGINATION, AND CREATIVITY.

God, thank You for stories that give me hope.

APRIL 2

PELÉ

1940–2022 • BRAZIL

SCORING GOALS

Every generous act of giving, with every perfect gift, is from above.

JAMES 1:17

At seventeen, a young soccer superstar named Pelé helped Brazil win its first-ever World Cup. Pelé not only kicked the ball powerfully—he also seemed to know what the other team's players would do! But Pelé knew where his talent came from: "God gave me the gift of knowing how to play football," he said. As one of the most famous players in the world, Pelé could have focused on money and fame. But he didn't. At the World Cup in 1970, Pelé led his teammates in prayer each night. Instead of praying to win games, they prayed for the sick, the poor, and those affected by the war in Vietnam. He even opened "Olympic villages" around Brazil so kids could learn to play soccer. Pelé knew winning wasn't the most important goal in the world—honoring God and caring for others was.

> PELÉ ALSO COMPOSED MUSIC, INCLUDING THE MUSICAL SCORE FOR A MOVIE ABOUT HIS LIFE!

God, help me keep my focus on what's really important: serving others in Your name.

APRIL 3

RENÉ DESCARTES

1596–1650 • FRANCE AND THE NETHERLANDS

TRUTH SEEKERS

I the L ORD speak the truth.

ISAIAH 45:19

René studied many things: math, science, philosophy. But one subject intrigued him more than any other: finding the truth. René believed that God gave people the ability to use their brains to learn if something was true. That might mean using a science experiment to explain what makes up a rainbow or using physics to explain how the earth moves around the sun. René also believed that sometimes humans wouldn't be able to find the answers to everything. But trying to find the answers would help them understand their infinite God a little bit better. And above all, he thought, humans should put their faith in God instead of in their own judgment. René's ways of thinking helped scientists and philosophers see their work in a whole new way.

> RENÉ COINED THE FAMOUS PHRASE "I THINK; THEREFORE, I AM."

God, thanks for my brain and that I can learn about the world You made.

APRIL 4

HANNAH MORE

1745–1833 • ENGLAND

LEARNING LIGHTS THE WAY

Make me to know your ways, O Lord; teach me your paths.

PSALM 25:4

Hannah loved to learn. Learning to read expanded the worlds she could explore. Learning math helped her calculate the supplies needed to survive a harsh winter. Learning about God grew her love for the world and for all people. Hannah's family had the money to hire her teachers, but many children weren't so lucky. In addition to her writings, Hannah and her sister opened schools where children could learn to read, study Scripture, and even master skills for their professions. Hannah persevered despite those who didn't want to bring education to women and the poor.

HANNAH WAS ALSO AN ACCOMPLISHED WRITER. ABOLITIONIST WILLIAM WILBERFORCE USED HER POEM "SLAVERY, A POEM" TO ARGUE IN PARLIAMENT AGAINST SLAVERY.

God, help me to keep learning about
You and the world You made.

APRIL 5

DONATELLO

C. 1386–1466 • ITALY

WHAT'S OLD IS NEW

Ask for the ancient paths, where the good way lies; and walk in it.

JEREMIAH 6:16

Donatello's art was so lifelike that viewers thought his sculptures might walk right off their pedestals! He was the first sculptor since the ancient Greeks and Romans to create a *freestanding* sculpture not attached to a building. The sculpture was carved all the way around, making the figure seem more lifelike. Donatello tried his hand at (and mastered!) sculpting with many kinds of materials: marble, wax, stone, glass, even bronze. He was passionate about bringing back older techniques from the Classical period. Thanks to Donatello, Bible characters weren't stuck on a page. His sculptures of people like David, John the Baptist, and Mary Magdalene helped Christians imagine what they must have been like in real life.

> DONATELLO RARELY REPEATED HIMSELF IN HIS ARTISTIC CREATIONS. HE ALWAYS WANTED TO EXPERIMENT WITH NEW SUBJECTS AND TECHNIQUES.

God, remind me to stay open to learning from others.

APRIL 6

CHIUNE SUGIHARA

1900–1986 • JAPAN AND LITHUANIA

STANDING UP FOR WHAT'S GOOD

Is not this the fast that I choose: to loose the bonds
of injustice . . . to let the oppressed go free?

ISAIAH 58:6

A government representative for his country, Japan, Chiune was sent to Lithuania in 1939 to set up a consulate. Part of his job was to help people get the correct paperwork to travel to Japan. Chiune became friends with many people in Lithuania, including Jewish people. When World War II began and the Nazi army invaded, the Jewish people weren't safe. Some asked Chiune to help them escape. Chiune loved God and knew that what the Nazis were doing was wrong. Even though Japan wouldn't approve the travel forms, Chiune knew he had to do something. He signed the travel forms and helped nearly 2,000 Jews escape Lithuania. Chiune ultimately lost his job for disobeying, but those lives were saved because of his effort.

> **CHIUNE KNEW RUSSIAN AND WAS THE FIRST JAPANESE DIPLOMAT IN LITHUANIA.**

*God, give me the courage to do what
is right, even when it's hard.*

APRIL 7

WILLIAM WORDSWORTH

1770–1850 • ENGLAND

NEVER ALONE

> Even though I walk through the darkest valley,
> I fear no evil; for you are with me.
>
> **PSALM 23:4**

William knew what it was like to feel alone. He lost his mom when he was seven years old, then his dad when he was thirteen. Back then, when children lost their parents, they were sent to live at different schools, even if they had siblings. As he grew older, William met others who missed people they'd lost. He didn't want anyone who was lonely to think they were alone. So he decided to write poems about his feelings, what he had gone through, and how God had helped him. William also loved nature and spent lots of time outside. He thought poems should address both the hard and beautiful things people experience. For 200 years, people have found hope and joy in William's poetry.

> AS AN ADULT, WILLIAM REUNITED WITH HIS SISTER DOROTHY. THEY WERE NEVER SEPARATED AGAIN.

God, thank You for the poems, stories, and people who remind us that we aren't alone.

APRIL 8

WOLFGANG AMADEUS MOZART

1756–1791 • AUSTRIA

MUSIC THAT HONORS YOU

It is good to give thanks to the Lord,
to sing praises to your name.

PSALM 92:1

"Come see the miracle which God let be born in Salzburg," said Leopold Mozart to audiences around Europe, as they waited to hear the boy at the piano begin to play. Leopold was talking about his son, Wolfgang Amadeus Mozart. By age four, little Wolfgang was playing songs on the harpsichord, an early form of the piano. By age five, he was writing his own music. Wolfgang became one of the greatest composers who ever lived. He wrote many pieces that could be played in churches. Some were songs of praise, about God's glory. Some pieces reminded people that God was with them in their grief. Wolfgang could have chosen to create music only for audiences in opera houses or royal courts. But he composed music that helped people grow closer to God.

> MOZART HAD A PET BIRD CALLED A STARLING. HE EVEN WROTE A SONG BY COPYING THE BIRD'S TUNE!

God, thank You for the special talents You have given me. I want to use them to honor You.

APRIL 9

OCTAVIA HILL

1838–1912 • ENGLAND

TURNING HARD INTO HOPE

> God . . . consoles us in all our affliction, so that we may be
> able to console those who are in any affliction with the
> consolation with which we ourselves are consoled by God.
>
> **2 CORINTHIANS 1:3-4**

Octavia was born into a comfortable home. But when she was thirteen, her father's business failed and everything changed. Octavia was suddenly sent to work with her mother, where she was saddened by the difficulties poor people faced. Later, Octavia had the opportunity to create better housing opportunities for the poor by renting out properties through a landlord. She worked to charge lower rents and helped tenants create community and find pride in their homes. She also knew that people needed places outside their homes where they could get fresh air. Octavia worked with others to create parks so people could enjoy nature. She turned something difficult—her dad losing their family's wealth—into a way of knowing how to help others.

> OCTAVIA'S WORK TO CREATE GREEN SPACES EVENTUALLY FORMED ENGLAND'S NATIONAL TRUST. TODAY THE TRUST MANAGES MORE THAN 500 OUTDOOR SPACES!

*God, open my eyes to the ways I can use
my hardships to help others.*

APRIL 10

FRED ROGERS

1928–2003 • UNITED STATES

A GOOD NEIGHBOR

Love your neighbor as yourself.

LEVITICUS 19:18

"Won't you be my neighbor?" Fred would sing at the beginning of his show, *Mister Rogers' Neighborhood*. Fred was a minister who believed two big truths: that television was a powerful way to reach people, and that loving our neighbor is the best thing we can learn to do. Even kids! Fred knew that sometimes life can feel confusing, lonely, and scary, especially when we try to deal with problems by ourselves. Fred wanted to show kids that it's okay to feel big feelings and that feelings are less scary when we talk about them. So he talked about hard things like war, divorce, and how we treat those who are different from us. For more than thirty years, Fred taught millions of children to love each other the way God loves us. He showed a generation how to be good neighbors.

FRED WROTE MORE THAN 200 SONGS, INCLUDING THE THEME SONG TO HIS SHOW!

God, help me love my neighbor as myself, just as You do.

APRIL 11

ANTOINE LAVOISIER

1743–1794 • FRANCE

DISCOVERY QUEST

Great are the works of the LORD, studied by all who delight in them.

PSALM 111:2

What happens to an object when you set it on fire? What is water made of? These questions about God's creation kept Antoine, a lawyer, up at night. Antoine spent most of his time at a desk, figuring out how to collect taxes or make the military more efficient. But Antoine's passion was looking for answers about the natural world. He'd build his own chemistry equipment, conduct experiments, and record his findings. His wife, Marie Anne, was a gifted artist who drew the equipment and experiments so other chemists could test the experiments too. No one did this back then! Antoine's work ultimately led chemists to create the periodic table of elements, which describes the small particles that make up the world we live in. Today Antoine is known as the "Father of Modern Chemistry."

> ANTOINE SERVED ON A COMMITTEE TRYING TO UNIFY SYSTEMS OF WEIGHTS AND MEASURES. THIS RESULTED IN THE METRIC SYSTEM.

God, I want to keep discovering more about You.

APRIL 12

HANK STRAM

1923–2005 • UNITED STATES

TEACHING BY EXAMPLE

Give instruction to the wise, and they will become wiser still.

PROVERBS 9:9

Coach Stram was more than a coach. To many he was known as "The Mentor." A coach might instruct you, but a mentor is someone trustworthy who *guides* you. And that's who Coach Stram was to his players. He knew his players' football careers wouldn't last forever, so he also coached them to become the best *people* they could be. He did that by teaching players to excel at the basics—in whatever they were doing. He taught them to think creatively about how they played (Coach Stram made many innovations in how the game of football was played that are still used today). He was adamant that all players have the opportunity to play, no matter the color of their skin. Coach Stram mentored by his example.

> COACH STRAM WAS KNOWN AS A SNAZZY DRESSER. ON GAME DAY, HE'D WEAR SUITS THAT COORDINATED WITH HIS TEAM'S COLORS!

God, thank You for the mentors in my life.

APRIL 13

LEWIS CARROLL

1832–1898 • ENGLAND

DOWN THE RABBIT HOLE

> He has filled him with divine spirit, with
> skill, intelligence, and knowledge.
>
> **EXODUS 35:31**

Lewis was a young math professor and church deacon. He had a big imagination and had grown up with younger siblings, so he was good at telling stories that would entertain his boss's three daughters. One day, he told a story about Alice, a girl at a picnic who spotted a rabbit with a pocket watch, then decided to follow the rabbit down his rabbit hole. Lewis described a world filled with a grinning cat, a Queen of Hearts, and even an unbirthday party. The girls were captivated by Lewis's story. Lewis wondered if the story could be turned into a book. He'd never written a book before—he worked with numbers! But Lewis took a leap of faith, followed his own imagination down a rabbit hole, and published the story. By the time he died, *Alice's Adventures in Wonderland* was the most popular children's book in England.

> THE OLDEST DAUGHTER OF LEWIS'S BOSS WAS NAMED . . . ALICE!

*God, thank You for my imagination—and
the courage to try something new.*

APRIL 14

BLESSED PETER GONZALEZ

1190–1246 • SPAIN

THE RIGHT REASONS

Humble yourselves therefore under the mighty hand of God, so that he may exalt you in due time.

1 PETER 5:6

Peter smiled as he rode into the town of Astorga. The new job his uncle, a bishop, had gotten for him at the cathedral would make him very respected. But as Peter rode through the city gates, his horse tripped! Peter fell into the mud just as people stepped outside their houses to admire the cathedral's newest clergyman. The embarrassing incident stayed in his mind for a long time. And then Peter realized—his attitude had been all wrong! Peter had made his new job all about how it made him look instead of about serving the church members. Peter decided to change his attitude. He became a priest and an insightful preacher. Eventually he began advising the Spanish king Ferdinand III. He reminded Ferdinand to treat everyone—Spanish citizens and their defeated enemies—with compassion.

> PETER IS ALSO KNOWN AS "SAINT ELMO."

God, help me remember to serve You for all the right reasons!

APRIL 15

SAINT CÉSAR DE BUS

1544–1607 • FRANCE

THE RIGHT LIFE FOR ME

*Do not swerve to the right or to the left;
turn your foot away from evil.*

PROVERBS 4:27

Like so many young people, César had no idea what to do with his life. When he finished school, he came to a crossroads: either begin a quiet life surrounded by books and writing, or pursue a life of travel and adventure in the military. César first chose his pen and wrote a few plays. But he got bored and decided to fight with the army! But what awaited César at the battlefield made his stomach turn. The brutality of war was not for him *at all*. César fell ill and thought about his life again: He was going to become a priest. César began to teach the Bible to children and families in out of the way places. César ended up doing what he loved—working with words while on an adventure, with God by his side!

> CÉSAR ESTABLISHED TWO NEW RELIGIOUS COMMUNITIES TO SHARE IN THE WORK OF TEACHING KIDS AND FAMILIES ABOUT GOD!

God, show me which path is right for me.

APRIL 16

FLOYD PATTERSON

1935–2006 • UNITED STATES

GOLD-HEARTED CHAMPION

The integrity of the upright guides them.

PROVERBS 11:3

Floyd was committed to do things the right way. If one of his boxing opponents fell, Floyd was quick to help them up. If he saw a rival practicing before a match, Floyd didn't stick around. He thought it would be unfair to study the boxer's moves. This integrity extended outside the ring too. Floyd stood alongside Martin Luther King Jr. to fight for civil rights. When Floyd had begun his boxing career, many arenas weren't integrated. A crowd in Arkansas one time refused to let him into the arena—until a priest intervened. Meeting that priest was a turning point in Floyd's faith. He became active in his community's Catholic church. He even volunteered to distribute Holy Communion at a local nursing home. Floyd was committed to being the best man he could be, inside and out.

> AT AGE TWENTY-ONE, FLOYD BECAME THE WORLD'S YOUNGEST HEAVYWEIGHT BOXING CHAMPION.

God, help me commit to doing right, no matter where I am.

APRIL 17

BERNHARD RIEMANN

1826–1866 • GERMANY

I'M NERVOUS!

When I am afraid, I put my trust in you.

PSALM 56:3

Young Bernhard was shy. He didn't like to speak up in class or spend time with people he didn't know well. But he did love one thing, besides his family: math! In high school, he solved equations faster than his teachers. They gave him a complex 900-page book about math. Bernhard read it in six days! As he grew older, Bernhard kept studying math and felt it was his way to serve God. But how would he make money doing it? His profes-

> BERNHARD'S WORK IN GEOMETRY HELPED ALBERT EINSTEIN DISCOVER HIS FAMOUS THEORY OF RELATIVITY!

sors encouraged him to teach. This meant Bernhard would have to talk in front of students. And before *that*, he'd have to give a long talk about math in front of his professors. Bernhard was so nervous. But he gave the talk anyway. And his professors were blown away!

God, help me to be brave when I'm scared.

APRIL 18

BLESSED JAMES OLDO

1364–1404 • ITALY

WHAT REALLY MATTERS

This is my prayer, that your love may overflow more
. . . to help you to determine what is best.

PHILIPPIANS 1:9–10

James had always had plenty of everything: food and books, luxury and comfort. He and his wife, Caterina, had three children, and a life of never-ending good times seemed to stretch before them. But then a disease began to spread among the town. When two of James's children died, he suddenly realized they had been living all wrong. Instead of living for pleasure, they needed to help others. James decided to turn their house into a hospital. At first, Caterina objected. How could they stay safe if they invited sick people into their home? But she saw what God was doing in her husband. Later, after Caterina died, James became a priest. His house was transformed again, this time into a place where groups of people could pray. He inspired many others to dedicate their lives to God.

> JAMES IS BURIED IN THE CHURCH OF SAINT JULIAN, WHICH HE HAD GIVEN THE MONEY TO BUILD.

God, help me realize what really matters in life: serving You.

APRIL 19

BILLY SUNDAY

1862–1935 • UNITED STATES

CHANGE OF CALL

> I heard the voice of the Lord saying, "Whom shall I send, and who will go for us?" And I said, "Here am I: send me!"
>
> **ISAIAH 6:8**

Billy was a baseball player for the Chicago White Sox when he became a Christian. But over the next seven years, he felt God calling him to preach to crowds instead of playing baseball in front of them! When Billy left his career as a center fielder, he began to preach to some of the largest groups any preacher had been in front of in America. Some estimate that Billy preached to as many as 100 million people! How did Billy draw so many people? He spoke with simple words and energetic gestures to convey his sermon message. Billy listened to what God had called him to do and changed his entire life to follow God's leading.

> AS A PREACHER FOR THE YMCA, BILLY MADE ONE-THIRD THE SALARY HE HAD MADE AS A PROFESSIONAL BASEBALL PLAYER. BUT FOLLOWING GOD'S CALL WAS PRICELESS!

God, help me hear the calling You have for me.
And give me the courage to follow it.

APRIL 20

MICHELANGELO

1475–1564 • ITALY

I KNOW WHO I AM

Beloved, we are God's children now.

1 JOHN 3:2

Michelangelo knew exactly who God had made him to be: a sculptor. Put a piece of marble in his hands, and he could find the sculpture within it. But when the pope asked him to paint the ceiling of the Sistine Chapel, he said yes. He spent four years on his back, high off the floor, painting beautiful pictures of Bible stories on the ceiling of the sacred chapel. Many thought this was his best work. Others thought his drawings, showing the human form in pencil, were Michelangelo's greatest talent. But he always saw himself first as a sculptor. He used all the talents God gave him (and there were many!), but he stayed true to the gift that meant most to him—sculpting.

> MICHELANGELO LIVED TO BE EIGHTY-EIGHT—ALMOST TWICE AS LONG AS PEOPLE LIVED DURING THAT TIME.

God, thank You for giving me abilities—
and the ability to enjoy them.

APRIL 21

WILLIAM WILBERFORCE

1759–1833 • ENGLAND

USE YOUR GIFTS

Now there are varieties of gifts but the same Spirit.

1 CORINTHIANS 12:4

William loved to talk—and he was good at it. Since others liked what he had to say, William went to work in Parliament, a branch of government in England. When William became a Christian, his faith changed how he believed others should be treated. He realized that buying and selling enslaved people was wrong. For eighteen years, William asked Parliament to abolish the slave trade. Every year, he asked other Parliament members to support a bill to end the slave trade. He made speeches about why slavery was wrong. Each year, he convinced more people to join his efforts. Finally, in 1807, Parliament passed a bill that outlawed the slave trade in the British Empire. William had used his gifts for good.

> AT THE UNIVERSITY OF CAMBRIDGE, WILLIAM MET HIS LIFELONG FRIEND (AND FUTURE PRIME MINISTER) WILLIAM PITT THE YOUNGER. THEY'RE BURIED NEXT TO EACH OTHER AT WESTMINSTER ABBEY.

God, I want to use my gifts for Your glory. Please show me how.

APRIL 22

GUSTAVO GUTIÉRREZ

1928–2024 • PERU

LIKE A GOOD NEIGHBOR

[Jesus asked], "Which of these three, do you think, was a neighbor to the man who fell into the hands of the robbers?" He said, "The one who showed him mercy." Jesus said to him, "Go and do likewise."

LUKE 10:36–37

"We love God by loving our neighbor," Gustavo used to say. Gustavo's neighbors lived in one of the poorest areas of Lima, Peru. He was a priest who believed Christians had a duty to help their neighbors in need—especially those who didn't have enough to eat, or a place to live, or who didn't feel safe. He encouraged people to think about the way Jesus lived. Not only did Jesus share messages of hope and lessons in parables; He also healed sick people and fed the hungry. Gustavo taught that it's important to show God's love to people by helping to meet their needs. Because when Christians respond to the world's deepest suffering, they are doing their most important job: being good neighbors.

> MANY PEOPLE AROUND THE WORLD WERE INFLUENCED BY GUSTAVO'S TEACHINGS, INCLUDING AMERICAN DOCTOR PAUL FARMER (YOU CAN READ ABOUT PAUL ON PAGE 262!)

God, I want to be a good neighbor. Please show me how.

APRIL 23

BROWNIE WISE

1913–1992 • UNITED STATES

JUST TRY IT

In the morning sow your seed, and at evening do not let your hands be idle; for you do not know which will prosper, this or that, or whether both alike will be good.

ECCLESIASTES 11:6

Brownie worked hard to figure out what products would make life easier for her customers. She thought about her life as a mom and businessperson. What would make *her* life easier? And then she found a brand-new product—Tupperware! These plastic bowls with sealing lids made storing leftovers easier. Tupperware was new, and many people didn't know how to use it. So Brownie decided to throw parties to show other busy women how Tupperware could help them. The parties were a hit, and the product began to sell! Then Brownie started a company where other people could sell Tupperware too. At a time when many moms didn't work outside the home, selling Tupperware gave them an opportunity to make money. Brownie encouraged her new sales staff, reminding them that they could do anything they put their minds to.

> IN 1954, BROWNIE BECAME THE FIRST WOMAN ON THE COVER OF *BUSINESS WEEK* MAGAZINE.

God, I'm glad I get to accomplish cool things with You by my side every step of the way.

APRIL 24

TONY GWYNN

1960–2014 • UNITED STATES

THE RIGHT KIND OF WORK

Be kind to one another.

EPHESIANS 4:32

Tony was one of the best-ever hitters in baseball. When Tony came to the plate wearing his San Diego Padres uniform, everyone knew he'd get a hit. But being a great hitter didn't happen overnight. He knew God had given him ability, but he worked hard to earn his lifetime .338 batting average. Tony recorded his games to see how he could get better. And he was kind to everyone. He'd wave to fans, team owners, and kids picking up dirty socks in the locker room. He treated reporters with kindness, whether they were from the *New York Times* or a school paper. The day Tony was inducted into the Baseball Hall of Fame, he called to encourage a coworker before surgery. This hall-of-famer's greatest achievement was being kind to others.

> TONY WAS SUCH A GOOD ATHLETE THAT HE ALSO HAD THE OPTION TO PLAY IN THE NBA! HE CHOSE BASEBALL INSTEAD.

God, thank You for Tony's example of kindness. Help me work hard to show Your love to others.

APRIL 25

FRANZ JOSEPH HAYDN

1732–1809 • AUSTRIA

FILLED BY JOY

In your presence there is fullness of joy.

PSALM 16:11

Every time Franz sat down to write music, he thought about how his faith made him feel: happy! Franz wanted others to feel that happiness too. Through his music, he could help people feel a sense of awe about time with God. Franz did this especially in his musical piece called *The Creation*. With blaring trumpets, sighing strings, booming bassoons, and the beautiful voices of a choir, Franz brought his audience to "in the beginning," when God created the heavens and the earth. Franz believed his purpose was to bring people comfort and said, "Perhaps your labor will become a source in which the [worried] man . . . will for a while find peace and rest."

> FRANZ ENDED EACH OF HIS PIECES WITH "GOD BE PRAISED" OR "FOR THE GLORY OF GOD ALONE."

God, thank You for filling my life and faith with joy!

APRIL 26

ARISTIDES

C. 101–C. 200 • GREECE

A BIG APOLOGY

Conduct yourselves wisely toward outsiders. . . .
Let your speech always be gracious.

COLOSSIANS 4:5–6

After Jesus rose from the dead and returned to heaven, His followers went all over the world telling people about Him. Some people didn't listen. But others did! One of those people was a man named Aristides. He was a deep thinker who wrote lots of books. When Aristides heard about Jesus, he thought and thought about what His followers were saying. And it all made sense! So Aristides wrote a book called *Apology for the Christian Faith*. But he wasn't saying "sorry" for what he was writing. An "apology" can also mean talking about why you believe something. Aristides became one of the first Greek thinkers to write about his Christian beliefs. He sent his beliefs to the Roman emperor so he could also know why Jesus was the real deal.

> ARISTIDES'S APOLOGY WENT MISSING FOR HUNDREDS OF YEARS. HIS WRITINGS WEREN'T REDISCOVERED UNTIL THE LATE 1800S!

*God, give me courage to tell others
about why I believe in You.*

APRIL 27

ANTHONY VAN DYCK

1599–1641 • SPANISH NETHERLANDS (NOW BELGIUM)

SHINE YOUR LIGHT

"Let your light shine before others."

MATTHEW 5:16

Anthony wasn't afraid to show off his skills as an artist, even at a young age. Anthony was apprenticed to an older painter at just ten years old! Early on, Anthony showed he was talented at painting portraits—a desired skill since there were no cameras. His oldest-surviving portrait, *Portrait of a Man*, was created when Anthony was just fourteen. Word of Anthony's skill got around, and he gained a brand-new mentor: the already famous Peter Paul Rubens. Anthony worked as an assistant, but before long, Anthony's work was standing on its own! Anthony went on to be one of the greatest portrait artists in Europe. He created moving religious pieces that inspired devotion and faith.

ANTHONY BECAME THE OFFICIAL PORTRAIT ARTIST FOR TWO ENGLISH KINGS: JAMES I AND CHARLES I.

God, thank You for my talents! Help me to be brave enough to show them to the world.

APRIL 28

JOHN DONNE

1572–1631 • ENGLAND

YOU'RE GOOD ENOUGH

For we are what he has made us, created in Christ Jesus for good works.

EPHESIANS 2:10

John had a way with words. His friends knew it. His wife knew it. Everyone knew it—except John. He loved God with all his heart and knew he would enjoy working for the church. But he felt he wasn't worthy. Sometimes people hired John to write for them, everything from theology to poetry to funeral speeches. And people were amazed by what he wrote. John asked the king for a job at court. "I won't employ you anywhere outside the church," the king said. John accepted, but

> JOHN WAS HEAD OVER HEELS IN LOVE WITH HIS WIFE, ANNE. HIS POEMS TO HER ARE CONSIDERED THE GREATEST LOVE POEMS IN THE ENGLISH LANGUAGE.

he was nervous. He eventually became dean of Saint Paul's Church in London, where he was the favorite preacher of kings James I and Charles I. John had doubted his gifts were enough. But when he finally had the courage to say yes, he impacted many—even kings.

God, I know You made me good enough, just as I am! Help me use the gifts You gave me.

APRIL 29

GREGOR MENDEL

1822–1884 • AUSTRIAN EMPIRE (MODERN-DAY CZECH REPUBLIC)

DIFFERENT TRAITS

There are varieties of services, but the same Lord.

1 CORINTHIANS 12:5

Gregor had always excelled at science and math. But his family didn't have money to send him to school. Instead, Gregor joined a monastery for different opportunities to use his gifts. First, the priests sent Gregor to visit the sick, but that job was too stressful for him. The priests sent him to be a substitute teacher. Gregor loved this job, and his students loved him. To become a full-time teacher, Gregor needed to pass an exam. But Gregor got nervous taking tests. He failed the teaching exam—twice. Although he was sad about the results, Gregor still pursued his studies. Eventually he discovered how pea plants pass down certain traits to new pea plants they create. And today Gregor is known as the father of modern genetics.

BECAUSE OF GREGOR'S WORK, NOW WE KNOW HOW ANIMALS AND HUMANS PASS DOWN TRAITS TOO!

*God, help me remember that it's okay
not to be good at everything!*

APRIL 30

CONSTANTINE I

C. 280–337 • ROME

FOREVER CHANGED

"I am exalted among the nations, I am exalted in the earth."

PSALM 46:10

In AD 312, Constantine was the first Roman emperor to become a Christian. And because of that, the entire Western world changed forever. Constantine outlawed crucifixion as a punishment. He asked for new copies of the Bible to be made for churches. People began recognizing Sunday as a holy day. He built churches in countries on three different continents: modern-day Italy, Germany, Türkiye, Israel, Palestine, Egypt, Tunisia, and Libya, among other places. Because this leader became a believer, life changed for many people. People started teaching their kids and grandkids to follow these new beliefs. Christianity spread around the world and became an important part of many people's lives, which is the reason you're reading this book right now!

> CONSTANTINE ORDERED A CHURCH TO BE BUILT IN ROME, SAINT PETER'S BASILICA. IT WAS THERE FOR MORE THAN 1,200 YEARS BEFORE A NEW ONE OPENED IN 1615.

*God, I am so thankful I know about You
and share Your love with others.*

MAY 1

MARTIN LUTHER KING JR.

1929–1968 • UNITED STATES

WORKING FOR A DREAM

In Christ Jesus you are all children of God.

GALATIANS 3:26

Martin had a dream that, one day, people of all races would live together peacefully. He worked hard to make this dream come alive in America. Based on his beliefs from his Christian faith, Martin felt that peacefully protesting against laws that segregated, or separated, people was the best way to show how wrong the laws were. He encouraged people to boycott the bus system in Montgomery, Alabama, after Rosa Parks was arrested for refusing to give up her seat to a white passenger. He sat with Black young men and women at lunch counters usually reserved for white customers. He led marches and gave speeches to thousands of people, all because he believed that each person, no matter their race, is God's creation. The year after Martin shared his dream, a law overturning segregation was passed.

> MARTIN'S FAMOUS "I HAVE A DREAM" SPEECH WAS IMPROVISED! PARTWAY THROUGH THE SPEECH, GOSPEL SINGER MAHALIA JACKSON SHOUTED, "TELL THEM ABOUT THE DREAM!" AND HE DID!

God, thank You for showing us how You want us to live peacefully with others.

MAY 2

FRANCES RIDLEY HAVERGAL

1836–1879 • ENGLAND

A NEW WAY TO SEE

"Blessed are the pure in heart, for they will see God."

MATTHEW 5:8

Sometimes all it takes to change our minds is to hear the same information from someone else. That's what Frances discovered. Her entire life, Frances had gone to church, read the Bible, and talked about God with her parents and sisters. But when she left for boarding school, Frances started to look at faith in a completely new way. The woman who took care of the students, Mrs. Teed, spent lots of time praying with the girls. She passed her excitement for following Jesus onto her students. The girls began to see that they could talk to Jesus anytime. And the more they talked to Him, the more real their relationship with Him felt. By the time she went home for Christmas, Frances couldn't wait to share that excitement for her faith with her family.

> FRANCES GREW UP TO BE A HYMN WRITER. HER MOST FAMOUS SONG IS CALLED "TAKE MY LIFE AND LET IT BE."

God, thank You for mentors who help me see You in a new way!

MAY 3

DR. MARY MCLEOD BETHUNE

1875–1955 • UNITED STATES

CLEARING PATHS FOR OTHERS

Commit your work to the LORD, and your plans will be established.

PROVERBS 16:3

Little Mary had sixteen siblings. When her parents heard about a school for Black children, they could only afford to send one child; they chose Mary. Mary became a teacher and in 1904 started a school for Black girls. It became so successful that people started listening to Mary's thoughts on world events. When women received the right to vote in 1920, Mary encouraged them to push for equal rights for women *and* people of color. She worked to end segregated education and improve health care for Black children. In 1935, President Franklin D. Roosevelt appointed Mary director of the National Youth Administration, and she became the first Black woman to lead a federal agency. Mary wrote, "Faith is the first factor in a life devoted to service." And she never stopped working so people of color, women, and girls could have more opportunities.

> MARY HAD A ROLE IN THE FOUNDING OF THE UNITED NATIONS AND THE UNITED NEGRO COLLEGE FUND.

God, help me open paths for others to have opportunities to learn and grow like I do.

MAY 4

JOHNNY UNITAS

1933–2002 • UNITED STATES

PLAYING WITH PERSISTENCE

We also boast in our sufferings, knowing that
suffering produces endurance.

ROMANS 5:3

Whatever Johnny lacked in size and skill at football, he made up for with persistence. *Persistence* means trying again and again, even when you face obstacles. Johnny was just 145 pounds in high school. Several colleges passed on him before he landed at the University of Louisville. After college, Johnny was chosen by the NFL's Pittsburgh Steelers, but he was quickly cut from the team. He played for a semi-pro team for six dollars a game, waiting for a chance to go pro. He got a backup spot on the Baltimore Colts. But Johnny's first pass was caught by the other team for a touchdown—a huge mistake! Two weeks later, the starting quarterback broke his leg, and Johnny had to play the rest of the season. He began to break NFL records! In 1973, Johnny retired as one of the most-awarded players ever.

> JOHNNY SET A RECORD FOR MAKING A TOUCHDOWN PASS FOR FORTY-SEVEN GAMES! HIS RECORD STOOD FOR MORE THAN FIFTY YEARS.

*God, whenever I come to an obstacle,
please help me keep going.*

MAY 5

SAINT HILARY

401–449 • GAUL (MODERN-DAY FRANCE)

SET AN EXAMPLE

How can young people keep their way pure? By
guarding it according to your word.

PSALM 119:9

Hilary was born into a family of wealth and received a good education. During his schooling, Hilary met his relative Honoratus, a bishop. Honoratus had dedicated his life to God and asked for Hilary to do the same. Hilary left his riches behind to join Honoratus's monastery and lived a quiet life filled with prayer. When Honoratus died, Hilary was made bishop in his place. Hilary was only twenty-nine years old! He would be leading people in the church two or three times his age. But he happily took on his new role. He worked hard and donated to the poor. He traveled on foot and wore simple clothing. Although he was young, Hilary set an example for the people he was leading.

HILARY'S NAME IN LATIN IS . . . "HILARIUS." NO JOKE!

God, let me set an example on how to live for You.

MAY 6

ROBERT BOYLE

1627–1691 • ENGLAND

UNDERSTANDING GOD'S WORLD

It is he who made the earth by his power, who
established the world by his wisdom.

JEREMIAH 51:15

You can be a scientist *and* have deep faith in God. That's what Robert thought! To him, discovering new chemical compounds in the soil or measuring the volume of gases under pressure—actually, any part of science that helped him understand more about the world around him—meant he was understanding more of God's greatness. Robert found that the more he studied science, the deeper his faith was. Back then, many scientists made big statements based on hunches. But Robert thought there was a better way to draw conclusions: through detailed experiments and observation. With these practices, he helped modern scientists create methods of experimentation that are still used today. And in turn, Robert could describe how God created a world that works in great harmony.

> ROBERT ALSO HELPED A GROUP OF MEN, INCLUDING ARCHITECT CHRISTOPHER WREN, FOUND THE ROYAL SOCIETY OF LONDON, THE OLDEST SCIENCE SOCIETY IN THE WORLD.

God, I love learning more about the world You made!

MAY 7

EDMONIA LEWIS

C. 1844–1907 • UNITED STATES AND ITALY

WORK OF ART

We are the clay, and you are our potter; we
are all the work of your hand.

ISAIAH 64:8

Edmonia stared at the photograph of President Lincoln, studying the shape of his jaw, the angle of his nose. Then she picked up her tools and began to carve the marble in front of her. An American living in Rome, Edmonia created beautiful sculptures. She'd come a long way from living with her aunts near Niagara Falls. She'd gone to college, then learned to sculpt the head and shoulders, called *busts*, of prominent people. She used the sales of those busts to travel to Rome to study classic artists and practice her faith. Influenced by her Black and Ojibwe heritage, Edmonia would sculpt famous people or beloved Bible characters. Many from around the world traveled to view her work. Edmonia's work showed her pride in all that contributed to the unique and talented person God made her to be.

> EDMONIA WAS THE FIRST BLACK AND NATIVE AMERICAN SCULPTOR TO RECEIVE INTERNATIONAL RECOGNITION.

God, thank You for making me a perfectly unique work of art!

MAY 8

DOROTHY SAYERS

1893–1957 • ENGLAND

REAL GOD

[Jesus], though he was in the form of God . . . being found in human form, he humbled himself and became obedient.

PHILIPPIANS 2:6–8

Dorothy knew that the story of Jesus was the greatest story ever told. But no one was telling it the way it *needed* to be told! Many people who had gone to church all their lives were used to stuffy teachings about Jesus. They didn't seem to remember that Jesus wasn't a made-up character. He had come to earth as a real person! Dorothy was a fantastic storyteller who wrote books and radio shows. So she wrote a radio show about Jesus called *The Man Born to Be King.* She had to fight for the apostles and Jesus to speak using common language and accents (not stuffy words!). To Dorothy, having these men sound like people listeners knew would bring the story to life in a brand-new way—and draw them closer to Jesus.

> IN 1915, DOROTHY BECAME ONE OF THE FIRST WOMEN TO GRADUATE FROM THE PRESTIGIOUS OXFORD UNIVERSITY.

God, thank You for being so real to me!

MAY 9

MINCAYE ENQUEDI

C. 1935–2020 • ECUADOR

AN OPEN HEART

Be transformed by the renewing of your minds.

ROMANS 12:2

Mincaye grew up in a village in the Amazon rainforest. His tribe, the Huaorani, had never heard about Jesus. They were fierce warriors who defended their village from enemies. One day, a group of missionaries came to tell them about Jesus. The Huaorani believed the men were enemies, so they killed them. A few years later, a wife and a sister of the missionaries came back to the village to talk about Jesus. This time, Mincaye listened. And his life was transformed by Jesus. Where he had once felt fear and guilt, now he had been freed. Mincaye learned that one of the men he had killed had a son named Steve. Mincaye decided to act as Steve's father. After Steve grew up, he brought his family to live in the village with Mincaye. God's love made that possible.

> MINCAYE LIVED AND PREACHED THE GOSPEL IN HIS VILLAGE AND BLESSED MANY PEOPLE.

God, thank You for the radical transformation Your forgiveness brings.

MAY 10

WANG ZHIMING

1908–1973 • CHINA

LOVE YOUR NEIGHBORS

Let us love one another, because love is from God.

1 JOHN 4:7

Wang watched as his country began to change. A new government had taken over. They didn't like foreign countries and thought religion was dangerous. Wang, a pastor, didn't agree. But he tried to live in peace with everyone, including the Red Guards, who carried out the government's policies. But when the Red Guards began to humiliate people who owned land and say hateful things about people in foreign countries, Wang refused to join them, then began to speak out, saying this was wrong. The government began to put Christians in jail, and the Red Guards arrested Wang and his family. Four years later, they sentenced Wang to death. But the government couldn't get rid of Christians! Today there are more than 30,000 believers in Wang's hometown.

> IN 1981, A MEMORIAL WAS ERECTED NEAR WANG'S HOME. IT'S THE ONLY MONUMENT KNOWN IN CHINA TO COMMEMORATE SOMEONE KILLED FOR THEIR FAITH DURING THE CULTURAL REVOLUTION PERIOD.

God, when people pressure me to hate others or say bad things about them, help me say no.

MAY 11

SAINT CYRIL AND SAINT METHODIUS

CYRIL: C. 827–869 • METHODIUS: C. 815–884 •
BYZANTINE EMPIRE (MODERN-DAY GREECE)

SPEAK MY LANGUAGE

Every tongue should confess that Jesus Christ is Lord.

PHILIPPIANS 2:11

Cyril and Methodius, brothers, grew up in a part of Greece where many Slavic people lived. Slavic people spoke a different language from Cyril, Methodius, and other Greek people. But the brothers could speak to their Slavic friends. Cyril and Methodius wondered how they could teach their Slavic friends about Jesus. They decided to translate the Bible! But the Slavic people didn't have an alphabet. They communicated only by speaking. So the brothers used the Greek alphabet as inspiration and added new letters to symbolize sounds in the Slavic language.

> THE ALPHABET CYRIL AND METHODIUS CREATED BECAME THE BASIS FOR THE CYRILLIC ALPHABET. IT'S STILL USED TODAY IN RUSSIAN AND OTHER SLAVIC LANGUAGES.

The brothers used this new alphabet, the Glagolitic alphabet, to translate the Bible into a language known as "Old Church Slavonic." For their impact on the Slavic people, the brothers are known as "the Apostles of the Slavs."

God, help me to break through boundaries to reach people for You!

MAY 12

ROGER BANNISTER

1929–2018 • ENGLAND

TOGETHER IT'S POSSIBLE

Iron sharpens iron, and one person sharpens the wits of another.

PROVERBS 27:17

At the 1952 Olympics, twenty-three-year-old Roger crossed the finish line of the 1,500-meter run, which measures just under a mile. But he wasn't happy with his fourth-place finish. Roger asked his Olympic teammates Chris Brasher and Chris Chataway to train with him and give pointers. Roger and the Chrises ran and ran, all while Roger attended medical school, studying neurology. In May 1954, Roger was ready for a new race at Oxford. At the starting signal, he exploded into his run. He collapsed at the finish line as the crowd cheered. He had broken the world record for the fastest mile—under four minutes! He grabbed the Chrises and celebrated. "We had done it—the three of us!" Roger wrote in his memoir. Together they did what many thought was impossible.

> ROGER BELIEVED HIS CAREER AS A NEUROLOGIST WAS A GREATER ACHIEVEMENT THAN HIS WORLD-RECORD RUN.

God, thank You for the friends who lift me up!

MAY 13

LEONHARD EULER

1707–1783 • RUSSIA

SEEING A NEW WAY

*Who is a rock besides our God?—the God who girded
me with strength, and made my way safe.*

PSALM 18:31–32

Leonhard was a math genius. He could solve complicated problems even his *teachers* couldn't solve and made discoveries in geometry and calculus. He believed math helped him understand God's creation. Leonhard's reputation earned him places in royal courts across Europe to advance academies for different countries and empires. Leonhard would work late into the night, with oil lamps that didn't give much light. He began to lose sight in one eye, then developed a cataract in the other. Before long, Leonhard lived in total blindness. But he refused to stop working. He kept making discoveries in math and science, keeping the computations in his head. Though he wasn't a classroom teacher, he helped establish math education in Russia. He kept using his mind to accomplish great things.

> LEONHARD POPULARIZED THE USE OF "PI" TO DESCRIBE THE CIRCUMFERENCE OF A CIRCLE.

*God, when I meet obstacles, please help
me find a way around them.*

MAY 14

ANTONÍN DVOŘÁK

1841–1904 • BOHEMIA (MODERN-DAY CZECH REPUBLIC)

HEART AND HUSTLE

Whatever your hand finds to do, do with your might.

ECCLESIASTES 9:10

Antonín's twenties were difficult. After graduating from the prestigious Institute for Church Music in Prague, he struggled to find success. Antonín had to hustle to make money, playing the viola in local inns and theater bands and giving music lessons to young students. Since he had to do so many jobs, Antonín didn't have much time to write music. He couldn't afford paper to write on, let alone a piano to compose on. But he believed God had given him this talent, and by the time he was twenty-three, he had written two symphonies, an opera, and many other songs. Antonín kept writing, and finally, ten years later, Austria recognized his talent and gave him money so he could focus on writing. Today he's known as one of the Romantic period's greatest composers.

> **ANTONÍN MET GREAT COMPOSERS PYOTR TCHAIKOVSKY AND JOHANNES BRAHMS, WHO BECAME FRIENDS AND HELPED HIM PERFORM HIS WORKS PUBLICLY.**

God, sometimes it's hard to keep working when I don't see results. Help me keep hustling for my dreams.

MAY 15

ALBRECHT DÜRER

1471–1528 • GERMANY

THAT WAY IS BETTER

The wise listen to advice.

PROVERBS 12:15

Albrecht looked at the artwork on the walls around him, his mouth open in awe. The way artists in Italy created, whether they were painting or making engravings, was so different from the artists back home in Germany. *There are so many ways to make art*, Albrecht thought. *I'm going to try some of their techniques!* He was inspired by the way Italian artists showed bodies in motion—the way people moved in real life! Instead of painting the way he always had, Albrecht allowed himself to try something new, to become a beginner again and test new techniques. From then on, Albrecht considered Italy his second home. He enjoyed getting to know a new culture and learning new ways to depict the art that God had inspired him to do.

AT ONLY THIRTEEN YEARS OLD, HE CREATED A SELF-PORTRAIT IN A FORM CALLED "SILVERPOINT" THAT IS THE EARLIEST ATTRIBUTED SURVIVING SELF-PORTRAIT BY A EUROPEAN MASTER.

God, let my curiosity open my mind to new ideas and ways to do things.

MAY 16

SAINT JOHN OF NEPOMUK

C. 1345–1393 • BOHEMIA (MODERN-DAY CZECH REPUBLIC AND POLAND)

FOREVER FAITHFUL

"Blessed are you when people . . . utter all kinds of evil against you falsely on my account."

MATTHEW 5:11

Saint John was a priest who served every person equally, no matter who they were. Rich or poor, peasant or royal, John treated them all the same. Because he was a priest, people confessed their sins to John, and it was John's job to keep that information to himself. People felt like they could tell him anything, no matter how bad their sin was. One day, the king of Bohemia suspected that his wife had confessed some kind of sin to John. He went to John and asked what his wife had confessed, but John refused to tell him. This angered the king, and he punished John for disobeying. But John refused to break his promise. Even though John's decision put him in danger and ended his life, he stayed faithful to the people he served.

> THERE ARE MORE THAN 12,000 STATUES OF SAINT JOHN OF NEPOMUK ACROSS EASTERN AND CENTRAL EUROPE.

God, please help me stay true to You and the people I love, no matter what.

MAY 17

THOMAS MERTON

1915–1968 • UNITED STATES

WHICH PATH?

Make me to know your ways, O LORD; teach me your paths.

PSALM 25:4

Thomas wanted to do what God wanted him to do. But he wasn't always sure *where* God was leading him! Thomas was a priest who belonged to a Trappist monastery. The Trappist brothers didn't speak much, so that they could focus on doing what God wanted. Thomas was an excellent thinker and writer. He wrote books that inspired many and brought them closer to God. But the more Thomas wrote, the more people wanted to hear from him. They invited him to travel away from the monastery to speak to their groups.

> THOMAS WAS A CHAMPION OF PEACE. HE STRONGLY BELIEVED IN THE CIVIL RIGHTS MOVEMENT OF THE 1960S.

What was Thomas supposed to do? Stay at the monastery and write, or go away and talk to people? Thomas wasn't always sure. He prayed and asked God what to do. He knew that God would lead him on the right path.

God, please help me know the right thing to do.

MAY 18

PAYNE STEWART

1957–1999 • UNITED STATES

THE GREATEST TROPHY

"This is my commandment, that you love
one another as I have loved you."

JOHN 15:12

Payne was one of the best golfers in the world, and he had the trophies to prove it. But something was missing. Payne had friends and family who loved him, but being the best golfer seemed like the only goal worth living for. But one day his friend Paul called: Paul had cancer. Over the next few months, Payne watched Paul grow weaker as he bravely fought the disease. But Paul didn't give up his hope in Jesus. In fact, Paul said he knew that Jesus was with him always—even in cancer. This changed the way Payne looked at his life. Instead of being the best golfer, he wanted to be the best husband, dad, and friend. He wanted to spend time with Jesus. Soon Payne realized what had been missing all along—loving his Savior and his people.

> PAYNE WORE A BRACELET WITH THE LETTERS WWJD, WHICH STANDS FOR "WHAT WOULD JESUS DO?"

God, thank You for the love that fills my life!

MAY 19

SAINT CELESTINE V

1215–1296 • ITALY

DIFFERENT GIFTS

We have gifts that differ according to the grace given to us.

ROMANS 12:6

Before Celestine V was elected pope, he was known as Peter. And Peter loved his time alone, reading the Bible and talking to God. Starting at age twenty, Peter spent his days alone with God. When Peter was eighty-four, he was shocked to learn that he'd been elected pope. For two years, the church had been without a pope. They finally settled on Peter, who took the name Celestine V. Despite his devotion to God, Celestine didn't think God had given him the gifts needed to lead others. After five months, he told church leaders how he felt and stepped down. He knew God had given him other gifts and was humble enough to realize that the church might do better under a different leader.

> CELESTINE WAS THE FIRST POPE TO *ABDICATE*, OR STEP DOWN FROM, HIS POSITION.

*God, help me to recognize my gifts
and use them to glorify You.*

MAY 20

ARTHUR HOLLY COMPTON

1892–1962 • UNITED STATES

WHICH PATH?

He guides me on the right paths for the honor of his name.

PSALM 23:3

When Arthur graduated from college, he had no idea what to do with his life. He'd graduated with a degree in science. But he also loved God so much. Should he be a scientist? Or go into ministry? "Your work in science may become a more valuable Christian service than if you were to enter the ministry or become a missionary," his dad said. So Arthur enrolled at Princeton to study physics. His studies led to new discoveries in quantum mechanics (from which we get lasers, medical imaging machines, electron microscopes, and more!). Eventually Arthur developed the first self-sustaining atomic chain reaction. This helped scientists realize how to control the release of nuclear energy, which powers our world today. Arthur's scientific service helped to change the world.

> IN 1927, ARTHUR WON THE NOBEL PRIZE FOR PHYSICS.

God, when I'm at a crossroads, help me see how I can serve You.

MAY 21

DANNY THOMAS

1912–1991 • UNITED STATES

POWERFUL PRAYER

The prayer of the righteous person is powerful.

JAMES 5:16

Danny sat in the church pew, his heart overflowing with love for God. He had seven dollars in his pocket and had decided to give all of it to the church, hoping his offering might be put to good use. But later, when Danny reached in his pocket to pay a hospital bill, he realized he didn't have any money. He decided to pray. *Please, God, help me find a way to pay this hospital bill.* The next day, Danny, an entertainer struggling to find work, booked a job that paid ten times

> DANNY'S HOSPITAL, ST. JUDE, IS LOCATED IN MEMPHIS, TENNESSEE.

what he had put in the collection box! Over the next few years Danny's fame grew. He even had a television show named after him! Through it all, he prayed for God to show him how to live. Danny built a hospital called St. Jude Children's Research Hospital, where no family would receive a bill.

God, when I'm facing an impossible task, help me turn to You first.

MAY 22

WALTER WANGERIN JR.

1944–2021 • UNITED STATES

TRUTH STORIES

"The reason I speak to them in parables is
that 'seeing they do not perceive.'"

MATTHEW 13:13

Throughout his life, Walter was many things: a father, a pastor, a professor. But perhaps the title most knew him by was as a storyteller. Walter's stories won important awards, like the National Book Award. But Walter didn't tell stories to win awards. He told them so others could learn God's truth in ways they didn't expect. Walter believed that people need to see *why* things are true and how their lives can be made better by those truths—such as understanding how God is close to us in dark times, even when we can't see Him. And through those stories, readers learned more about who God is—kind of like the way Jesus told parables to help people know more about God too.

> WALTER WROTE ALL KINDS OF STORIES: SCIENCE FICTION, CHILDREN'S BOOKS, EVEN BOOKS ABOUT PRAYER, GRIEF, CHILDHOOD, AND MARRIAGE.

God, help me find You in the stories I hear and read.

MAY 23

RALPH HOUK

1919–2010 • UNITED STATES

NEXT BEST THING

> Be still before the LORD, and wait patiently for him; do not fret over those who prosper.
>
> **PSALM 37:7**

Ralph was on the bench—again. He was a back-up catcher for the New York Yankees. And every night for seven seasons, he watched Yogi Berra, the main catcher, settle in behind the plate instead of him. Since he wasn't playing, Ralph would study the players. He noted each pitcher's best throws and which balls the batters were hitting. He saw how well each fielder made plays. He talked to relief pitchers to learn their strategy. Although Ralph wished

RALPH'S NICKNAME WAS "THE MAJOR," WHICH HE EARNED DURING HIS ARMY SERVICE IN WORLD WAR II.

he was playing, he did the next best thing: He became a student of the game. Then he used that knowledge to become a coach! That's how Ralph became the first Yankees coach to lead his team to back-to-back World Series titles the first couple years as manager.

*God, when one dream doesn't work out,
help me see where You're leading me.*

MAY 24

LUDWIG VON BEETHOVEN

1770–1827 • AUSTRIA

HERE, THERE, EVERYWHERE

"You are the light of the world. A city built on a hill cannot be hid."

MATTHEW 5:14

Faith is something we can take with us wherever we go. And wherever we are, our faith can be inspired. That's what Ludwig believed! Ludwig was one of the greatest musical composers who ever lived. He wrote many kinds of musical pieces. Many were to be played at church, but he also wrote *concertos* to be performed in concert halls. When someone asked where one of his newest pieces was meant to be performed, Ludwig said that his goal was to strengthen the faith of everyone who heard the music—the performers, the audience, everyone! To him, where the music was performed didn't matter. Everything he wrote reflected his awe and appreciation of the world God created.

> MANY OF BEETHOVEN'S IDEAS CAME DURING HIS LONG WALKS IN THE COUNTRY.

God, no matter where I am, please help me reflect who You are.

MAY 25

SAINT BEDE THE VENERABLE

C. 672–735 • NORTHUMBRIA (MODERN-DAY ENGLAND)

SHARE WHAT YOU KNOW

The fear of the Lord is the beginning of knowledge.

PROVERBS 1:7

Before information became easy to find in books and on the internet, people shared new ideas mostly by talking to others. Bede, a priest in a land called Northumbria, was known for writing his thoughts about the Bible. But he also believed that writing down a history of his land might help people know what life had been like and also learn from their stories. Sharing information he thought was true, Bede wrote a history of Northumbria, starting when Julius Caesar arrived in 55 BC, all the way up to his own lifetime around AD 700. Because of Bede's creativity and perseverance, we know how Christianity in England came to be.

> BEDE DATED EVENTS ACCORDING TO HOW MUCH TIME HAD PASSED SINCE JESUS' BIRTH. THE LATIN PHRASE *ANNO DOMINI*, OR "AD," BECAME POPULAR BECAUSE OF BEDE.

Thank You for giving us the Bible, which teaches us how to follow You.

MAY 26

CHARLES HARD TOWNES

1915–2015 • UNITED STATES

POINT BACK TO GOD

I will tell of all your wonderful deeds.

PSALM 9:1

On an April morning in 1951, Charles was sitting on a park bench in Washington, DC. He was a scientist and was trying to develop better communications and radar systems for the military so people could see and talk to each other from far away. Then suddenly—*aha!*—Charles felt like God had placed a revelation in front of his eyes. He'd create a device called a *maser*, which would concentrate microwaves into a powerful beam. Eventually, the microwaves in the maser were swapped with light and became the *laser*. Charles went on to win a Nobel Prize for his discovery. But he never took the credit alone. Whenever anyone praised him, Charles pointed his discovery back to God.

> BECAUSE OF CHARLES'S DISCOVERY OF THE LASER, WE CAN SCAN PRICES AT THE SUPERMARKET, MEASURE TIME PRECISELY, CUT STEEL, AND EVEN WATCH STARS BEING BORN!

God, I give You the glory for everything I do!

MAY 27

ANTHONY TROLLOPE

1815–1882 • ENGLAND

WRITING A NEW STORY

All scripture is inspired by God and is useful for teaching . . . in righteousness.

JEREMIAH 24:6

Sixteen-year-old Anthony was making the long six-mile trek to school once again. Anthony didn't like school. He didn't like how other students made fun of him for not having as much money. He never knew if his parents would be home when he returned or if they'd be off trying to make money in yet another harebrained scheme that was sure to fail. The only escape Anthony had was to daydream on these long walks. Anthony could go where he wanted in his imagination, spend time with who he wanted, have money and fame and friends. Decades later, Anthony realized that his habit of daydreaming had helped him become one of the most successful novelists of the nineteenth century with fans such as Saint John Henry Newman.

> ANTHONY WROTE FORTY-SEVEN NOVELS IN HIS LIFETIME WHILE ALSO WORKING FOR THE BRITISH POST OFFICE.

God, help me use the hard times in my life to heal hurts and bring glory to You.

MAY 28

JOHN WYCLIFFE

C. 1330–1384 • ENGLAND

GOLDEN RULES

God has breathed life into all Scripture. . . . It is
useful for training us to do what is right.

2 TIMOTHY 3:16

John was a scholar and theologian who thought one book was more important than any other book in the world: the Bible. Why? John believed the Bible showed everyone, from peasants to kings, how to live. He thought the best way people could learn about the Bible was to read it themselves. At the time not many people could read. And the few who did couldn't read Latin, the language that books were written in during the Middle Ages. So John thought of a new idea: *Why not translate the Bible into English?* John began to organize a project to translate the Bible into everyday English. Ten years after he died, the English translation of the Bible was complete.

JOHN'S IDEAS SOON SPREAD TO OTHER SCHOLARS AND PREACHERS IN CENTRAL EUROPE—INCLUDING JAN HUS, WHO YOU CAN READ ABOUT ON PAGE 318!

God, thank You for the Bible that guides our lives.

MAY 29

JIMMY CARTER

1924–2024 • UNITED STATES

BUILDING UP OTHERS

"I will show you what someone is like who comes to me, hears my words, and acts on them. That one is like a man building a house, who dug deeply and laid the foundation on rock."

LUKE 6:47–48

Jimmy was the thirty-ninth president of the United States. Many presidents go back to their regular lives at the end of their presidency. But Jimmy, inspired by his belief that God calls us to serve others, got to work. In 1984, Jimmy and his wife, Rosalynn, began to volunteer with an organization called Habitat for Humanity. They grabbed a hammer and nails, and alongside other volunteers, the Carters began to help build houses for people in need. They enjoyed it so much that they kept doing it for more than thirty years! They worked alongside more than 100,000 volunteers in fourteen countries, helping to build and renovate more than 4,000 homes for people who needed them. Jimmy attended builds with Habitat well into his nineties, offering a smile and an encouraging word.

> AFTER HE WAS PRESIDENT, JIMMY WENT BACK TO SERVING AT HIS CHURCH. HE TAUGHT SUNDAY SCHOOL EVERY WEEK.

God, I want to bring You glory by serving others.
Please show me how I can get started today!

MAY 30

BART STARR

1934–2019 • UNITED STATES

ROLE MODELS

What does the Lord require of you but to do justice, and to love kindness, and to walk humbly with your God?

MICAH 6:8

Many kids look up to athletes as role models. But who do *athletes* look up to? For Green Bay Packers quarterback Bart Starr, the answer was easy: Jesus! Bart was one of the first great quarterbacks in modern NFL history. But no matter his success, if Bart wasn't showing Jesus' love to others, his life felt a little less meaningful. On the field, he tried to display good sportsmanship. Off the field, he tried to help others. In 1965, Bart started a ranch to help boys and their families get needed mental health services. Bart showed Jesus' love so much that an NFL award is named after him! The Bart Starr Award is given to the player who shows outstanding character on and off the field. In showing Jesus' love, Bart became a role model for others.

BART HELPED THE PACKERS WIN THE VERY FIRST SUPER BOWL!

God, I want to show Your love to others! Please show me how.

MAY 31

MARY JACKSON

1921–2005 • UNITED STATES

TAKE ON THAT CHALLENGE

Cast your burden on the Lord, and he will sustain you; he will never permit the righteous to be moved.

PSALM 55:22

Mary loved new challenges. And in 1953, this gifted mathematician got one—conducting experiments on a high-speed wind tunnel that would help the US send people to space! This tunnel could blast winds at almost twice the speed of sound! Mary's boss suggested she join a training program to become an engineer. Mary would need permission to join the white students. And in 1958, Mary became the first Black female engineer in NASA history. For much of her career, Mary focused on the layer of air surrounding an airplane and how that air affects a plane when it's flying. When she wasn't working, Mary and her husband, Levi, opened their home to other women looking to become engineers. She helped kids in the local science club so they could see that they, too, could become mathematicians and engineers.

MARY'S STORY HELPED INSPIRE THE BOOK AND MOVIE *HIDDEN FIGURES*.

God, thank You for standing by me in every single challenge.

JUNE 1

ANDREI TARKOVSKY

1932–1986 • SOVIET UNION (MODERN-DAY RUSSIA)

GREAT MOVIE!

Above all, maintain constant love for one another.

1 PETER 4:8

"Lord, I want to see the world as You made it, and Your people as You would have them be," Andrei said in his prayers one day. Andrei was a filmmaker. His movies got people to *think*. His characters searched for and found meaning and purpose in an unexpected place: love. The government of Andrei's country was opposed to his movies. But people liked Andrei's movies and asked him to keep making them. He knew the world was on a concerning path, focused on getting more stuff and being amazed by the latest technology instead of on building relationships with others and with God. Andrei's movies showed that there is a better way to build a life—by living to reflect God's love.

ANDREI'S DAD, ARSENY, WAS A POPULAR RUSSIAN POET.

God, I'm praying Andrei's prayer today: I want to see the world as You made it, and Your people as You would have them be!

JUNE 2

EUSEBIUS OF CAESAREA

C. 260–C. 340 • CAESAREA MARITIMA (MODERN-DAY ISRAEL)

SACRED HISTORY

Encourage one another and build each other up.

1 THESSALONIANS 5:11

Eusebius was one of the world's smartest people at the time he lived. He collected different pieces of writing like some people collect jewelry. Information was precious to him! Eusebius was a Christian and wanted to learn what believers before him had said, believed, and experienced. So he decided to write a big book that told the story of the church. He called it *Ecclesiastical History*. From the years 312 to 324, he kept adding to the book—because new things happened in the church all the time! *Ecclesiastical History* is one of the most important books in Christianity. It has been passed down for almost 2,000 years. Because of Eusebius, we know about some of the earliest Christians and how the church grew and grew.

EUSEBIUS LIVED DURING THE TIME OF THE ROMAN EMPEROR CONSTANTINE I, WHO ALSO BECAME A CHRISTIAN! EUSEBIUS EVEN BAPTIZED HIM.

> *God, thank You for the Christians who came before me! Help me to listen to their wisdom.*

JUNE 3

BESSIE COLEMAN

1892–1926 • UNITED STATES

TRY TO FLY

I can do all things through him who strengthens me.

PHILIPPIANS 4:13

Bessie, a young Black woman, didn't know of any pilots who looked like her. She wanted to become one! Bessie applied to flying schools in America, but she was rejected. Bessie's brother had fought in World War I in France and told her about women flying planes. So Bessie learned French, saved up her money, and applied to flying schools in France. And she was accepted at the *best* flying school! She

> **BESSIE WAS THE FIRST BLACK WOMAN TO EARN A PILOT'S LICENSE.**

learned not only how to fly but also how to complete tricky maneuvers like tail spins, figure eights, and loop de loops. Bessie traveled across Europe and America as a stunt pilot. She drew huge crowds wherever she went, showing everyone what is possible when you have the courage to keep trying.

God, when I'm up against a roadblock, give me the courage to keep trying.

JUNE 4

MARY KAY ASH

1918–2001 • UNITED STATES

SHARE THE WEALTH

"Love your neighbor as yourself."

JAMES 2:8

When Mary Kay was a young girl, her mother would always tell her, "You can do it, Mary Kay!" When she grew up, Mary Kay wanted to help other women feel that way too. After being treated poorly at her workplace, she decided to launch her own cosmetics company with the Golden Rule as her guide: "Treat others how you want to be treated." She often imagined the people she interacted with having a sign around their necks that said, "Make me feel important." That's how Mary Kay treated each person she met, whether they were a customer or someone she worked with. She listened if someone had concerns. And when the company did well, Mary Kay shared the success with her employees! Mary Kay knew success is sweeter when it's shared.

> MARY KAY WAS KNOWN TO SAY, "GOD FIRST, FAMILY SECOND, CAREER THIRD."

God, help me treat others the way I want to be treated.

JUNE 5

CLAUDIO MONTEVERDI

1567–1643 • ITALY

SING A NEW SONG

I will sing to the Lord as long as I live.

PSALM 104:33

Claudio was an Italian priest and composer who was one of the first people to develop a new art form: opera! An opera is a performance that tells a story like a play but uses singers and musical instruments. Before Claudio, the tone of music didn't always match the lyrics of a musical piece. Claudio thought that was silly! If a character was sad, Claudio would direct strings to play softly. If a character was happy, the accompanying music would be loud and bright!

> CLAUDIO WAS A MUSICAL PRODIGY. HE WAS PUBLISHING VOCAL WORKS BY AGE FIFTEEN!

Claudio worked tirelessly to see music in a new way—and to carry out that vision. This can be difficult. But thanks to pioneers like Claudio, people can discover and enjoy new forms of art. And art helps us understand what it's like to experience emotion and be human.

God, give me the vision to see Your will for me.

JUNE 6

IDA LEWIS

1842–1911 • UNITED STATES

RESCUE ME

"You are the light of the world."

MATTHEW 5:14

Ida lived in a lighthouse by the ocean. Her job was to keep the light shining so sailors wouldn't crash their boats into the rocky shore. Before electricity was discovered, keeping the light burning all night was a challenge. But Ida didn't mind. She became famous worldwide as one of the only female lightkeepers—and for her amazing rescues! When she saw sailors in trouble, Ida would take her rowboat out to rescue the sailors. One time, she even rescued sheep that had gone overboard! Ida received awards and medals, and President Ulysses S. Grant even visited her. But Ida didn't need the spotlight. She could be found reading her Bible outside the light station, watching for anyone who needed help.

IDA WAS SIXTY-THREE YEARS OLD WHEN SHE MADE HER FINAL RESCUE!

God, help me keep my eyes open for anyone who might need help.

JUNE 7

MICKEY MANTLE

1931–1995 • UNITED STATES

WINNING PEACE

"I have said this to you so that in me you may have peace."

JOHN 16:33

Mickey was one of the most talented people to ever play baseball. He played with the New York Yankees from 1951 to 1968 and won many awards: three American League MVP titles, four-time home run leader, seven World Series, entrance into the Baseball Hall of Fame. But even though he found success, he still felt like something was missing from his life. Years later, he was battling with cancer and called one of his former teammates, Bobby Richardson. Bobby had always seemed so upbeat and hopeful. Bobby began to read from the Bible in Philippians 4 to encourage his friend. A month later, Bobby went to visit Mickey again. "I want you to know I've become a Christian," he told Bobby. Mickey lived the rest of his life with a peace he'd never had before.

> MICKEY HIT ONE OF THE FARTHEST-RECORDED HOME RUNS IN HISTORY—565 FEET! THAT'S NEARLY FOUR SCHOOL BUSES LONGER THAN THE AVERAGE HOME RUN!

God, help me try to win what really matters: peace in my life with You.

JUNE 8

JOHANNES VERMEER

1632–1675 • THE NETHERLANDS

HIDDEN MESSAGES

I treasure your word in my heart, so that I may not sin against you.

PSALM 119:11

Johannes created stunning works of art, bathed in light and rich colors, that still capture hearts around the world four centuries later. We don't know much about Johannes or why he decided to become a painter. But his paintings reflect images and lessons that point to a life of faith. One of Johannes's earliest paintings is of Jesus spending time with Mary and Martha. In fact, many of Johannes's paintings feature women and girls doing everyday things, though sometimes with a hidden message. Vermeer would place an object in the painting that completely changed the meaning—like putting imagery depicting biblical scenes in the background to remind viewers of Bible lessons. Vermeer didn't *tell* people about his faith; he *showed* them.

> JOHANNES'S MOST FAMOUS PAINTING IS CALLED *GIRL WITH A PEARL EARRING*. GOOGLE IT!

God, I know You're everywhere if I take the time to look.

JUNE 9

WALKER PERCY

1916–1990 • UNITED STATES

BIG QUESTIONS

Before they call I will answer.

ISAIAH 65:24

Walker was a doctor working in New York City when he contracted tuberculosis, a highly contagious infection that affects a person's lungs. To keep from spreading the disease, Walter stayed away from others for several months. He passed the days resting by reading books. He had a realization. All his life he'd depended on science to answer questions. But science couldn't answer questions like *What is the purpose of our lives?* or *How should we live when life is hard?* But some of the books Walker was reading tried to answer these tough questions. After he recovered, Walker decided to become a writer. With his faith as a guide, Walker used his stories to try to answer these big questions for readers.

> WALKER THOUGHT PEOPLE COULD FIND MEANING IN THE SMALLEST THINGS—EVEN IN THE MOVIES THEY WATCH.

God, thank You for helping me answer the big questions I have.

JUNE 10

BLESSED MARÍA DEL TRÁNSITO DE JESÚS SACRAMENTADO

1821–1885 • ARGENTINA

SERVING HOWEVER YOU CAN

"I will be your father, and you shall be my sons
and daughters, says the Lord Almighty."

2 CORINTHIANS 6:18

María was so sad. She loved God with all her heart. But every time she tried to join a new group dedicated to Him, within a few months she would get sick and hardly be able to get out of bed. How was she supposed to serve God if she could hardly function? But then she had an idea. María had always wanted to find a way to serve children in need. If her body wouldn't cooperate, maybe she could serve God in other ways—like with her brain and her connections! María asked several church friends about this idea, and they agreed that it was a good one! Together with a few friends and a priest, María established a congregation committed to serving the poor, the orphaned, and the abandoned in Argentina.

MARÍA'S GROUP ALSO FOUNDED A FEW COLLEGES IN ARGENTINA!

*God, thank You for giving me opportunities
to serve You every single day!*

JUNE 11

IRENA SENDLER

1910–2008 • POLAND

TRUE HEROES

He delivered me because he delighted in me.

PSALM 18:19

Irena Sendler was a Catholic social worker in Warsaw, Poland, in the early 1900s. She helped to give medicine, clothing, and other goods to people in need. When the Nazis invaded Warsaw in 1939, they forced more than 400,000 Jews out of their homes and into a small neighborhood that no one could leave. However, they let Irena in to do her social work. Irena began to sneak Jewish children out of the neighborhood, who were sometimes carried in potato sacks or riding in an ambulance. She sent them to live in convents, where Catholic nuns live, or with non-Jewish families. Irena and her fellow social workers saved more than 2,500 children. When people called Irena a hero, she replied, "The heroes were the babies, the parents and grandparents who gave up their children."

> IRENA KEPT TRACK OF EVERY CHILD SHE SAVED AND HELPED REUNITE THEM WITH THEIR PARENTS AFTER THE WAR.

God, give me the courage to be brave enough to help others, even in the face of danger.

JUNE 12

BLESSED JOLENTA OF POLAND

C. 1235–1298 • POLAND

LIVE TO SERVE

Outdo one another in showing honor.

ROMANS 12:10

Jolenta's life started out like a fairy tale. Her father was the king of Hungary! When Jolenta grew older, she married into another royal family. Her husband was the duke of Poland and was very wealthy. But instead of staying tucked away in a castle, Jolenta decided to help others. She looked for people who were poor or sick, for widows and orphans. She and her husband not only gave them money but also built hospitals, churches, and convents where people could continue to receive help they needed. When Jolenta's husband died, she was sad. But she didn't stop doing good. In fact, she decided that instead of living in her big house, she would live in a convent. That way, she could live and work alongside people who were doing good things in the world.

> JOLENTA WAS MADE THE *ABBESS*, OR LEADER, OF THE CONVENT WHERE SHE LIVED.

God, help me do all the good I can wherever You place me in the world.

JUNE 13

JOSEPHINE BUTLER

1828–1906 • ENGLAND

STAND UP FOR OTHERS

Those who are kind to the needy honor [God].

PROVERBS 14:31

Josephine Butler and her new husband, George, moved to Oxford, England, so he could go to Oxford University. In her new town Josephine began to notice that men didn't treat women with much respect, and she wanted to help. She opened Butler's House of Rest, a safe place for women to earn money and not be judged. Josephine also campaigned for women's education. She also fought for women to earn the same amount of money as men for doing the same job. Talking about these kinds of topics wasn't considered polite at the time. Josephine lost many friends, but she knew God wanted her to do this work. Because of her efforts, lives and laws were changed.

ONE YEAR, JOSEPHINE ATTENDED MORE THAN A HUNDRED PUBLIC MEETINGS AND TRAVELED MORE THAN 4,000 MILES TO TALK ABOUT HER WORK!

God, help me to see who needs help. Then open my eyes to how I can serve them.

JUNE 14

SAINT ALBERT CHMIELOWSKI

1845–1916 • POLAND

LOOK TO HELP

Contribute to the needs of the saints.

ROMANS 12:13

Albert knew he was a gifted artist even at a young age. His teachers knew it too. He traveled from Poland to study art in Germany and France. As a painter, he had a talent for seeing the world around him. Albert was also kind and looked for ways to help others. Albert noticed how many people seemed to be suffering, whether they didn't have money for food or were sad that a loved one had died. Albert didn't see how his paintings could help. But maybe he could help with their physical and spiritual needs! So Albert decided to leave his art career behind. He gathered groups of people to serve those in need. He organized food pantries and shelters for people without homes. He spent the rest of his life encouraging people to help others.

> ALBERT'S LIFE INSPIRED A POLISH BOY NAMED KAROL WOJTYLA, WHO GREW UP TO BE KNOWN AS POPE JOHN PAUL II!

God, remind me to keep my eyes open for someone I can help today.

JUNE 15

JOHN MILTON

1608–1674 • ENGLAND

THE REAL HERO

In him we might become the righteousness of God.

2 CORINTHIANS 5:21

When you think of a hero, you might picture someone who fought on a battlefield, maybe who conquered a great enemy. But not John. In his epic poem *Paradise Lost*, John's hero was a humble Son who loved His people so much that He decided to give His life for them. John recognized that Jesus was the most courageous hero who ever lived, fiercer than any heroes from classic literature like Achilles or Odysseus. Instead of fighting on a battlefield, Jesus willingly died on a cross to save humankind, even as people called Him a criminal. John's writings helped people look at the Bible in a new way. Because the Bible isn't just a book of rules. It's the story of a great hero who came to save the world—including you!

> JOHN IS CONSIDERED THE SECOND GREATEST ENGLISH AUTHOR, AFTER WILLIAM SHAKESPEARE. MILTON HIMSELF WAS A HUGE SHAKESPEARE FAN!

God, thank You for sending Jesus, the greatest hero of all!

JUNE 16

ALTHEA GIBSON

1927–2003 • UNITED STATES

THE REAL WIN

In all these things we are more than conquerors
through him who loved us.

ROMANS 8:37

"I knew I was an unusual, talented girl through the grace of God," Althea once said. Decades before Serena and Venus Williams took the court by storm, Althea was breaking barriers for Black players. Many people thought Althea was "too" many things for tennis: too skinny, too rowdy, too focused. But she didn't care. She just wanted to play the sport she loved! Through her passion and dedication, Althea was the first Black athlete to earn several titles. In the 1950s, she became the first Black player to win the French Open, the US Open, and Wimbledon. In 1957, she became the first Black athlete to win the Associated Press's Athlete of the Year Award—then she won it again the next year! She showed the world what one talented yet determined athlete can accomplish.

> ALTHEA'S JEWISH TENNIS PARTNER, ANGELA BUXTON, BECAME HER BEST FRIEND. THEY WON THE DOUBLES CHAMPIONSHIP AT WIMBLEDON.

God, when others tell me I'm "too much" or "not enough," help me listen to You instead.

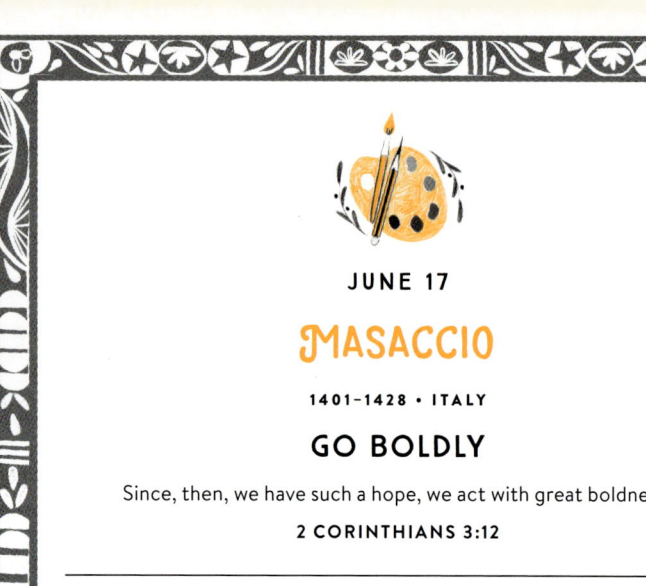

JUNE 17

MASACCIO

1401–1428 • ITALY

GO BOLDLY

Since, then, we have such a hope, we act with great boldness.

2 CORINTHIANS 3:12

Masaccio tilted his head as he studied the *fresco*, the painting he'd begun on the wall of the church. Jesus and the apostles looked so real that they could've walked off the wall and sat in a pew! That was the young painter's goal. Masaccio had made the bold decision to try a brand-new style of art that no one in his lifetime had done before. Most artists painted people in 2D, but Masaccio's characters were in 3D. Masaccio probably didn't mean to change the way people painted for the next 450 years. But his bold decision to be different inspired many others to create beautiful paintings that showed people in realistic, lifelike ways!

> MASACCIO'S MOST FAMOUS PAINTING IS *THE TRIBUTE MONEY*. IT SHOWS THE STORY OF PETER FINDING A COIN IN A FISH'S MOUTH TO PAY A TAX COLLECTOR.

God, help me to be bold and stand out from the crowd for You!

JUNE 18

SIGRID UNDSET

1882–1949 • NORWAY

EVERYONE'S STORY MATTERS

So God created humankind in his image . . .
male and female he created them.

GENESIS 1:27

*W*hat was it like to be a woman in Norway during medieval times? Sigrid wondered. To some, this question seemed odd. But not to Sigrid. Sigrid thought the stories of women from long ago were interesting and also gave insight into life in her time. Back then, many novelists didn't write books about women. Most featured men going on exciting adventures. But Sigrid thought stories about women were worth sharing. The characters in her novels lived hundreds of years before. They wore and ate different things. And they were smart, independent thinkers who readers could relate to. These women faced hard choices, endured complex emotions, and weathered difficult seasons. For the way Sigrid wrote about women, she received a Nobel Prize for Literature in 1928.

> SIGRID'S WRITING AGAINST THE NAZIS LED TO HER FLEEING TO THE US DURING WORLD WAR II.

God, help me remember that everyone's story is worth telling.

JUNE 19

SØREN KIERKEGAARD

1813–1855 · DENMARK

TRUE LOVE

God is love, and those who abide in love abide in God, and God abides in them.

1 JOHN 4:16

Søren was a writer who thought a lot about what it meant to be a true Christian. He thought that believing in God was no good if people didn't act on that belief by showing His love to others. Jesus said to love our neighbor as we love ourselves. To Søren, the story of the Good Samaritan showed this idea perfectly. The injured Jewish man on the side of the road wasn't the Samaritan's *actual* next-door neighbor. But the Samaritan thought this man's life was so important that he deserved help. Søren thought that's how Christians should treat every person they meet: as important and special. Because each of us would want to be treated in the same way. For Søren, the way to be a true Christian was to embody the love God has for each of us.

SØREN WASN'T WELL-KNOWN DURING HIS LIFETIME. HIS WRITINGS BECAME POPULAR NEARLY A HUNDRED YEARS AFTER HIS DEATH.

God, help me to see my neighbors as You see them.

JUNE 20

MARTIN NIEMÖLLER

1892–1984 • GERMANY

SPEAK UP, SPEAK OUT

You, O Lord, do not be far away! O my help, come quickly to my aid!

PSALM 22:19

Martin didn't know what was happening to his country. Adolf Hitler was gaining power and was even trying to get churches in Germany to support what the Nazis were doing. But Martin thought what Hitler was doing was wrong. The Nazis hated the Jews so much that they wanted to take the Old Testament and Paul's letters in the New Testament out of the Bible because they were written by Jewish people. So Martin tried to organize churches to protest. Martin kept preaching even though he knew he was in danger. In 1937, he was arrested by the secret police. He was placed in concentration camps for eight years, until the end of World War II. He then helped rebuild churches in Germany and worked the rest of his life to achieve peace around the world.

> MARTIN IS KNOWN FOR APOLOGIZING TO THE JEWISH PEOPLE ON BEHALF OF GERMANS EVERYWHERE. HE SAID GERMANS SHOULD HAVE DONE MORE TO STOP WHAT WAS HAPPENING.

God, please give me courage to speak up when I see evil.

JUNE 21

JOHANN SEBASTIAN BACH

1685–1750 • GERMANY

TRUST AND LET GO

It was the duty of the trumpeters and singers to make themselves heard in unison in praise and thanksgiving to the Lord.

2 CHRONICLES 5:13

"Where there is devotional music, God with His grace is always present," Johann declared. As a classical music composer, organ player, and church music director, Johann had dedicated his life to using music to connect listeners to beauty, emotion, and even God Himself. Johann wrote many pieces called *cantatas*, where a choir sings alongside instruments, and many of these were for the church. Bach produced more work in some seasons than in others. Sometimes he created one cantata a week! Johann knew that you don't have to make a perfect composition to please God. Your effort alone is enough. Johann trusted the gifts he was given, did his work, and then released it into the world.

> YOU'VE PROBABLY HEARD ONE OF BACH'S MOST FAMOUS ORGAN WORKS, MAYBE IN A MOVIE THAT GAVE YOU THE HEEBIE-JEEBIES: *TOCCATA AND FUGUE IN D MINOR*. LOOK IT UP!

*God, thank You for the gifts You've given me!
Help me use those gifts to bring You glory.*

JUNE 22

EDDIE ROBINSON

1919–2007 • UNITED STATES

DREAM IT–THEN DO IT

In all toil there is profit.

PROVERBS 14:23

Young Eddie had a dream—he wanted to be a football coach! In college, he played quarterback and was an assistant coach for his team. And after graduation, he got his dream coaching job! When Eddie was playing and coaching, segregation still existed, meaning Black people and white people were kept separate, including in sports. But Eddie's dream of coaching meant more than just winning games. He encouraged his players to work hard, to attend church, and to be good citizens to change people's attitudes about Black players.

> EDDIE COACHED AT THE SAME COLLEGE FOR FIFTY-FIVE YEARS, WINNING A RECORD-BREAKING 408 GAMES!

Eddie and his players were respected on and off the field. Over the years, more than 200 of his players were drafted into the NFL. And most important, Eddie never forgot why he wanted to coach in the first place—to change people's lives.

God, help me work hard to make my dreams come true!

JUNE 23

FRANCISCO DE ZURBARÁN

1598–1664 • SPAIN

MAKE IT ALL REAL

*He was revealed in flesh . . . seen by angels . . .
believed in throughout the world.*

1 TIMOTHY 3:16

Francisco was a painter with a particular gift. He could make Bible characters appear so lifelike that they seemed to pop off the canvas and into real life! From paintings of Mary and Joseph taking baby Jesus to Egypt to Jesus dying on the cross, Francisco's paintings hung on the walls of churches in Spain and even all the way to Lima, Peru, in South America. Francisco worked to make his paintings as lifelike as possible so viewers could gaze on them and realize that the people they read about in their Bibles and heard about at church weren't made-up characters. They were real people, just like them! That realization might help their faith feel more real too.

> FRANCISCO USED SHADOWS AND LIGHT TO HIGHLIGHT THE SUBJECTS IN HIS PAINTINGS. BECAUSE OF HIS STYLE, HIS NICKNAME IS "THE SPANISH CARAVAGGIO."

*God, thank You for every person, story, and piece
of art that makes Your Word more real to me!*

JUNE 24

BLESSED JUTTA OF THURINGIA

C. 1200–1260 • PRUSSIA (MODERN-DAY GERMANY)

SEEING GOD IN OTHERS

In humility regard others as better than yourselves.

PHILIPPIANS 2:3

Jutta was so excited. She and her husband loved God and were starting the long journey from their home in Europe to the holy city of Jerusalem! But along the way, something unimaginable happened: Jutta's husband died. Rather than go back to her old life, Jutta decided to make a change. She got rid of all her clothes, jewels, and furniture. Jutta chose to wear simple clothes and live simply so she could focus on serving God. From then on, Jutta spent her days helping others. She cared for the sick, especially people living with leprosy. Many people wouldn't go near lepers because they were afraid of getting sick. But not Jutta. She also opened up her home to people who were blind or crippled. She saw God in the face of every person she served.

> SOME PEOPLE FROM JUTTA'S OLD LIFE LAUGHED AT WHO SHE BECAME. BUT JUTTA DIDN'T CARE. SHE ENJOYED SPENDING TIME WITH HER NEW FRIENDS.

God, remind me that when we serve others who need help, we're really serving You.

JUNE 25

GEORGE WASHINGTON CARVER

1861–1943 • UNITED STATES

GOD'S CREATION PROVIDES

Open my eyes, so that I may behold wondrous things out of your law.

PSALM 119:18

George was in awe of the world God had made. He especially enjoyed learning about plants and studied hard to become a botanist (a plant scientist). George became a teacher and researcher at the famous Tuskegee Institute in Alabama. Through his scientific studies, George discovered many new facts about plants, especially peanuts and sweet potatoes. George found that those two crops didn't take too many nutrients out of the soil, which meant farmers could plant them in the same place for many years. Peanuts and sweet potatoes also provided nutrition for those who ate them. George was loved not only by his students but also by the general public. He taught people how to use nature to help others and that God can be seen in His wondrous creation.

> GEORGE ALWAYS WORE A FLOWER OR A SPRIG OF GREEN ON THE LAPEL OF HIS COAT.

God, thank You for creating such a beautiful world.

JUNE 26

BOB HOPE

1903–2003 • UNITED STATES

SPREADING JOY

He will fill your mouth with laughter, and your lips with shouts of joy.

JOB 8:21

Bob Hope loved to make people laugh! His joy was infectious, and he wasn't afraid to laugh at himself. Bob wanted to make everyone laugh but especially those in the military. He knew how hard it must be to be away from home. So Bob traveled all over the world doing comedy shows for people in the military. He entertained troops during World War II in the 1940s, the Korean War in the 1950s, the Vietnam War in the 1960s and 1970s, and even the Persian Gulf War in the 1990s. Bob could have stayed in Hollywood, but he didn't. He chose to serve those who were selflessly serving their country.

> IN 1997, CONGRESS DECLARED BOB THE FIRST "HONORARY VETERAN" FOR HIS COMEDY TOURS FOR THE MILITARY.

God, thank You for the gift of laughter!
Help me spread joy to others today.

JUNE 27

JOHN WOODEN

1910–2010 • UNITED STATES

A FIRM FOUNDATION

He will be the stability of your times, abundance
of salvation, wisdom, and knowledge.

ISAIAH 33:6

John was a college basketball coach at UCLA. He coached for forty years, and for every five games, his team won four times. That's a lot of winning! But John knew that the secret to winning wasn't just having talented players. Each player needed a strong foundation of good character to support their talent. Every season, John showed the team his famous "pyramid of success." The pyramid was made of character "building blocks" that would make a player stronger, like loyalty, enthusiasm, self-control, and friendship. Near the top were patience and faith, which were central to John's beliefs as a Christian. John knew players needed to believe in themselves, learn patience, and grow spiritually. And since John's team won games 80 percent of the time, maybe he was onto something!

> DURING COACH WOODEN'S FINAL YEARS COACHING, HE LOST 22 GAMES—AND WON 335!

*God, I want to share Your love with
others. Please show me how.*

JUNE 28

SAINT IRENAEUS

C. 120–C. 200 • LUGDUNUM (MODERN-DAY FRANCE)

TRULY HELPING

So then, putting away falsehood, let all of us speak the truth
to our neighbors, for we are members of one another.

EPHESIANS 4:25

It's fun to be right, isn't it? When someone has a different opinion, proving them wrong can feel like we're winning a game. But Saint Irenaeus didn't like to be right to feel like he'd won something. When it came to talking about Jesus, Saint Irenaeus wanted to be right so that people understood the truth about Jesus and how to live their lives. When Saint Irenaeus was living, some people were saying that Jesus had told them some secrets that only *they* knew and were trying to get people to follow them. But Saint Irenaeus showed those people scriptures and talked to them about why that wasn't true. Saint Irenaeus was more concerned about helping people know Jesus than he was about being right.

IN 2022, POPE FRANCIS NAMED SAINT IRENAEUS AS A DOCTOR OF THE CHURCH.

*God, help me care more about helping
others than simply being right.*

JUNE 29

JESSE BUSHYHEAD

1804–1844 • UNITED STATES

A LOYAL LEADER

Who can find one worthy of trust? The righteous walk in integrity.

PROVERBS 20:6-7

Jesse was a member of the Cherokee Nation. His family had lived in East Tennessee for many years. Jesse had become a Christian when he was twenty-six years old and preached every Sunday. One day, the government said the Cherokee people had to move hundreds of miles away to Oklahoma. Back then, they had to walk or take a wagon to make this big trip. Jesse was sad—his people didn't want to leave their home. But if they had to go, he would lead them. Against cold winter winds, Jesse led more than 800 people through Tennessee, Kentucky, Illinois, Missouri, and finally into Oklahoma. After they arrived, Jesse built a new church where his people could worship. People remember Jesse's loyalty to the Cherokee Nation even today.

NO MATTER WHERE HE WENT, JESSE ALWAYS CARRIED HIS BIBLE.

God, help me to be a loyal friend like Jesse.

JUNE 30

GINGER SMOCK

1920–1995 • UNITED STATES

MAKING TIME FOR THANK-YOUS

Bless the Lord, O my soul, and do not forget all his benefits.

PSALM 103:2

Concertgoers at the Hollywood Bowl couldn't believe their ears. Who was this remarkable ten-year-old playing the violin? Ginger could play not only rehearsed pieces; she could also *improvise* and create new worlds with her music. Ginger's improvising skill helped her become a respected jazz violinist. By the age of twenty-three, she was playing across Southern California with an all-female jazz trio called the Sepia Tones. In 1951, the Sepia Tones even became the first Black band to headline their own TV show on a major network. Through it all, Ginger always made time for her church. Even after late Saturday night performances, early on Sunday morning Ginger would climb the stage at church to play. Playing at church was a way to thank God for giving her the gift of music.

> IN HER LATER YEARS, GINGER WAS A *CONCERTMASTER* IN MANY ORCHESTRAS. THE CONCERTMASTER IS THE MOST KNOWLEDGEABLE VIOLIN PLAYER AND SECOND-IN-COMMAND AFTER THE CONDUCTOR.

*God, no matter what's going on in my life,
I want to make time to thank You.*

JULY 1

DAVID WILKERSON

1931–2011 • UNITED STATES

HAPPY AND HEALTHY

The LORD is my chosen portion and my cup.

PSALM 16:5

As a young pastor, David left his small hometown in Pennsylvania to go to New York City to tell people about Jesus. David quickly realized that many of the young people he spoke with were struggling. They thought they needed alcohol and drugs to survive. David wanted to help these teens feel happier and healthier, so he started a program called Teen Challenge. Young people who attended Teen Challenge learned how to take better care of their bodies. They also talked with counselors about their struggles. Sharing our struggles with others can make a problem less scary. David also shared how to have a relationship with Jesus. Over the next several decades, David and Teen Challenge helped thousands of people live happier, healthier lives.

DAVID WROTE A BOOK ABOUT HIS LIFE CALLED *THE CROSS AND THE SWITCHBLADE*. IT'S BEEN TRANSLATED INTO MORE THAN THIRTY LANGUAGES!

> *God, help me learn to take care of the body You gave me while also growing closer to You.*

JULY 2

VINCE LOMBARDI

1913–1970 • UNITED STATES

TACKLING THE LITTLE THINGS

"You have been trustworthy in a few things, I
will put you in charge of many things."

MATTHEW 25:23

"Gentlemen, this is a football," coach Vince Lombardi told his team, holding up the pointed brown ball. The burly NFL football players looked at each other through their face guards, cracking smiles. They knew what a football was. They were the Green Bay Packers! What was Coach Lombardi getting at? It was the first practice of the season, and Coach Lombardi knew, based on his strong faith in God, that being faithful with the small things is so important. Even though the team had almost won a championship the year before, they needed to go back to basics. Because mastering the basics—like blocking, tackling, and memorizing plays—would help the team win games! Vince was right. His team was so good at the small things that their big wins added up to big championships!

> VINCE HELPED THE PACKERS WIN THE FIRST TWO SUPER BOWL TROPHIES. NOW THE TROPHY IS NAMED AFTER VINCE!

*God, show me the small things I need to get
right so I can do great things for You.*

JULY 3

JOHN LEWIS

1940–2020 • UNITED STATES

WALK TO FREEDOM

> To do righteousness and justice is more
> acceptable to the LORD than sacrifice.
>
> **PROVERBS 21:3**

On March 7, 1965, John and about 600 others were preparing to march peacefully over the Edmund Pettus Bridge in Selma, Alabama. They were marching for equal voting rights for every American citizen, no matter their race. Partway across the bridge, John and his friends were confronted by law enforcement and others who had been told by Alabama's governor to stop their peaceful march. They were attacked with tear gas, whips, and clubs. Many, including John, went to the hospital with serious injuries. John called for President Johnson to do something. Later that year, the president signed the Voting Rights Act, which ensured the right to vote for every American. John's faith continued to guide his activism for years to come. "Without prayer, without faith in the Almighty, the civil rights movement would have been like a bird without wings."

> JOHN WENT ON TO SERVE IN THE US HOUSE OF REPRESENTATIVES FOR THIRTY-THREE YEARS.

God, thank You for the people who are brave
and speak out about what is right.

JULY 4

GALILEO GALILEI

1564–1642 • ITALY

SHARING YOUR DISCOVERIES

O Lord, how manifold are your works! In
wisdom you have made them all.

PSALM 104:24

Whether using math equations to explain the way objects fall or a telescope to discover the moons of Jupiter, Galileo stayed in awe of God's creation. For as long as he lived, he never quit studying, experimenting, and sharing what he learned about the world God made. Sometimes Galileo's discoveries were different from what others believed. For thousands of years, many believed the Bible said the universe revolved around the earth. But Galileo discovered that the earth and all the planets revolve around the sun. Many told Galileo to stop sharing his discoveries or he'd get into trouble. But Galileo didn't care. He wanted to tell the truth about the way God's creation worked so that people could understand God's world a bit more.

> GALILEO BUILT HIS OWN TELESCOPE AND DISCOVERED MORE STARS THAN WE CAN SEE WITH JUST OUR EYES—AND THAT THE MOON'S SURFACE IS ROCKY!

*God, give me the courage to keep
sharing what I learn about You.*

JULY 5

J. B. PHILLIPS

1906-1982 · ENGLAND

I GET IT NOW!

"Do you understand what you are reading?" [Philip asked]... "How can I, unless someone guides me."

ACTS 8:30-31

J. B. sat with the teens in his parish, reading Bible verses aloud from the King James Bible. But instead of comforting the teens, the scriptures seemed to confuse them. "What does that mean?" they'd ask the young Anglican priest. So J. B. decided to translate the book of Colossians into the plain, modern English the teens spoke. When he read from his new translation, the youth group was ecstatic. "We get it now!" they exclaimed. J. B. was so excited that he translated the whole New Testament into the same plain English. Eventually, it wasn't just J. B.'s youth group who was excited to read and understand the Bible this way; it was people across the globe.

> J. B. SENT A COPY OF HIS COLOSSIANS TRANSLATION TO C. S. LEWIS. HE ENJOYED THE WORK AND ENCOURAGED J. B. TO KEEP GOING!

*God, thank You for those who help
me understand Your words.*

JULY 6

THEOPHILUS OF ANTIOCH

UNKNOWN–C. 180 • ANTIOCH (MODERN-DAY TÜRKIYE)

TELL ME WHY

Always be ready to make your defense to anyone who demands from you an accounting for the hope that is in you; yet do it with gentleness and reverence.

1 PETER 3:15–16

Theophilus paused, thinking of what else to say to his friend Autolycus. When Theophilus was growing up, he had learned to worship the gods and goddesses of Greece. But when he was older, he heard about Jesus and became a Christian. Autolycus didn't understand why his friend had changed. He made fun of Theophilus's new faith. Theophilus wanted to explain why he believed in Jesus. He was patient with Autolycus—it had taken a while for Theophilus to truly believe in Jesus too. Theophilus wrote at least three times to his friend, explaining his beliefs. We don't know if Autolycus ever changed his mind. But we do know that Theophilus tried his hardest to share Jesus with his friend.

> THEOPHILUS WAS THE FIRST WRITER TO USE THE GREEK WORD *TRIAD* TO SAY "FATHER, SON, AND HOLY SPIRIT."

God, help me tell all my friends about You. I want them to know You!

JULY 7

GORDIE HOWE

1928–2016 • UNITED STATES

CHASING JOY

May the God of hope fill you with all joy.

ROMANS 15:13

Do you think your grandpa could play professional hockey? If you just laughed, think again! At fifty-two years old, Gordie Howe was still skating on the NHL ice. Gordie was a talented player who helped the Detroit Red Wings win four championships. He hung up his skates when he was in his early forties, when many players do. But after a couple of years, he grew bored. When someone asked if he wanted to play professional hockey on a team with his sons, Gordie thought it might be fun. *But what will other people think? Will they make fun of me?* He decided to go for it anyway. Playing with his sons brought Gordie lots of joy! And he became the oldest NHL player ever.

> IN HIS CAREER, GORDIE RACKED UP MANY INJURIES: A BROKEN WRIST, BROKEN RIBS AND TOES, A DISLOCATED SHOULDER, AND MORE THAN 300 STITCHES. BUT HE KEPT PLAYING WITH A SMILE!

God, thank You for giving me gifts that bring me joy and bring You glory!

JULY 8

HÉLDER PESSOA CÂMARA

1909–1999 • BRAZIL

GOD'S HUMBLE SERVANT

"All who exalt themselves will be humbled, and all
who humble themselves will be exalted."

MATTHEW 23:12

Hélder was a bishop with a particular mission: helping the poor. He'd visit poor areas of Rio de Janeiro where people didn't have much to eat or didn't have access to electricity and water. From the pulpit and on television, Hélder would ask people to donate to help them. He asked people to think about how to help others in need. Because of his position, Hélder could have lived in a nice house. He could've worn fancy clothing and a gold cross around his neck. But Hélder turned down all of it. He wore a simple brown robe and a wooden cross. He asked people not to call him "Eminence," the title he would have earned as bishop. Why? Because he wanted to be seen as no better than the people he was serving. Hélder was a humble servant for God.

> EVEN AFTER HÉLDER RETIRED FROM HIS POSITION, HE STILL HELPED THE POOR AT HIS LOCAL CHURCH.

*God, I want to humbly serve the people
around me. Please show me how.*

JULY 9

MARY ANNING

1799–1847 • ENGLAND

SPECIAL DISCOVERY

You are . . . God's own people.

1 PETER 2:9

Mary wasn't like the other girls. By five years old, she was tagging along with her dad to look for fossils, which he sold at their cabinet shop. Mary's dad taught her to look for fossils on the beach and delicately clean them up. As she grew older, Mary read books on geology and anatomy, and after her father died, Mary searched for fossils even more. At age twelve, she found an *Ichthyosaurus*, a marine dinosaur. She also was the first to find a complete skeleton of a *Pleiosaurus* and a *Pterodactyl*. Male scientists at the time were hesitant to recognize her; some didn't give her credit for her discoveries. But Mary kept searching anyway. Her discoveries laid the foundation of the field of paleontology.

> MARY ALSO PIONEERED THE STUDY OF *COPROLITES*—OR FOSSILIZED POOP!

God, thank You for making me different and unique!

JULY 10

ANDRÉ TROCMÉ

1901–1971 • FRANCE

A BIG HELP

> I command you today, by loving the LORD your
> God and walking always in his ways.
>
> **DEUTERONOMY 19:9**

André was a pastor who faced a big problem. His home country of France was occupied by the Nazis, who were persecuting the Jewish people. Helping Jews was illegal, but André knew that was wrong. He encouraged his congregation to shelter Jews who asked for help. Word began to spread quietly that the village of Le Chambon-sur-Lignon, where André lived, was a place where Jews could find help. The villagers eventually helped hundreds of Jews find homes or escape to Switzerland, where it was safe. André was arrested and pressured to sign a document saying he wouldn't help the Jews anymore, but he refused. He stood firm in what he believed. André knew that God wanted him to help others, even when it cost him his safety.

> RESEARCHERS ESTIMATE MORE THAN 5,000 REFUGEES PASSED THROUGH LE CHAMBON-SUR-LIGNON, THANKS TO ANDRÉ'S ENCOURAGEMENT TO HELP.

God, I want to help those in need, even when it is hard. Please show me how.

JULY 11

TOM LANDRY

1924–2000 • UNITED STATES

CONCENTRATE!

*Let your eyes look directly forward and
your gaze be straight before you.*

PROVERBS 4:25

The Dallas Cowboys were a brand-new football team playing in the NFL. Their first season, they didn't win any games. *How can we fix this?* Coach Landry wondered. Over the next three decades, Coach Landry transformed the Cowboys into a winning team. How did he do it? By making his players practice more? Or bench-press more weights? Nope. Coach Landry taught them to discipline their *minds* to pay attention to what was happening on the field without getting caught up in mistakes or big plays. If players weren't "getting" a lesson, Coach Landry would often use a Bible story to make his point. Several championship appearances and two Super Bowl rings proved that perhaps Coach Landry was right about this whole "discipline" thing.

> COACH LANDRY'S PRIORITIES WERE "GOD, FAMILY, AND FOOTBALL." DURING THE OFFSEASON, HE TAUGHT SUNDAY SCHOOL AT HIS CHURCH.

*God, when I'm trying to accomplish a big goal,
help me to be disciplined to reach it.*

JULY 12

FANNY CROSBY

1820–1915 • UNITED STATES

HIDDEN TALENT

Humble yourselves before the Lord, and he will exalt you.

JAMES 4:10

Fanny Crosby wrote thousands of *hymns*, which are songs of praise to God. No one knows exactly how many, because she often published them under a different name. She had only one wish: that her songs would help others see God. She didn't care if she got credit; she just wanted people's faith to grow. Even more amazing, Fanny had been blind since she was a baby! At fifteen, she enrolled in the New York Institution for the Blind, where she excelled in her studies and wrote poetry. As she got older, Fanny saw how much people needed help. She did mission work in New York City, helping the poor and new immigrants. The people she met inspired the messages of love, grace, and redemption in her songs.

> FANNY WAS THE FIRST WOMAN TO FORMALLY SPEAK IN THE US SENATE, WHERE SHE WAS ASKED TO READ ONE OF HER POEMS.

God, help me use my talents to honor You.

JULY 13

SAINT TERESA OF THE ANDES

1900–1920 • CHILE

NEVER TOO YOUNG

Let no one despise your youth, but set the believers an example in speech and conduct, in love, in faith, in purity.

1 TIMOTHY 4:12

Growing up, Teresa was known as Juanita. She was a typical child who enjoyed the outdoors, played sports, and sometimes fought with her siblings. When she was fourteen, she read a book by a young French nun named Thérèse and learned the importance of following God. Juanita realized she could help others, just like Thérèse! When she was fifteen, Juanita saw a child shivering in the cold and took him home. She fed the boy and got him clothes and shoes. Later, Juanita spent vacations teaching kids about God. At nineteen, Juanita became a nun and took the name *Teresa*. She wrote letters to friends and family to share her thoughts about God. Many who read her letters dedicated their lives to Him. Even though she died less than a year later, Teresa's great love for God touched many lives.

> **TERESA IS THE FIRST SAINT FROM CHILE. PEOPLE ARE STILL INSPIRED BY HER LETTERS TODAY!**

God, help me show Your love to others, no matter how old I am.

JULY 14

LOUIS ZAMPERINI

1917–2014 • UNITED STATES AND JAPAN

FREEDOM IN FORGIVENESS

Forgive each other; just as the Lord has forgiven you.

COLOSSIANS 3:13

It was 1949, and Louis Zamperini didn't know how to stop feeling so angry and so sad. At age nineteen, he had run in the 1936 Olympics. After college, he joined the Army Air Corps. While serving, his plane plunged into the ocean. Louis spent forty-seven days lost at sea before being found by the Japanese and imprisoned for two years. When Louis finally came home, he couldn't stop thinking about the torture and loneliness he'd gone through in the war. He argued with his wife and drank alcohol to try to forget his pain. But then he heard a sermon from Billy Graham that changed his life. Louis became a Christian and returned to Japan to forgive the men who had hurt him. He spent the rest of his life telling people about the freedom he found by forgiving others.

LOUIS WAS GIVEN THE HONOR OF CARRYING THE OLYMPIC FLAME THREE TIMES: IN 1984, 1996, AND 1998.

God, please help me forgive others who wrong me.

JULY 15

KATHERINE JOHNSON

1918–2020 • UNITED STATES

OUT-OF-THIS-WORLD GIFTS

Serve one another with whatever gift each of you has received.

1 PETER 4:10

Katherine Johnson's favorite subject in school was math. She was so good at it that by age ten, she was solving high school math problems. In the 1950s, scientists asked Katherine to help them study how to send people to space. Katherine calculated the path for *Freedom 7*, which sent the first US astronaut into space. The next year, an astronaut named John Glenn asked Katherine to check if computer calculations for his spaceflight were correct (computers were brand-new, and people were nervous to trust them!). Katherine crunched the numbers and said the calculations were correct. A few days later, John Glenn became the first person to orbit the earth. Katherine also helped send the first astronauts to the moon! All the while, she knew that God's grace had opened doors for her, and she used her gifts for His glory and to help make history.

> KATHERINE'S WORK WAS SO IMPORTANT THAT NASA NAMED A BUILDING AFTER HER: THE KATHERINE G. JOHNSON COMPUTATIONAL RESEARCH FACILITY.

Lord, help me use the gifts You've given me to do Your will.

JULY 16

GEORGES ROUAULT

1871–1958 • FRANCE

TURN AROUND

With the Lord there is steadfast love, and with him is great power to redeem.

PSALM 130:7

Georges was a French artist who dedicated his career to creating paintings that revealed his faith. Georges became a Christian as a young man. He was touched by God's undeserved grace for him. While at the French courts, Georges saw people struggling in the worst times in their lives. He began to paint these people, depicting them as people whose lives could be turned around by God. Georges had trained to create glass for churches. The bright colors in his paintings mimicked the beautiful light that would come through those church windows. He hoped that the people looking at his paintings would feel transported to a big cathedral so that they too could feel hope that their lives could be redeemed by God.

> ONE OF GEORGES'S ART SCHOOL CLASSMATES WAS THE FAMOUS ARTIST HENRI MATISSE.

God, thank You for turning my life around and giving me hope!

JULY 17

JESSE OWENS

1913–1980 • UNITED STATES

RUN YOUR RACE

Run in such a way that you may win.

1 CORINTHIANS 9:24

At a young age, Jesse could breeze past competitors on the track. He set world records during high school and eventually earned a spot on the US Olympic Track and Field team. But the 1936 Olympics were being hosted by Germany. Adolf Hitler ruled the country, and he wanted to show the world that his German people were the fastest and strongest athletes. He thought this could convince others that his policies against people based on skin color or background were a good idea. Many people disagreed with Hitler and wanted to boycott the Olympics. As a young Black man, Jesse thought about boycotting too, but he decided to show Hitler he was wrong by putting his speed to the test. Jesse won four gold medals during the games and bravely showed the world that anyone can achieve great things, no matter their skin color.

> JESSE LOVED TO RUN BECAUSE IT WAS A SPORT HE COULD DO ALL BY HIMSELF, NO MATTER WHERE HE WAS.

God, thank You for giving me Your power and strength. I want to use them for Your glory.

JULY 18

J. J. THOMSON

1856–1940 • ENGLAND

WORK HARD, PLAY HARD

There is nothing better for mortals than to eat and drink, and find enjoyment in their toil.

ECCLESIASTES 2:24

J. J. was a professor at Cambridge and a pioneer in the field of physics. With the discovery of electrons, he completely changed the way people thought about the structure of atoms. His discovery was so important that he won a Nobel Prize in 1906 and was knighted by Britain's King Edward VII in 1908. You might expect such an important man of science to live at the lab. Not J. J.! He spent time outside the lab reading popular fiction, attending plays, keeping up with politics, and following Cambridge's cricket and rugby teams. He enjoyed long walks in the countryside and looked for rare plants to take back to his elaborate garden. He made a point to meet young people who weren't scientists so he could learn more about the world outside his lab.

> THOMSON ALSO HAD A KNACK FOR DISCOVERING TALENTED STUDENTS. SEVEN OF HIS PUPILS WON NOBEL PRIZES.

God, thank You for giving us important work—and hobbies we love.

JULY 19

LUCY MAUD MONTGOMERY

1874–1942 • CANADA

YOU BELONG WITH ME

You are no longer strangers, but you are . . . also
members of the household of God.

EPHESIANS 2:19

Hmm, what should I write about? Lucy wondered. Lucy's childhood had been different from many others her age. Born in a small Canadian province called Prince Edward Island, Lucy had lost both parents before she was two years old and lived with her grandparents. Now a young woman working as a teacher, Lucy realized her story could help some of her students feel less alone. So Lucy wrote a story about Anne, a redheaded orphan with freckles, a cheerful spirit, and a wild imagination. *Anne of Green Gables* became an instant bestseller. Many readers saw themselves in Anne, who sometimes didn't know quite where she belonged. Lucy's writing showed that we all feel a little different sometimes. But we can find "family," whether they're related to us or are people we meet later.

> LUCY'S CLOSEST FRIENDS CALLED HER "MAUD."

God, thank You for giving us people who love us.

JULY 20

MAGGIE LENA WALKER

1864–1934 • UNITED STATES

BIG BRAIN, BIG HEART

> Whoever is kind to the poor lends to the Lord.
>
> **PROVERBS 19:17**

Maggie had a head for business, and God had given her a heart to help others. She could see what people needed and how to help them. Maggie worked at Order of Saint Luke's, an organization that helped Black members in need. Members paid a little money every month. Then, if a family member couldn't work, Saint Luke's would give the family money to live on until the sick or injured person was better. But Saint Luke's was giving away more money than they had. They couldn't keep going if they ran out of money!

> THE SAINT LUKE PENNY SAVINGS BANK WAS THE FIRST US BANK OPENED BY A BLACK WOMAN.

So Maggie figured out how to get more members. She also opened the Saint Luke Penny Savings Bank, where members could get home or business loans. Maggie used her business brain and big heart to help others.

God, help me use the brain You gave me to help others.

JULY 21

JOHANN PACHELBEL

1653–1706 • GERMANY

PLANTING SEEDS

You reap whatever you sow.

GALATIANS 6:7

If you've attended a wedding, you've likely heard Johann's most famous work: *Canon in D*. The piece starts slow, with just an organ or cello. The same melody is repeated, and each time, more and more strings join the tune, until the beautiful, lush piece ends! Johann couldn't have known how many people would enjoy his music hundreds of years later. Although Johann composed many pieces for the church, during his life he was known more for his talents as an organ teacher. One of his students was Johann Christoph Bach, the older brother of the famous Johann Sebastian Bach. As a teacher and a composer, Johann was planting seeds into his students and generations beyond.

> THE WORLD FORGOT ABOUT PACHELBEL UNTIL 1919, WHEN A MUSIC SCHOLAR PUBLISHED *CANON IN D*. THE SONG APPEARED IN AN OSCAR-WINNING 1980 MOVIE AND EXPLODED IN POPULARITY.

God, I want to plant seeds of goodness. Give me faith that they'll sprout joy for others someday!

JULY 22

JOHN NAPIER

1550–1617 • SCOTLAND

WATCH YOUR WORDS!

> Let no evil talk come out of your mouths, but
> only what is useful for building up.
>
> **EPHESIANS 4:29**

In a small town in rural Scotland, villagers talked about the mysterious man who lived in the biggest house in town. He didn't leave his home much. The only thing he did, some said, was study numbers. "Perhaps he is a wizard," the people would whisper. But John didn't care. He was too busy inventing! John was a mathematician who not only read religious texts in Greek but also invented *logarithms*, a new way of doing calculations. Logarithms allowed people to solve long math problems much faster than traditional methods. This was useful for anyone navigating a long journey or for astronomers studying the stars. By the time he died, John had earned the respect of his fellows Scots and was lauded by mathematicians and scientists around the globe.

> JOHN ALSO INVENTED THE FIRST FORMS OF PORTABLE CALCULATORS AND EVEN POPULARIZED THE USE OF THE DECIMAL POINT.

God, when people say unkind and untrue things about me, please help me ignore them and keep on going.

JULY 23

WALTER PAYTON

1954–1999 • UNITED STATES

BLESSED TO BE A BLESSING

God loves a cheerful giver.

2 CORINTHIANS 9:7

NFL running back Walter Payton won many awards during his thirteen years in the NFL. He was named Most Valuable Player in 1977. He helped the Chicago Bears win their first Super Bowl title. But Walter's favorite award he ever won was the Man of the Year Award, given for showing excellence both on and off the field. The Payton family's motto was "We are blessed to be a blessing." They ran restaurants in Chicago, and every year they invited children in foster care to a Christmas party at their restaurants (Santa came too!). The Payton family was thankful for their blessings and wanted to share with others. The smiles they received from the children they helped were better than any trophy Walter could have won.

> THE "MAN OF THE YEAR AWARD" IS NOW GIVEN IN WALTER'S NAME. IT'S ONE OF THE HIGHEST HONORS AN NFL PLAYER CAN RECEIVE.

God, thank You for all the blessings You've given me! Please help me share them with others.

JULY 24

SAINT SHARBEL MAKHLOUF

1828–1898 • LEBANON

A QUIET LIFE

The eyes of the LORD range throughout the entire earth,
to strengthen those whose heart is true to him.

2 CHRONICLES 16:9

You don't have to do big things to make a huge impact. At age twenty-three, Sharbel joined a monastery. He spent his days praying and working in the fields with his fellow brothers. After twenty-four years, Sharbel asked to move to a smaller home nearby, where only three people lived. In such a quiet home, Sharbel would be able to spend even more time in prayer, just like the saint he admired most, Saint Maroun. Word spread about Sharbel's holiness. People traveled to receive a blessing from him and ask to be remembered in his prayers. He gladly said yes. Sharbel lived twenty-three more years as a monk, showing others that a quiet life devoted to God can still be an impactful one.

> SAINT MAROUN MONASTERY, WHERE SHARBEL'S TOMB IS LOCATED, IS ONE OF THE MOST-VISITED CHRISTIAN PILGRIMAGE SITES IN LEBANON.

God, thank You for allowing us to choose how
to live for You—in big and small ways.

JULY 25

ENDŌ SHŪSAKU

1923–1996 • JAPAN

MY POINT OF VIEW

See what love the Father has given us, that we should be called children of God.

1 JOHN 3:1

When Endō was about ten years old, his mother became a Christian—then Endō did too. Endō didn't expect his decision to follow Jesus to give him a new way to see the world. In Endō's native Japan, there weren't many Christians, so he stuck out. As a young man, he traveled to France, excited to be in a place with more Christians. But in France, many people treated Endō differently because he was from Asia. Endō didn't know where he fit in. So he wrote many novels that showed what happens when people in Eastern cultures like Japan meet people in Western cultures like Europe and the United States. His books showed what it was like to be a Christian in different places around the world.

> ENDŌ'S MOST FAMOUS BOOK, *SILENCE,* WAS ADAPTED INTO A MOVIE BY THE FAMOUS DIRECTOR MARTIN SCORSESE.

God, help me welcome everyone who follows You with open arms.

JULY 26

TIYO SOGA

1829–1871 · SOUTH AFRICA

CONNECT THE DOTS

"You will be my witnesses in Jerusalem, in all Judea
and Samaria, and to the ends of the earth."

ACTS 1:8

Tiyo closed the book he was reading, *The Pilgrim's Progress* by John Bunyan. *So many of my people back in South Africa would enjoy this book*, he thought. At the time, Tiyo was studying the Bible in Scotland so he could one day become a preacher. Tiyo loved *The Pilgrim's Progress*. It mirrored the way many people felt (and still feel!) throughout their lives: excited to start a journey, confused and sad when they get lost, joyful when they find their way. He thought his people, the Xhosa, back in South Africa, could relate and might find it helpful in their Christian walk. So he translated it into his native Xhosa language. Tiyo's big brain connected the dots between continents, and his love for God allowed hearts to be changed.

TIYO EVENTUALLY ACHIEVED HIS DREAM TO BECOME A PREACHER AND MOVED BACK TO SOUTH AFRICA TO PREACH.

> *God, help me see different ways to
> connect Your love to others.*

JULY 27

SAINT TITUS BRANDSMA

1881–1942 • THE NETHERLANDS

WHAT'S RIGHT OR WHAT'S EASY?

*If you endure when you do right and suffer
for it, you have God's approval.*

1 PETER 2:20

For heroes, doing what's right is more important than what they might lose because of it. That's how Titus felt. He was a priest and a journalist who helped other Catholic journalists create newspapers in The Netherlands. When the Nazis invaded during World War II, they wanted newspapers to print articles that spread lies about the Jews, saying they did bad things they didn't do. But Titus knew the truth: The Nazis were lying so that people would grow to distrust the Jews. That way, people wouldn't protest when Nazis persecuted the Jews. So Titus wrote a letter to other Catholic journalists not to print what the Nazis told them to, but the Nazis found out and arrested Titus. He stood up for what he believed.

> TITUS WAS TAKEN TO A NAZI CONCENTRATION CAMP. HE GAVE A WOODEN ROSARY TO A NURSE THERE, AND SHE BECAME A CHRISTIAN.

*God, when I must decide between what's right and
what's easy, help me choose to do what's right.*

JULY 28

MARY PRINCE

C. 1788–1833 • ENGLAND

BREAKING CHAINS

He destined us for adoption as his children through Jesus Christ.

EPHESIANS 1:5

Mary was born to an enslaved woman in Bermuda and was tragically separated from her mother and sold into slavery. Growing up, Mary wanted to join a church so she could worship God alongside others, but her owners forbade it. But at twenty-nine, she secretly joined a church anyway. At church she learned the slave trade in England was illegal. Her owners were traveling to England and planned to take Mary. *Will I be free if I go there?* she wondered. Once there, Mary learned that although trading enslaved people was illegal, owning them was still legal. Many people believed the lie that enslaved people enjoyed their lives and didn't want to be free. So in 1831, Mary published her autobiography, *The History of Mary Prince*, about the life she had endured. Two years later, England outlawed slavery altogether.

> MARY WAS THE FIRST WOMAN TO PRESENT AN ANTISLAVERY PETITION IN FRONT OF PARLIAMENT.

God, give me courage to meet each obstacle I face.

JULY 29

ALLAN ROHAN CRITE

1910–2007 • UNITED STATES

USE THE TOOLS YOU HAVE

"Give, and it will be given to you."

LUKE 6:38

By day, Allan worked at the Boston Naval Shipyard. He made detailed drawings of the propulsion systems that moved big ships across the ocean. His work helped US Navy shipbuilders visualize new designs.

But when he wasn't at his drafting desk in the navy yard, Allan created all kinds of art for churches and Christians. He painted murals for churches in New York, Detroit, and Washington, DC. He created Stations of the Cross for churches in the US and Mexico.

> ALLAN OFTEN GAVE AWAY HIS ARTWORK. THE BOSTON ATHENAEUM, ONE OF THE COUNTRY'S OLDEST LIBRARIES, HAS MORE THAN SEVENTY ITEMS DONATED BY ALLAN.

He even transformed some well-known hymns—"Nobody Knows the Trouble I've Seen" and "Swing Low, Sweet Chariot"—into visual drawings. No matter where he was, Allan used his artistic gifts to help and inspire others.

God, please help me use the gifts You gave me to aid others.

JULY 30

SAINT PETER CHRYSOLOGUS

C. 400–C. 450 • RAVENNA (MODERN-DAY ITALY)

THE GOLDEN WORDS

How are they to call on one in whom they have not believed . . . to believe in one of whom they have never heard?

ROMANS 10:14

Peter was a bishop in a town called Ravenna. He loved God so much and wanted everyone to know Him too! Peter believed the best way to tell others about God was through short messages that people could understand quickly and easily. Peter told people how much God loved them and how much better their lives would be if they followed Him. He preached that a life with God means forgiving someone when they hurt you— and that freedom comes with forgiveness. Being a Christian means showing love for others—not waiting for them to show love to you. People thought Peter's messages were so good that they copied his words onto paper. They kept these writings, and many of his sermons still survive today.

> PETER'S NAME TRANSLATES TO "PETER OF THE GOLDEN WORDS."

God, help me use my words to tell others about Your great love!

JULY 31

HENRYK GÓRECKI

1933–2010 • POLAND

CONSTANT COMPANION

Do not fear, for I am with you . . . I will strengthen you, I will
help you, I will uphold you with my victorious right hand.

ISAIAH 41:10

Henryk experienced many dark times in his life. His mother died when he was only two years old. His father and stepmother discouraged his musical gift and banned him from playing his mother's piano. He lost friends and family members during the Nazi occupation of Poland during World War II. Then he lost the country he knew when Poland came under Communist rule. There was so much change and upheaval in Henryk's life. But the one constant, besides composing music, was God. He knew that God was with him through all these dark times. "Faith, for me, is everything," he once said in an interview. "If I did not have that kind of support, I could not have passed the obstacles in my life."

> AS A CLASSICAL MUSIC COMPOSER, HENRYK WROTE MANY PIECES INSPIRED BY HIS FAITH.

*God, no matter what I go through, help me remember
that You are with me every step of the way.*

AUGUST 1

MARTYN LLOYD-JONES

1899–1981 • ENGLAND

IT'S OKAY TO BE SAD

Why are you cast down, O my soul.... Hope in God.

PSALM 42:5

Martyn woke up one morning in 1954, stretched his arms, and began to get ready for the day. That's when a surprising Bible verse popped into his head: "My spirit, why are you so sad?" He realized that many people struggle with feeling sad, even Christians who believe in God. Martyn decided to start talking about these feelings in his sermons. Back then, many people didn't talk about mental health—because they didn't know how and because it was uncomfortable. But Martyn, who was also a medical doctor, knew from his training and from the Bible that people could place their hope in Jesus when hard things happen, especially if they were sad. Martyn knew that taking care of people's minds and souls mattered and wanted people to know that Jesus was always with them.

> FOR THIRTY YEARS, MARTYN PREACHED AT WESTMINSTER CHAPEL. THAT'S JUST AROUND THE CORNER FROM BUCKINGHAM PALACE, WHERE THE KING OF ENGLAND LIVES!

God, thank You for always loving me, no matter what.

AUGUST 2

OLIVIER MESSIAEN

1908–1992 • FRANCE

MUSIC OF THE HEART

It is he whom we proclaim . . . teaching everyone in all wisdom.

COLOSSIANS 1:28

Olivier was a kid with a knack for playing piano. He made a promise: "In all the work I ever do, I'm going to make God the foundation of it all." And Olivier kept his word! At just eleven years old, he went away to school to study organ and writing music. He became the organ player for Church of the Trinity in Paris. Olivier was sure that music was connected to God in a big way. And he was inspired by music and rhythm from other cultures like China, Japan, Bolivia, and Bali. He even recorded singing birds to include their rhythms in his pieces! Though sometimes he got discouraged playing religious music for people who didn't share his views, he kept playing and composing, fulfilling his promise.

> IN 1939, OLIVIER JOINED THE FRENCH ARMY TO FIGHT IN WORLD WAR II. HE WAS CAPTURED AS A PRISONER OF WAR BUT KEPT WRITING MUSIC WHILE IMPRISONED.

God, in everything I do, help me to show You to others.

AUGUST 3

SAINT THEOPHILUS OF CORTE

1676–1740 • CORSICA (MODERN-DAY FRANCE)

A QUIET PLACE

In returning and rest you shall be saved; in quietness
and in trust shall be your strength.

ISAIAH 30:15

Theophilus wasn't a big, tough man. He didn't speak with a loud, booming voice. Instead, he was drawn to the quiet. He loved to spend time by himself so he could talk to God in prayer. When Theophilus became a priest, he was asked to spend time at a retreat house in Italy. A retreat house is a place where people can spend time in silence to focus on their relationship with God. It was a perfect place for Theophilus to work! He answered questions for anyone at the retreat house. People who visited felt much better after spending time alone with God, so Theophilus decided to open up a couple more retreat houses!

> THEOPHILUS BECAME KNOWN FOR SPENDING TIME WITH PEOPLE IN THE CONFESSIONAL, AT THEIR SICKBEDS, OR BESIDE A LOVED ONE'S GRAVE.

God, I'm so glad I can talk to You anytime through prayer.

AUGUST 4

SAINT JOHN VIANNEY

1786–1859 • FRANCE

STAY COMMITTED

Lead a life worthy of the calling to which you have been called.

EPHESIANS 4:1

When John was a child, France was going through a scary time. The people in charge said being a Christian was wrong. But John saw many priests and nuns who continued to believe and help others. John thought these people were heroes. He wanted to be a priest too. But to be a priest, he had to learn Latin, which was really hard! John studied until he finally understood the language. He eventually became a priest and was so committed to helping others that he would work up to fifteen hours a day. He refused to turn anyone away. He also helped create a home for girls who didn't have one. Many people traveled to confess their sins to John and receive his advice. He remained dedicated to those he served for his entire life.

> BY THE TIME JOHN DIED, MORE THAN 20,000 PEOPLE A YEAR CONFESSED THEIR SINS TO HIM.

God, when You give me a mission, give me the strength to follow Your will.

AUGUST 5

PHIL RIZZUTO

1917–2007 • UNITED STATES

GOOD FRIENDS

Bear one another's burdens.

GALATIANS 6:2

Phil Rizzuto was the reigning Most Valuable Player in baseball's American League when he met twelve-year-old Ed Lucas. Ed was blind, but he loved Yankees baseball. He and Phil were from the same hometown in New Jersey and became fast friends. Ed eventually began attending Saint Joseph's School for the Blind, and Phil began supporting the school. Years later, long after Ed had graduated, he came to Phil with a problem. "We need to build a new school," Ed said. Phil decided to do something about it. He'd seen that golf tournaments could be good ways to raise money. People would pay to attend or donate on behalf of a player, and it was *extra* helpful if the participants were celebrities! Phil launched his own celebrity golf tournament and raised more than $2 million, enough to build a new school.

> PHIL PLAYED ON YANKEES TEAMS THAT WON SEVEN WORLD SERIES TITLES! AFTER BASEBALL, HE ANNOUNCED YANKEES GAMES FOR FORTY YEARS.

God, thank You for my friendships!

AUGUST 6

HANK AARON

1934–2021 • UNITED STATES

REAL STRENGTH

The Lord is my strength and my shield; in him my heart trusts.

PSALM 28:7

Hank was one of baseball's best hitters. His love of baseball started when he was a kid who couldn't afford a bat and ball, so he'd hit bottle caps with a stick. Hank slowly worked his way up through the baseball ranks, eventually playing for the Milwaukee Braves. He was winning batting championships and World Series titles with his team. In 1974, Hank broke Babe Ruth's home run record. Hank could've taken credit for his accomplishment. After all, he had worked very hard to get from hitting bottle caps to breaking records. But Hank knew who was really behind his talents. "I need to depend on Someone who is bigger, stronger, and wiser than I am," Hank said. "I don't do it on my own. God is my strength."

> HANK HIT 755 HOME RUNS IN HIS CAREER. HIS RECORD STOOD FOR MORE THAN THIRTY YEARS.

God, help me remember that You are my strength, and I can always rely on You.

AUGUST 7

RAPHAEL

1483–1520 • ITALY

PORTRAIT OF KINDNESS

Let your gentleness be known to everyone.

PHILIPPIANS 4:5

Raphael loved getting to know people. He liked talking with kings and princes in the royal halls of court. He enjoyed getting to know the dignified people whose portraits he painted. He spent time in churches across Italy, talking with clergy about art pieces they wanted him to create. Raphael was kind and paid attention to people's emotions. God had given him the ability to tell if someone was happy or sad, perhaps even angry or simply thinking deeply. This trait also helped Raphael show emotion in his artwork—something he is known for. His paintings of religious scenes, inspired by his deep faith, and of regular citizens alike were infused with the emotion he so carefully observed in others.

> RAPHAEL PAINTED MORE THAN 300 "MADONNAS," PAINTINGS OF GENTLE, GRACEFUL WOMEN, TYPICALLY DEPICTING THE VIRGIN MARY.

God, no matter what I choose to be,
above all, I choose to be kind.

AUGUST 8
JANE AUSTEN
1775–1817 • ENGLAND

BOOKS ARE MIRRORS

Love is patient; love is kind.
1 CORINTHIANS 13:4

Jane sat at her desk, pen in hand, thinking about the new scene she was writing. Jane wrote novels that told stories about people in her native England. She was especially gifted at telling stories about people—particularly, young women. Her heroines were smart and funny. Most of the time, they tried to do the right thing, but they also made mistakes. The way Jane wrote about women made them seem like real people a reader might have known herself. In this way, many women saw themselves in the heroines Jane wrote about. They also saw the 1 Corinthians 13 kind of love that Jane's heroines looked for—and got!—at the end of her stories, whether a heroine found romance, a friendship, or a love for family.

> JANE'S BOOKS WERE ALL PUBLISHED ANONYMOUSLY UNTIL AFTER SHE DIED.

God, thank You for stories that show me more about myself—and You!

AUGUST 9

CHRISTY MATHEWSON

1880–1925 • UNITED STATES

GOOD REPUTATION

Favor is better than silver or gold.

PROVERBS 22:1

In 1936, Christy became one of the first five players elected to the Baseball Hall of Fame. Many players donate bats, balls, and gloves to be enshrined in the hall. Christy donated his Bible. That's the kind of player—and person—Christy was. Growing up, Christy listened eagerly to sermons about using our gifts from God and how hard things make us stronger. Christy would scribble these lessons in the margins of his Bible. Christy's nickname became "The Christian Gentleman." Once, he wouldn't give an interview to a sportswriter who treated his wife badly. His actions earned him such a good reputation that many preachers used him as an example in sermons. His manager Connie Mack once said, "He gave dignity and character to baseball." That's high praise!

> CHRISTY STILL RANKS NEAR THE TOP OF ALL PITCHERS WHO HAVE EVER PLAYED BASEBALL.

God, I want the reputation of someone who follows You.

AUGUST 10

WALTER RAUSCHENBUSCH

1861–1918 • UNITED STATES

OPEN HANDS

"Open your hand to the poor and needy neighbor in your land."

DEUTERONOMY 15:11

Walter, a twenty-four-year-old pastor at Second German Baptist Church in New York City, was distressed by what he saw around him. Unemployment. Poverty. Disease. Malnutrition. Crime. The people in his neighborhood needed their physical needs met, in addition to being cared for spiritually. After all, Walter believed, Jesus healed the sick and fed the hungry, didn't He? Walter began to live out these ideas in his church, helping many people in his community. He wrote a book called *Christianity and the Social Crisis* so Christians in other places could learn how his church had fed, clothed, and healed people. It became the bestselling religious book for the next three years. Walter ended up helping more people than he could've imagined.

MARTIN LUTHER KING JR. ADMIRED WALTER'S WORK. "HIS WRITINGS LEFT AN INDELIBLE IMPRINT ON MY THINKING," HE WROTE.

God, open my eyes to what the people around me need.
Give me the wisdom to help meet those needs.

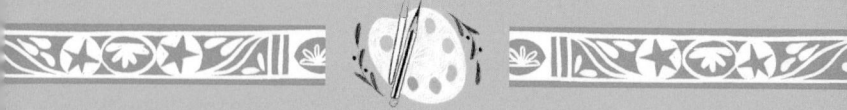

AUGUST 11

DUKE ELLINGTON

1899-1974 • UNITED STATES

STRONGER TOGETHER

> The eye cannot say to the hand, "I have no need of you." ... The members of the body that seem to be weaker are indispensable.
>
> **1 CORINTHIANS 12:21-22**

Duke was one of the most talented jazz composers and band leaders of all time. His music also reflected his deep faith, including a series of "Sacred Concerts." Duke had an amazing ability to blend different melodies, instruments, and people together beautifully. He could listen to a band and hear what was working and even what might be missing—like an instrument that would make their sound bigger, fuller, and richer. He also wasn't afraid to include other talented people in his band. In fact, the more expressive a performer was, the more Duke wanted to work with them! Duke knew that, together, they could create something better than if they played alone. Duke and the band traveled the world to share their sound, and many of Duke's band members stayed with him for decades.

> DUKE PERFORMED WITH LEGENDS WHO WEREN'T IN HIS BAND, SUCH AS SINGER ELLA FITZGERALD AND TRUMPETER AND SINGER LOUIS ARMSTRONG.

*God, thank You for the people in my life!
I know we are stronger together.*

AUGUST 12

GEORGE MÜLLER

1805–1898 • ENGLAND

GOD WILL PROVIDE

"Ask, and it will be given you; search, and you will find."

MATTHEW 7:7

When a pastor named George walked through London, he saw many children living on the streets and without parents. George asked God to give the children a home. "God will provide," he said. People began sending money to George, even though he didn't ask for it. Then he found a building that could serve as a home. People donated food and furniture. Some even volunteered to help run the home and teach the children. Over the years, more than 10,000 children came to live in George's home. From the start, he believed that God could turn a bad situation into a blessing. Through George's prayers and hard work—and the people in his community—that belief became real.

> IN 1857, CHARLES DICKENS VISITED ONE OF GEORGE'S HOMES. HE WAS SO IMPRESSED WITH THE CARE THE CHILDREN RECEIVED THAT HE WROTE A NEWSPAPER ARTICLE ABOUT IT.

God, thank You for always giving me what I need and listening when I pray.

AUGUST 13

SAINT DULCE OF THE POOR

1914–1992 • BRAZIL

DO WHAT YOU CAN WHERE YOU ARE

Happy are those who are kind to the poor.

PROVERBS 14:21

In her younger years, Saint Dulce was known simply as "Maria." When Maria was thirteen, her aunt took her through a poor area of the city. Maria realized how much more she had compared to others who lived just streets away. She began to help others how she could—right in her own neighborhood. Maria offered free haircuts and treated injuries. When she was eighteen, Maria decided to dedicate her life to God and became a nun. She took the name "Dulce" after her mother.

SAINT DULCE IS THE FIRST BRAZILIAN FEMALE SAINT.

Right away, Sister Dulce began to tend to the poor, especially those who needed food and medicine. She asked her Mother Superior if she could turn the convent's chicken yard into a safe place for people. This eventually became a hospital, and today it sees 3,000 patients a day—for free!

> *God, with Your help I know I can do good things for people right where I am! Please show me how.*

AUGUST 14

SAINT MAXIMILIAN KOLBE

1894–1941 · POLAND

IN HIS PLACE

Always seek to do good to one another.

1 THESSALONIANS 5:15

When Maximilian was twenty-three, he and six friends dedicated their lives to God and started teaching about Him. They published journals and even traveled from Poland to Japan to share about God. Maximilian was back in Poland when World War II broke out. The Nazis began to send Jews to concentration camps. They also sent other people they didn't like, especially outspoken Christians like Maximilian. Maximilian told his friends to hide while he stayed behind. He was eventually captured and sent to a concentration camp called Auschwitz. Maximilian shared his food, even as he grew sick. He heard people's confessions and celebrated Mass. When a prisoner escaped, the Nazis sentenced another prisoner named Franciszek to death as punishment. "I want to die in place of this prisoner," Maximilian said. Franciszek's life was spared, and Maximilian died a hero.

THE CELL WHERE MAXIMILIAN DIED IS NOW A SHRINE.

God, thank You for the example of Maximilian's selflessness.

AUGUST 15

YOGI BERRA

1925–2015 • UNITED STATES

WINNING WITH KINDNESS

Whoever pursues righteousness and kindness will find life and honor.

PROVERBS 21:21

Yogi played catcher for the New York Yankees. After eighteen seasons, he had shattered records and racked up plenty of World Series victories and MVP awards. Many people might say Yogi had accomplished enough, but he wasn't done! After he retired from playing, he spent the next twenty years as a coach and manager. He taught players about the game, but more importantly, Yogi, a devout Catholic, taught them how to treat others. "I believe his finest quality was how he treated everyone with sincerity and kindness," said legendary Yankees shortstop Derek Jeter. "He always made you feel good inside," said Yankees catcher Jorge Posada. "He embraced me the first day I met him," said Yankees pitcher Andy Pettitte. Yogi knew the greatest accomplishment wasn't just winning but treating others with kindness.

> YOGI WAS PART OF TEN WORLD SERIES–WINNING TEAMS. HE'S THE ONLY MLB PLAYER WITH A CHAMPIONSHIP RING FOR EACH FINGER!

God, help me show kindness to everyone I meet.

AUGUST 16

TYCHO BRAHE

1546–1601 • DENMARK

SPARK JOY

[The Lord made] the moon and stars to rule over the night.

PSALM 136:9

Tycho was *pumped* to learn about astronomy. When he was fourteen, he saw a solar eclipse that set his mind ablaze. *What else might be happening in space?* he wondered. During the day, he studied his normal subjects, but at night he spent hours looking at the starry skies. Soon his enthusiasm for astronomy bubbled over into his daytime studies. His math teacher helped him find an astronomy book from the ancient astronomer Ptolemy. Other teachers helped Tycho make small planet globes. Tycho used these makeshift solar systems to plot star positions. Before the invention of the telescope, Tycho was able to correctly plot the positions of 777 stars and paved the way for future scientists to discover more in space.

IN 1566, TYCHO LOST HIS NOSE IN A DUEL WITH HIS THIRD COUSIN. HE WORE A PROSTHETIC BRASS NOSE FOR THE REST OF HIS LIFE.

God, I love learning new things about the world You made!

AUGUST 17

FRANÇOIS MAURIAC

1885–1970 • FRANCE

GOOD INFLUENCING

Show yourself in all respects a model of good works.

TITUS 2:7

In 1954, François was one of the most celebrated novelists in France. A devoted Christian, François met a young Jewish man named Elie Wiesel. Elie had survived the horrors of the Holocaust. François listened to Elie describe his time in a Nazi concentration camp and the suffering he saw. François was moved to tears and told Elie he'd learned that people need to speak out and share the stories of those who suffer so that fewer people will hurt others in the future. Elie took François's words to heart.

> ELIE'S BOOK *NIGHT* HAS SOLD MORE THAN 10 MILLION COPIES AND HELPED ELIE EARN THE NOBEL PEACE PRIZE IN 1986.

He wrote a book about his experience called *Night*. François wrote the foreword, using his well-known name on the cover to tell others they needed to read this book. François used his influence for good.

God, please help me use my influence for good.

AUGUST 18

SAINT HELENA

C. 248–C. 328 • ROME (MODERN-DAY ITALY)

ALL IN

Love the Lord your God with all
your heart, and with all your soul.

DEUTERONOMY 6:5

Helena didn't learn about God until she became an adult. Her son, Roman Emperor Constantine, taught her about God. And once she believed, she was all in on her faith! One time, Helena took a long trip from Rome to Jerusalem. Today that trip takes a few days by car. But back then, it took months! Along the way, Helena built many churches so people would know about God and have a place to worship Him. As soon as she arrived in Jerusalem, she asked where people thought Jesus had died. Constantine built a church at that place, and it's still there. Today people visit the Church of the Holy Sepulchre and worship there.

> **HELENA LOVED TO HELP THE POOR. WHEN SHE VISITED A CHURCH, SHE'D LEAVE A LARGE DONATION FOR THOSE IN NEED.**

*God, when I'm all in on faith, it's amazing
what You can help me do.*

AUGUST 19

RICHARD ALLEN

1760–1831 • UNITED STATES

YOU ARE WELCOME!

I am not ashamed of the gospel; it is the power of
God for salvation to everyone who has faith.

ROMANS 1:16

As a young man, Richard Allen had a fire in his belly to become a preacher. And when a new denomination called the Methodist Episcopal Church opened, church members agreed: Richard would make a *great* preacher. Richard moved to Philadelphia and joined Saint George's Methodist Episcopal Church, where leaders occasionally asked him to preach. He also led prayer meetings for other Black congregants. Church leaders limited the number of attendees. Richard didn't understand; God's kingdom was open to everyone. So Richard left and formed his own congregation. And in 1787, he founded the first church in the US for Black members. It eventually became the African Methodist Episcopal (AME) Church, which is still around today.

> YOU CAN FIND AME CHURCHES ON FIVE CONTINENTS AND IN OVER THIRTY-NINE COUNTRIES!

*God, thank You for making Your kingdom open
to everyone. I want to be the best welcoming
committee for people who seek You.*

AUGUST 20

JESSE BOOT

1850–1931 • ENGLAND

HELP ME HELP YOU

*Do not withhold good from those to whom it is
due, when it is in your power to do it.*

PROVERBS 3:27

When Jesse was a boy, his parents ran an herbalist shop, which sold medicines made from plants. When Jesse was only ten years old, his father died, so Jesse helped his mother run the shop. Over time Jesse noticed that doctors sometimes prescribed medicines patients couldn't afford. He decided to sell those medicines at a lower price so everyone could get treatment. The business grew, and Jesse opened more shops. Jesse also took care of his employees. Besides paying them fair wages, he also paid for their doctor visits, college education, membership to an athletic club, and even breakfast each day! Jesse knew that being a good businessperson didn't have to benefit just himself; his business could also impact others for good.

> WANT TO SHOP AT A BOOTS STORE? YOU CAN! THERE ARE MORE THAN 1,800 BOOTS STORES ALL OVER EUROPE AND ASIA.

*God, when I am successful, I want to help
others too! Please show me how.*

AUGUST 21

JANANI LUWUM

1924–1977 • UGANDA

SPEAK NOW

Lift up your voice with strength . . . do not fear.

ISAIAH 40:9

When he was twenty-four years old, Janani found Jesus—and his joy was infectious! He couldn't stop telling others about Jesus. But his joy was seen as a nuisance by government leaders. They warned him to stop talking about Jesus so much. But Janani was determined to help as many people as he could. Janani went back to school to become a priest. Eventually, in 1974, he was elected archbishop of Uganda. At the time, a brutal dictator named Idi Amin ruled the country. He spent all the country's money for himself and killed anyone who spoke out against him. But Janani said that what Amin was doing was wrong. Janani's courage eventually cost him his life. "I am prepared to die in the army of Jesus," he said.

> JANANI'S LIFE IS HONORED AT WESTMINSTER ABBEY. HIS STATUE, ALONG WITH NINE OTHERS, IS AMONG THE MODERN MARTYRS OUTSIDE THE CHURCH.

God, give me the courage to share how
You have changed my life.

AUGUST 22

FREDERICK BUECHNER

1926–2022 • UNITED STATES

GLIMMERS OF GOD

Then the glory of the LORD shall be revealed,
and all people shall see it together.

ISAIAH 40:5

Frederick believed that no matter what happens, God can give people opportunities to change and grow—even if they've made bad choices in the past. Frederick was a writer and created many characters who experienced this in their lives. And Frederick himself had gone through a big change! By his twenties, Frederick had already graduated from Princeton and written two novels. He was considered a success. But he found himself in a church pew in Manhattan one Sunday, listening to a sermon that inspired him to make God a bigger part of his life. He even went to seminary and became an ordained minister. From then on, Frederick wrote books that showed how glimmers of God's truth can show up in everyday life, even when people aren't sure if they believe in God.

> THROUGHOUT HIS LIFE FREDERICK WROTE THIRTY-NINE BOOKS!

God, help me look for glimmers of Your truth in my life.

AUGUST 23

HENRY PURCELL

C. 1659–1695 • ENGLAND

FEEL FEELINGS, SHARE FEELINGS

For everything there is a season . . . a time
to mourn, and a time to dance.

ECCLESIASTES 3:1, 4

Henry's heart soared when he heard performers sing a soulful *aria* from an Italian opera. *We should have this in England*, he thought. Most operas were written hundreds of miles south of England, in Italy, where the art form began. But Henry thought operas should be created in the English language as well. He was moved by characters whose emotion matched the swelling music. So this talented organist for Westminster Abbey went to work writing a landmark opera in English called *Dido & Aeneas*, a tragic love story filled with more emotion than the English had seen since Shakespeare's plays nearly a century earlier. And Henry brought a whole new experience in the English language in this format!

HENRY COMPOSED HIS FIRST WORK FOR KING CHARLES II'S BIRTHDAY WHEN HE WAS ONLY ELEVEN!

*God, You filled me with emotions that connect
me to others—thank You for that!*

AUGUST 24

ALVIN YORK

1887–1964 • UNITED STATES AND GERMANY

COURAGE ON THE BATTLEFIELD

Keep alert, stand firm in your faith, be courageous, be strong.

1 CORINTHIANS 16:13

Alvin didn't want to go to war. He believed the Bible taught that fighting others was wrong. But he was forced to go anyway. When Alvin arrived in Germany, his unit was asked to stop a group of enemy soldiers from shooting at them. Half of Alvin's fellow soldiers were killed in the fighting. No one was left to lead them, so Alvin stepped up. Even though he was scared, Alvin told the men to stay behind and guard the German soldiers they had taken captive. Alvin completed the mission by himself and captured more than 132 enemy soldiers. He arrived home a hero, though he didn't think of himself that way. He was simply defending his brothers when they needed him most.

> IN 1941, *SERGEANT YORK*, AN OSCAR-WINNING MOVIE ABOUT ALVIN'S LIFE, WAS RELEASED IN THEATERS.

God, help me step up and be brave when it matters most.

AUGUST 25

SAINT LOUIS IX OF FRANCE

1214–1270 • FRANCE

PROMISED PEACE

Whenever we have an opportunity, let us work for the good of all.

GALATIANS 6:10

When Louis became king of France, he vowed to be a king of peace. The last two kings had brought chaos. Louis wanted his people to do well. He built libraries, hospitals, orphanages, and churches. Louis himself visited the sick and even cared for those with leprosy. During Advent and Lent, anyone who asked for a meal received one, and Louis often served them himself. He kept a list of people's needs and personally made sure those needs were met. Louis treated all people with kindness and respect. Everyone loved Louis—peasants, knights, lords. They trusted and listened to their king. For many years the nation was at peace. Louis had kept his promise.

> EVERY DAY, LOUIS INVITED THIRTEEN SPECIAL GUESTS FROM AMONG THE POOR TO EAT WITH HIM.

God, I want to treat everyone with kindness and respect. Please show me how.

AUGUST 26

BRANCH RICKEY

1881–1965 • UNITED STATES

EQUAL PLAYING FIELD

Everyone who loves is born of God.

1 JOHN 4:7

Who is the most influential person in twentieth-century sports? According to ESPN, it's someone you've probably never heard of: Branch Rickey. For many years, Branch was the manager for the St. Louis Cardinals, then for the Brooklyn Dodgers. By this time, Rickey's beliefs as a Christian had made him realize something: Black players needed access to the same opportunities as white players, whether that was playing on a team that could go to the World Series or earning a good salary. Branch decided to break "the color barrier" and invited a talented Black player named Jackie Robinson to play for the Dodgers. Jackie faced hardship in the brave decision he made with Branch. But Jackie's talent and integrity showed the world that every person deserves the opportunity to play on the same field.

> FOR HIS WON'T-TAKE-NO-FOR-AN-ANSWER ATTITUDE, BRANCH WAS KNOWN AS "BASEBALL'S FEROCIOUS GENTLEMAN."

*God, when I need to address a wrong,
please show me what to do.*

AUGUST 27

HENRY 'ŌPŪKAHA'IA

**1792–1818 • KINGDOM OF HAWAI'I
(MODERN-DAY UNITED STATES)**

SET SAIL TO LEARN

Good and upright is the Lord; therefore
he instructs sinners in the way.

PSALM 25:8

Henry had been orphaned during battles between rival Hawaiian clans, and he was ready to go anywhere else. At age fifteen, he boarded a trading ship that took him far away to the state of Connecticut. Henry stayed with the president of Yale University, who found him a tutor. Henry not only learned to read and write, but he also learned about God. He was the first person from Hawaii to become a Christian, and he was also the first person to write down the Hawaiian language. Henry was excited to return home to share what he had learned about God and language, but he passed away before he could. Henry's friends promised to take his knowledge to Hawaii, and that's exactly what they did.

> HENRY TRANSLATED THE BOOK OF GENESIS IN THE BIBLE INTO HAWAIIAN.

God, keep my mind open to learn new things about You.

AUGUST 28

GEORGE GABRIEL STOKES

1819–1903 • ENGLAND

GOD AND SCIENCE

All things came into being through him, and without him not one thing came into being.

JOHN 1:3

George was a groundbreaking scientist who studied how different solids move through liquid (which is more important to science than it sounds!). In fact, his fellow scientists thought his work was so important that he was elected secretary, then president, of the Royal Society, the great group of scientific researchers in Great Britain. In his role, George decided which new fields were worth funding and which findings should be shared with scientists around the world. But George didn't talk only about science. He also talked about how God was tied to science! George said that life on earth is one of the strongest arguments for a Creator. *Just look at how complex human beings are*, George thought. Many organs work together to help the body function, and our minds are capable of amazing things too!

GEORGE COINED THE TERM *FLUORESCENCE* (THINK: FLUORESCENT LIGHT BULBS IN THE CEILING!) AND WAS THE FIRST PERSON TO EXPLAIN HOW IT WORKS.

God, in my work, help me show You to others.

AUGUST 29

SANDRO BOTTICELLI

1445–1510 • ITALY

INSPIRATION IS EVERYWHERE

He has made everything suitable for its time.

ECCLESIASTES 3:11

Some artists paint events or figures from history. Others create from their imagination. Sandro did both! He looked back thousands of years to see how the ancient Greeks and Romans made art. He also thought about Bible stories he wanted to create as he painted frescoes and special round paintings, called *tondos*, showing stories especially about Jesus. He even painted characters from Greek myths, the first Western painter to do so in about a thousand years. But he also looked to modern books of his day for characters to paint! He knew he could find inspiration in many different places, old and new. People connected with Sandro's art—the beauty in the colors he chose, the characters filled with expression, and the stories they knew by heart shown in a new way.

> PEOPLE FORGOT SANDRO'S WORK SHORTLY AFTER HE DIED. 300 YEARS LATER, HIS WORK WAS REDISCOVERED BY ARTISTS IN ENGLAND.

God, Your inspiration is all around me.

AUGUST 30

DOROTHY DAY

1897–1980 • UNITED STATES

LIVING SIDE BY SIDE

"I was hungry and you gave me food, I was thirsty and you gave me something to drink, I was a stranger and you welcomed me."

MATTHEW 25:35

Dorothy believed that Christians could do small things to make a big difference for their neighbors in need. She spent much of her life working to help the poor. Dorothy encouraged Christians to open their spare rooms to people who needed them. And if they didn't have extra space, they could offer food or help those needing work to find a job. Before long, Dorothy began to open houses of hospitality in New York City that housed people from all walks of life. Dorothy knew that when people live with each other, they aren't strangers anymore; they become family who look out for each other. During the Great Depression, these hospitality houses brought people together who otherwise would have been alone and gave them others to care about them.

> DOROTHY'S MODEL FOR HOSPITALITY HOUSES SPREAD ACROSS THE COUNTRY. BY WORLD WAR II, THERE WERE THIRTY-FIVE HOSPITALITY GROUPS FROM VERMONT TO CALIFORNIA.

God, help me see the small things I can do to show Your love to others.

AUGUST 31

ATHENAGORAS

C. 101–C. 200 • ANCIENT GREECE

SHARE THE REAL STORY

Contend for the faith.

JUDE v. 3

Around 175 AD, rumors began to swirl around Rome about people who called themselves "Christians," saying they did horrible things. The people who heard these rumors didn't like Christians at all—and even started to persecute them. Athenagoras, a deep thinker from Greece, was also a Christian. He decided to tell the Roman emperor, Marcus Aurelius, and his son Commodus the *real* story about Christianity. He explained that Christians believed in the one true God and wanted to do right. He also addressed the rumors about Christians and proved why they weren't true. Then he asked Marcus Aurelius to treat Christians the same as other Roman citizens and to stop hurting them. Athenagoras bravely defended his faith to the highest ruler in the land.

> ATHENAGORAS ALSO TRAVELED TO ALEXANDRIA, EGYPT, TO ESTABLISH A CHRISTIAN ACADEMY THERE.

God, I want to show people who You are so they understand You.

SEPTEMBER 1

PAUL FARMER

1959–2022 • UNITED STATES AND HAITI

WORKING TOGETHER FOR HEALING

[The Lord] heals all your diseases.

PSALM 103:3

Every human has a right to good health care. And most of the best things humans accomplish happen when they work together. These two principles guided Dr. Paul Farmer. He was especially interested in helping people in countries without easy access to doctors or medicine.

Paul wanted to figure out *why* they didn't have access to doctors and medicine. He talked with leaders in those countries to come up with solutions. Paul's partnerships helped to build a teaching hospital in Haiti after a huge earthquake. They helped people in Peru receive treatment for tuberculosis. Across the world, people living with HIV got needed medicine. Paul pushed through obstacles, and his organization, Partners in Health, helped millions of people find healing they needed.

> PAUL'S WORK INSPIRED A DOCUMENTARY YOU CAN WATCH CALLED *BENDING THE ARC.*

God, help me work together with others to heal those in need.

SEPTEMBER 2

BOBBY BOWDEN

1929–2021 • UNITED STATES

STUDYING GOD'S PLAYBOOK

"God so loved the world that he gave his only Son, so that everyone who believes in him may not perish but may have eternal life."

JOHN 3:16

Coach Bowden is known as one of the top college football coaches ever. Under his coaching, the Florida State Seminoles went to *twenty-eight* postseason bowls in a row! But Coach Bowden was known among his team for something else: reading the Bible. Every morning, Coach Bowden made a point to read the Bible. He even kept a Bible on his desk so he could read it each day. Many players were inspired by Coach Bowden's habit, and some even came to know more about Jesus because of him. Whenever players had questions about their faith, they knew they could talk to Coach Bowden. They were sure he'd know the answer since Coach spent time with God every single day!

> WHEN COACH BOWDEN AUTOGRAPHED PHOTOS, HE'D ALSO WRITE "JOHN 3:16" UNDER HIS SIGNATURE.

God, I want to know You so well that others can say that I know You.

SEPTEMBER 3

JOHN J. EGAN

1916–2001 • UNITED STATES

STAND UP FOR OTHERS

Maintain the right of the lowly and the destitute.

PSALM 82:3

In 1965, Dr. Martin Luther King Jr. asked people from all over the country—especially people who worked at churches—to come to Selma, Alabama. Dr. King was planning a march to show that Black voters were not able to cast votes in Selma, which was illegal. John was a priest in Chicago. He had dedicated his life to supporting people who were treated unfairly. John's doctor had recently told him to avoid stressful situations because of his heart problems. But John traveled to Selma anyway. John was one of the first priests to march with Dr. King. TV cameras showed a priest in his collar marching alongside all kinds of people, standing up against unfairness. His presence helped other people realize they could stand up against inequality too.

> JOHN FOUNDED A GROUP THAT WORKED TO KEEP POOR PEOPLE FROM BEING EVICTED FROM THEIR HOMES.

God, when I see someone treated unfairly,
help me stand up for them.

SEPTEMBER 4

MOTHER THERESA MAXIS DUCHEMIN

1810–1892 • UNITED STATES

RIGHT PLACE, RIGHT TIME

"Who knows? Perhaps you have come to royal dignity for just such a time as this."

ESTHER 4:14

At nineteen years old, Theresa was excited to begin a new chapter as a founding member of the first Catholic congregation of Black women in the US. Theresa was serving as General Superior when she met Rev. Louis Gillet. He founded a new congregation in a new state called Michigan. Reverend Gillet hoped to serve the many French-Canadian immigrants there, especially children who needed education. Theresa's background had prepared her! She'd received an excellent education and was fluent in French,

> THERESA ALSO HELPED FOUND A SISTERS, SERVANTS OF THE IMMACULATE HEART OF MARY IN PENNSYLVANIA.

thanks to her Haitian background. She'd even helped found a new congregation. She agreed to go with Reverend Gillet to Michigan. Together they founded Sisters, Servants of the Immaculate Heart of Mary. It is still around today, helping people in multiple states in need of God's love.

God, I know You're preparing me to do good things for You!

SEPTEMBER 5

MOTHER TERESA

1910–1997 • INDIA

LOVE IN THE SMALL THINGS

"I give you a new commandment, that you love one another."

JOHN 13:34

After seventeen years of teaching children in Kolkata, India, Mother Teresa realized her true mission: to care for the sick and the poor. She saw many on the streets who were old, blind, ill, or disabled—or even had leprosy. So she opened locations where they could get help. People saw Mother Teresa's actions and decided they wanted to be helpers too. Many were in awe of her work, thinking a person must be special to do this work. But Mother Teresa shook her head: "Not all of us can do great things, but all of us can do small things with great love." At the time of her death, Mother Teresa was working with 4,000 nuns and thousands of others to help those in need.

> WHEN POPE PAUL VI VISITED INDIA, HE GAVE MOTHER TERESA HIS LIMO TO USE. SHE RAFFLED THE CAR AND GAVE THE MONEY TO THE POOR.

Jesus, I want to help people in need like Mother Teresa did.

SEPTEMBER 6

WANG MING-DAO

1900–1991 • CHINA

GOD CAN STILL USE YOU

[The Lord] said to me, "My grace is sufficient for
you, for power is made perfect in weakness."

2 CORINTHIANS 12:9

Sometimes we think that if we make mistakes, God can't use us. But that's not true! Wang was a pastor in China. The government said Wang needed to change the way he taught about Jesus to fit what the government wanted. Wang thought this was wrong. He and his wife were arrested! Wang's captors said his wife would suffer if Wang didn't do what they said, so Wang agreed, and he and his wife were released. But Wang felt bad and decided to preach about Jesus anyway—the full truth. Once again, Wang and his wife were imprisoned, this time for much longer. But Wang was committed to the truth! He continued sharing about Jesus, even while he was in prison. He had made a mistake, but Wang ultimately did what was right and was used by God.

> WHEN HE WAS IN PRISON, WANG WOULD PREACH THROUGH PIPES . . . OF THE *TOILET*, AND OTHERS COULD HEAR HIM SINCE THE PIPES WERE CONNECTED!

*God, thank You for choosing to use me for
Your good, even after I mess up.*

SEPTEMBER 7

MADAM C. J. WALKER

1867–1919 • UNITED STATES

GIVE IT AWAY

The one who sows sparingly will also reap sparingly, and the one who sows bountifully will also reap bountifully.

2 CORINTHIANS 9:6

As your resources grow, so should your generosity. That's what C. J. believed! She was generous from the time she was a washerwoman up until she became the first self-made female millionaire in the US. In her younger days, C. J. gave her time to causes she cared about. She also pooled money with friends, neighbors, and churchgoers to help people in the Black community who were sick, hungry, or had some other need. C. J. started a hair care line and beauty schools that earned lots of money. And as her wealth grew, so did C. J.'s generosity! She gave to organizations doing good around the nation. From funding schools to giving money to elder care facilities and the YMCA, C. J. followed her faith and gave with open hands to help others.

> C. J.'S COMPANY EMPLOYED THOUSANDS OF BLACK WOMEN, FROM SALESPEOPLE TO HAIRDRESSERS.

God, I want to give my time and money in ways that matter. Please show me how.

SEPTEMBER 8

ANTHONY ASHLEY COOPER, LORD SHAFTESBURY

1801–1885 • ENGLAND

THE PEOPLE'S EARL

"Just as you did it to one of the least of these who are members of my family, you did it to me."

MATTHEW 25:40

Lord Shaftesbury could have worked powerful positions in the English government. But he felt God calling him to help those in need. So instead, Lord Shaftesbury spent his life helping people who were poor, had mental health troubles, or were stuck in unsafe working or living conditions. He helped pass laws to ban children from working in dangerous underground mines. He shortened the workday in mills and factories so people could rest and spend time with their families. He helped more than 300,000 children go to school in a time when schools weren't free for everyone. He also said that working people needed cheaper and safe housing. Driven by his faith, Lord Shaftesbury was a voice for those who didn't often have one.

> WHEN LORD SHAFTESBURY DIED, THE WHOLE COUNTRY MOURNED "THE PEOPLE'S EARL."

God, show me those who need my help today.

SEPTEMBER 9

AMANDA SMITH

1837–1915 • UNITED STATES

IN WORD AND DEED

"Go into all the world and proclaim the good news to the whole creation."

MARK 16:15

Amanda Smith was heartbroken. It was 1869, and her husband had passed away, and she didn't know how she would recover. Over time, Amanda leaned on her faith to figure out what to do next. She was inspired by church leaders who shared their struggles and how God had helped them overcome. Amanda nervously but courageously began to follow in their footsteps and started to preach. Soon, Amanda became the first Black woman to be an evangelist overseas. She traveled around the world for twelve years, preaching in England, India, and Africa. In word and deed, Amanda used her life to share the love of God with others.

> **AMANDA'S FAMILY HOME IN PENNSYLVANIA WAS A STATION ON THE UNDERGROUND RAILROAD.**

God, help me to remember that I can use my struggles to share Your love with others.

SEPTEMBER 10

MADELEINE L'ENGLE

1918–2007 • UNITED STATES

YOU'RE NEVER ALONE

"I am with you always, to the end of the age."

MATTHEW 28:20

"If I've ever written a book that says what I believe about God and the universe," Madeleine wrote in her private journal, "this is it." That book was called *A Wrinkle in Time*. In it Madeleine tells the story of a young girl named Meg, who goes on a journey to search for her missing scientist father. Even though the story is filled with science, space, and strange creatures, it also shows how love is stronger than fear and how light will always win over darkness—just like Jesus always does. Madeleine believed God's love could shine bright anywhere, even in faraway galaxies. And she used her creativity and big imagination to honor God with her stories.

> DOZENS OF PUBLISHERS REJECTED *A WRINKLE IN TIME*. TODAY IT HAS SOLD MORE THAN 16 MILLION COPIES AND HAS BEEN TRANSLATED INTO MORE THAN THIRTY LANGUAGES.

God, thank You for staying by my side. With You, I know I am always safe and loved.

SEPTEMBER 11

JOHANNES KEPLER

1571–1630 • WÜTTEMBERG (MODERN-DAY GERMANY)

HEAVENLY SKIES

The heavens are telling the glory of God; and
the firmament proclaims his handiwork.

PSALM 19:1

As a scientist and a man of faith, Johannes believed that God could be seen both in the heavens and on earth. From a young age, Johannes was fascinated in looking for God, especially in the night sky. When he was six, his mother showed him a comet passing by their family's inn. A few years later, he saw a lunar eclipse. He was fascinated by the heavens! Johannes decided to study astronomy and discovered that planets move in elliptical orbits around the sun. To him this made sense. God is like the sun, and humans are like the planets. Humans move and change, while God remains in the center. He doesn't change or move! Johannes's ideas created a foundation for other scientists after him, especially Sir Isaac Newton.

KEPLER WROTE A FICTIONAL STORY ABOUT A JOURNEY TO THE MOON—PERHAPS ONE OF THE WORLD'S FIRST SCIENCE FICTION STORIES!

God, thank You for creating the beautiful night sky!

SEPTEMBER 12

FRANZ SCHUBERT

1797–1828 • AUSTRIA

A LITTLE HELP FROM MY FRIENDS

A friend loves at all times.

PROVERBS 17:17

In his teen years, Franz enjoyed two things more than anything: hanging out with his friends and playing and writing music. Franz's friends knew how talented he was, especially at composing. But Franz was shy about sharing his work, even with his trusted companions. A talented composer named Antonio Salieri (some might say Mozart's greatest rival!) worked at Franz's boarding school. Franz's friends knew if he got the courage to show his compositions to Salieri, the teacher would be impressed and would know how to help Franz. Finally, Franz got the courage to show his work to his friends—and then Salieri. Franz's friends were right! Salieri thought Franz's work was marvelous. The two worked together for a few years. Eventually Franz went on to become the last great composer of the classical music era.

FRANZ WROTE MORE THAN 600 SONGS!

God, thank You for my friends!

SEPTEMBER 13

STAN MUSIAL

1920–2013 • UNITED STATES

QUIET LIFE = THE GOOD LIFE

Aspire to live quietly.

1 THESSALONIANS 4:11

Sometimes people think that athletes' lives off the field must be as exciting as they are on the field. But that's not always true! Stan "The Man" Musial, who played baseball for the St. Louis Cardinals, was one of the best-ever hitters in the league. But when he came home, he was just Stan! He enjoyed spending time with his family. He never missed church on Sundays. He didn't get into fights or use drugs or foul language. When he was hurt, he didn't complain. When he excelled on the field, he didn't demand special treatment. After he helped the Cardinals win a World Series title in 1944, he enlisted in the navy to fight in World War II. Stan lived out his faith in a quiet life of service, no matter where he was.

> ONE OF THE HIGHLIGHTS OF STAN'S LIFE WAS GETTING TO KNOW A FELLOW POLISH PERSON: POPE JOHN PAUL II!

*God, when I get bored, remind me that
a quiet life can be a good life.*

SEPTEMBER 14

PETER PAUL RUBENS

1577–1640 • SPANISH NETHERLANDS (MODERN-DAY BELGIUM)

WORKING TOGETHER

Those who are taught . . . must share in all good things.

GALATIANS 6:6

Peter Paul produced more paintings than just about any artist of his time. How? By getting help. Many people had seen his paintings in churches and homes and wanted paintings of their own. It was more than one person could do, so Peter Paul hired younger painters and taught them how he created his art. Peter Paul would create an initial sketch with the main figures. Assistants would then fill in the work, and Peter Paul would come back at the end to finish. Not only did young painters learn the techniques of a great artist—they also got paid to make art and find connections to potential customers! Peter Paul shared his secrets and techniques and helped others get their own start in the art world.

PETER PAUL SPOKE SEVEN LANGUAGES FLUENTLY!

*God, remind me to share what I know
when it can help other people.*

SEPTEMBER 15

ISAAC WATTS

1674–1748 • ENGLAND

SING PRAISES!

Sing to God, sing praises to his name.

PSALM 68:4

Isaac was a preacher who wanted to help his congregation praise God. As a passionate poet, he wrote songs tied into his sermon themes so the congregation could sing together after the sermon was over. Without realizing it, Isaac had invented the modern *hymn*. A hymn is a song that praises God or gives thanks to Him for blessings. Isaac hoped that when people sang the words of his songs, not only would God be praised, but people would also enjoy the act of praising Him. And it worked! People enjoyed Isaac's songs, and soon many congregations in England and America were singing the words he had written. Isaac also inspired other talented songwriters to use their gifts of creativity to write hymns for God.

> ISAAC ALSO WROTE TEXTBOOKS ON GEOGRAPHY, ASTRONOMY, GRAMMAR, AND PHILOSOPHY. THEY WERE USED IN BRITAIN AND AMERICA THROUGHOUT THE 1700S.

God, I praise You for being a good and gracious God!

SEPTEMBER 16

SAINT LUDMILA

C. 860–921 • BOHEMIA (NOW CZECHIA)

A GENEROUS HEART

Train children in the right way, and when old, they will not stray.

PROVERBS 22:6

Ludmila and her husband, Bořivoj, ruled a kingdom in Europe called Bohemia. They were the first rulers in Bohemia to become Christians and wanted to share their faith with the people, so they built the first Christian church in their country. Ludmila and Bořivoj had a grandson named Wenceslas, whom they loved very much. Ludmila helped raise Wenceslas, teaching him about God and the importance of showing love to others and making sure they had plenty to eat and a place to sleep. Wenceslas grew up to be a kind ruler who looked out for his people. He even took a vow of poverty, choosing to share his royal wealth instead of keeping it for himself. He remembered his grandmother's teachings all his life, and the people of Bohemia flourished.

> THE CHRISTMAS SONG "GOOD KING WENCESLAS" IS ABOUT LUDMILA'S GRANDSON AND HOW HE HELPED A POOR MAN ON A COLD WINTER NIGHT, TAKING FOOD AND FIREWOOD TO THE MAN'S HOME.

Lord, help me to remember Your teachings so I can help others.

SEPTEMBER 17

POPE FRANCIS

1936–2025 • ARGENTINA

BIG OR SMALL, WE ALL BELONG

Live in harmony with one another; do not be
haughty, but associate with the lowly.

ROMANS 12:16

When Francis was elected pope, he decided he wanted to do things a little bit differently. Instead of fancy papal clothes, he dressed in simple robes. Instead of the grand palace he could have lived in, Francis chose a small apartment. After a long day of work, instead of having someone else prepare his supper, Francis cooked it for himself. Why did he choose to live this way? Because, as Francis said, "My people are poor, and I am one of them." He wanted people to feel like they belonged in the church, no matter who they were. He wanted people to see they were important enough to be cared for, no matter how much they had. Francis lived as a humble servant-leader.

> FRANCIS WAS THE FIRST POPE FROM THE WESTERN HEMISPHERE OF THE GLOBE—AND THE FIRST FROM SOUTH AMERICA!

*God, help me to be humble so that
others can see You through me.*

SEPTEMBER 18

WILLIAM GLADSTONE

1809–1898 • ENGLAND

USE WHAT YOU HAVE WHERE YOU ARE

You have been a refuge to the poor, a refuge
to the needy in their distress.

ISAIAH 25:4

William's parents taught him about the Bible from the time he was little. In fact, William enjoyed spending time with God so much that he thought about working for the church. William eventually decided he might do more good working in the government. For the next sixty years, William had various roles in the English government and even became prime minister. Because of his faith, William felt he had a duty to help the poor and sick. He supported a land act in Ireland that protected the poor who lived there. He helped more children go to school. He even introduced "secret ballots" so people could keep their voting choices private. William believed politics to be "a most blessed calling." Backed by his faith, William worked to help many people.

> WHEN WILLIAM TURNED EIGHTY-FOUR YEARS OLD, HE BECAME THE OLDEST PRIME MINISTER IN BRITISH HISTORY.

*God, thank You for putting me in places
where I can help others.*

SEPTEMBER 19

DR. LOUISE "LULU" FLEMING

1862–1899 • CONGO

HEALING HANDS

He heals the brokenhearted, and binds up their wounds.

PSALM 147:3

Lulu was born in Florida to parents who were enslaved. At only fifteen, her strong faith in God guided her steps. After graduating at the top of her class from Shaw University, Lulu became the first Black woman sent to Africa by the Woman's American Baptist Foreign Missionary Society. She went to Congo, a country in central Africa, where she saw great need for God and doctors. So she returned to the United States to attend medical school. After earning her degree, Lulu—now Dr. Fleming—returned to Congo and worked tirelessly to provide medical care. She even helped people who wanted an education to travel to the United States to attend Shaw University, like she had. Dr. Fleming's bravery allowed her to touch lives at home and abroad as she shared the love of Jesus.

> DR. FLEMING WAS THE FIRST BLACK WOMAN TO GRADUATE FROM THE MEDICAL SCHOOL SHE ATTENDED, WOMEN'S MEDICAL COLLEGE OF PENNSYLVANIA.

Lord, help me to be Your healing hands wherever someone is hurting.

SEPTEMBER 20

ERNEST THOMAS SINTON WALTON

1903–1995 • IRELAND

KNOWLEDGE FOR GOOD

The mind of one who has understanding seeks knowledge.

PROVERBS 15:14

Students took their seats at Trinity College, whispering excitedly to one another. They couldn't believe they landed a spot in Dr. Walton's class! Ernest was a popular physics teacher. Students appreciated how he made complex ideas understandable. That only made them want to learn more! Perhaps his teaching ability was because he understood physics more than just about anyone. In 1932, he and another physicist named John Cockcroft figured out how to prove Einstein's famous theory of relativity, $E=mc^2$, by splitting the nucleus of an atom for the first time. In 1951, Ernest and John won a Nobel Prize for their work. Ernest knew that his discovery could change the world forever. He spent the rest of his life teaching students and working to develop ways to use nuclear energy responsibly.

> ERNEST'S DAD WAS A MINISTER IN THE METHODIST CHURCH.

God, help me steward my knowledge in helpful ways.

SEPTEMBER 21

CONNIE MACK

1862–1956 • UNITED STATES

LEADING WITH KINDNESS

Above all, clothe yourselves with love, which binds
everything together in perfect harmony.

COLOSSIANS 3:14

For fifty-three years, a tall, thin man could be seen standing in the dugout for the Philadelphia Athletics baseball team, quietly coaching his players. In this era, managers believed they needed to be tough on players to get them to play their best. Connie thought the opposite. A committed Catholic with a strong focus on integrity and loyalty, Connie didn't scold or criticize players for making mistakes. He was kind to them. He wanted them to know that while he expected them to work hard, he was on their side. And by working together for the same goal, they'd get the results they wanted. Connie's players not only respected their manager; they loved him and wanted to work hard for him. And Connie's approach worked. His teams won several pennants and World Series titles.

> WHEN CONNIE FINALLY RETIRED AT AGE EIGHTY-SEVEN, HE'D BEEN THE ATHLETICS' MANAGER FOR SO LONG THAT HE'D OUTLASTED EIGHT US PRESIDENTS!

*God, thank You for people who show
me how to lead with kindness.*

SEPTEMBER 22

GEORG PHILIPP TELEMANN

1681–1767 • GERMANY

WHERE CURIOSITY LEADS

In all your ways acknowledge him, and he
will make straight your paths.

PROVERBS 3:6

Georg fell in love with music when he was just a boy. But Georg's dad didn't think becoming a musician was a good idea. How would he earn enough money? Georg's parents wouldn't pay for music lessons, so he decided to teach himself! He wrote music and learned to play the violin, oboe, viola, and a keyboard instrument called a *clavier*. Even though he went to college to study law, soon music took over Georg's life. He never looked back!

> ONE OF THE INSTRUMENTS GEORG LEARNED TO PLAY WAS THE RECORDER—JUST LIKE MANY STUDENTS TODAY!

Georg became most famous for his beautiful church music. Many people in Georg's time thought he was the greatest living composer. Georg followed not only his heart but also his curiosity, which led him to create music that people still enjoy today.

*God, help me follow my curiosity to
find the path You have for me.*

SEPTEMBER 23

PHOEBE PALMER KNAPP

1839–1908 • UNITED STATES

A HOLY HOBBY

Make melody to our God on the lyre.

PSALM 147:7

One of Phoebe's favorite hobbies was music. As a child, Phoebe learned to play the piano and organ. Phoebe's mom was a talented writer, and together they would write songs about Jesus! As she grew older, Phoebe kept writing music for Jesus. But now she wrote songs with her friends! One afternoon in 1873, Phoebe was playing a new tune and asked her friend Fanny Crosby what the music was saying. "Why, I think it says, 'Blessed assurance, Jesus is mine! O what a foretaste of glory divine!'" Fanny said. And within a few minutes, Phoebe and Fanny wrote a hymn that people still love today: "Blessed Assurance." Phoebe's willingness to use her hobby for Jesus has helped people grow closer to Him for more than 150 years.

> PHOEBE AND HER HUSBAND, JOSEPH, HAD A HUGE ORGAN THAT AT THE TIME WAS ONE OF THE LARGEST IN THE WHOLE WORLD!

God, thank You for showing me hobbies
I love that can honor You.

SEPTEMBER 24

FREDERIC EDWIN CHURCH

1826–1900 • UNITED STATES (AND BEYOND!)

WORLD OF WONDERS

> In his hand are the depths of the earth; the
> heights of the mountains are his also.
>
> **PSALM 95:4**

For Frederic, nothing was more exciting than traveling to a new location and painting the world God made. At Niagara Falls, he captured the misty beauty of the mighty waterfalls. In the arctic, he painted icebergs and the colorful Northern Lights. Frederic traveled around South America, capturing erupting volcanoes and the Andes Mountains. Later he visited the Middle East, taking in the Holy Land and ancient ruins like Petra, a city built entirely into canyon rock. Frederic noticed and captured the small details that make a place special: the way a volcano eruption changes the surrounding landscape over time, how greens and reds of an aurora filter through the arctic sky. No detail of God's world was too small for Frederic to capture and take awe in.

> FREDERIC WAS GREAT FRIENDS WITH FELLOW PAINTER THOMAS COLE (ON PAGE 85) AND WRITER MARK TWAIN.

God, thank You for all the beauty You created.

SEPTEMBER 25

LUCY GOODE BROOKS

1818–1900 • UNITED STATES

MEET THE NEED

My God will fully satisfy every need of yours.

PHILIPPIANS 4:19

In the years after the Civil War, Lucy couldn't believe how many Black children in Richmond, Virginia, couldn't find their parents or didn't have parents. After the Emancipation Proclamation, many enslaved people had traveled to Richmond to look for family members they'd lost contact with after being separated. Lucy had been born enslaved and was a mother. Her three sons were still with her, but she'd lost contact with her daughter when she'd been taken to Tennessee. So Lucy decided to help as many children as possible. Working with both Black and white churches and charities, Lucy was able to open an orphanage in 1871 for Black children who couldn't find their parents. Today Lucy's organization still supports families in the Richmond area.

> IF YOU'RE WALKING AROUND DOWNTOWN RICHMOND, LOOK UP! YOU MIGHT BE WALKING AROUND LUCY GOODE BROOKS SQUARE.

God, whenever I see a need in my community, show me how to help.

SEPTEMBER 26

HORACE PIPPIN

1888–1946 • UNITED STATES

A PEACEFUL KINGDOM

[Jesus] shall stand as a signal to the peoples.

ISAIAH 11:10

Horace came home from World War I a changed man. He had not only seen the horrors of fighting; he had also lost use of his right arm. But that didn't stop Horace from doing what he loved most: painting. And Horace's paintings often showed how much better the world would be if everyone lived at peace. Sometimes he painted images of peace from the Bible. His painting *Holy Mountain I* shows a field of creatures that don't usually belong together—lions and lambs, cows and bears, a child and a snake—in peaceful harmony. Horace was inspired by Isaiah 11, a prophecy about the peace that's possible after Jesus came to the earth. This beautiful image inspired people at the end of a long season of war.

> AT THE TIME OF HIS DEATH, HORACE WAS KNOWN AS THE GREATEST BLACK PAINTER OF HIS TIME.

God, help me to live in peace with everyone.

SEPTEMBER 27

ANTONI GAUDÍ

1852–1926 • SPAIN

HEAVENLY CONNECTION

Set your minds on things that are above, not on things that are on earth.

COLOSSIANS 3:2

In Antoni's mind, nature was God's finest creation. As an architect, Antoni considered his purpose to help people connect to God. Antoni decided the buildings he designed would reflect God's creation as much as possible. Where many buildings featured straight lines and sharp angles (like balconies, windows, and roof tiles), Antoni tried to incorporate curves—like the way leaves curl and oceans roll. He admired how medieval architecture brought color into churches using stained glass windows, so Antoni added stained glass to his churches to connect the earthly world to the heavenly one. Antoni also included crosses in his designs as a sign of devotion. In everything he did, Antoni used his talent to glorify God and connect people to Him.

> ANTONI'S MOST FAMOUS BUILDING IS THE SAGRADA FAMÍLIA CHURCH IN BARCELONA. HE BEGAN WORKING ON IT IN 1883—AND IT STILL ISN'T FINISHED!

God, help me use my talents to connect others to You.

SEPTEMBER 28

GIL HODGES

1924–1972 • UNITED STATES

NUMBER ONE JOB

We walk by faith, not by sight.

2 CORINTHIANS 5:7

Gil might have been prized for his Golden Glove–level defensive skills at first base for the Brooklyn Dodgers. But for Gil, his number one job was being a Christian! When the team played at home, he attended church with his family. If the team was on the road, he'd find a church to attend. His teammates often found him praying before games. And Gil made sure his teammates got along. Gentle giant Gil could silence a disagreement with a look. He also looked out for his good friend and teammate Jackie Robinson,

> GIL HAD HUGE HANDS. ONE OF HIS TEAMMATES JOKED THAT HE COULD HAVE PLAYED FIRST BASE BAREHANDED!

the first Black player to break the color barrier. If anyone—the opposing team, fans, *anyone*—tried to mess with Jackie, Gil would put a stop to it. No matter where he was or what he was doing, Gil let his faith guide him.

God, help me remember that my number one job is to follow You!

SEPTEMBER 29

BROOKS ROBINSON

1937–2023 • UNITED STATES

HUMBLE AND KIND

Humble yourselves before the Lord, and he will exalt you.

JAMES 4:10

What if you were so good at your job that your nickname was "the Human Vacuum Cleaner"? That's how good of a third baseman Brooks was! Brooks played professional baseball for the Baltimore Orioles for twenty-three years. He was such a great defensive player that he won a Gold Glove sixteen years in a row—the award for the best defensive players! But Brooks never boasted about his talent. His faith made him humble. If someone asked him to describe a big play he'd made, he'd shrug it off. "It's just a reflex action," he'd say. One sportswriter said it didn't matter how many times he asked Brooks a question, Brooks was always kind. "I always had the idea he didn't know he was Brooks Robinson!" the writer said. People were drawn to Brooks because of his kind and humble nature.

BROOKS WAS SO BELOVED IN BALTIMORE THAT MANY PEOPLE NAMED THEIR KIDS AFTER HIM!

God, help me to be humble about the gifts You've given me.

SEPTEMBER 30

SOR JUANA INÉS DE LA CRUZ

C. 1651–1695 • MEXICO

MANY WAYS TO SHARE HIM

Let us continually offer a sacrifice of praise to God.

HEBREWS 13:15

In the 1680s, readers in Spain marveled at the words of a new writer they had never heard of. "Who is Sor Juana?" they asked. The answer was sitting in a quiet room in a convent across the ocean. From the time Sor Juana was a little girl, people noticed how smart she was. She was so gifted at reading and writing that she decided she would dedicate her life to God and to words! Sor Juana became a nun, and when she wasn't teaching girls at a local school, she was reading and writing. She described how she saw God through the beautiful world He created—including all the creative ways people could talk about Him! Through plays and poems, books and essays, Sor Juana shared about God with the world.

> IF YOU GO TO MEXICO, LOOK FOR SOR JUANA IN YOUR WALLET! HER PICTURE IS ON THE 100-PESO BILL.

God, thank You for all the creative ways we can show what we're learning about You!

OCTOBER 1

JASPER FRANCIS CROPSEY

1823–1900 • UNITED STATES

FALL BEAUTY

Out of the ground the L%%ORD%% God made to grow every tree that is pleasant to the sight and good for food.

GENESIS 2:9

From Jasper's paintbrush, warm rays of sunshine poured down on the rolling hills of New England, trees dappled in deep red and fiery orange. Jasper grew up in New York and was home a lot due to poor health. He had lots of time not only to study the scenery around him but also to learn how to draw and create wooden architectural models. At fourteen, Jasper became an architectural apprentice. Later, while designing churches on Staten Island in New York City, Jasper learned how to paint with oils and watercolors. As he traveled north, he became enchanted by the gorgeous fall colors, which he believed reflected God, and began painting landscapes. The way he captured God's creation was admired across the globe—even by England's Queen Victoria!

> JASPER WAS PART OF A GROUP OF PAINTERS CALLED THE HUDSON RIVER SCHOOL. THEY WANTED TO PAINT THE NATURAL AMERICAN LANDSCAPE, UNTOUCHED BY BUILDINGS OR BUSINESSES.

God, thank You for the beautiful autumn season You made!

OCTOBER 2

FELIX MENDELSSOHN

1809–1847 • GERMANY AND ENGLAND

NEW ADVENTURES

> The LORD will keep your going out and your coming
> in from this time on and forevermore.
>
> **PSALM 121:8**

Felix was a talented musician from a young age. He traveled to play and compose music for audiences all over Europe. But his favorite place was England. He traveled to England at least ten times in his life! He happily endured the cold winds off the coast of northern Scotland. Many a time, he found himself sitting at a piano bench playing for Queen Victoria and Prince Albert. He was inspired by every corner of the kingdom. He even wrote music about his favorite landscapes! Felix was inspired by God's creation, by new people and new experiences. Each trip helped him learn more—and inspired nearly 750 musical works he composed.

> QUEEN VICTORIA SO LOVED FELIX'S "WEDDING MARCH" THAT HER DAUGHTER WALKED DOWN THE AISLE TO IT. BRIDES STILL DO TODAY!

*God, I love to go on new adventures! I
can't wait to see what's next.*

OCTOBER 3

ERNIE DAVIS

1939-1963 • UNITED STATES

TEAM PLAYER

Two are better than one, because they have a good reward for their toil.

ECCLESIASTES 4:9

In 1961, running back Ernie Davis became the first Black football player to win college football's highest honor: the Heisman Trophy. But the people who knew Ernie best say that his biggest accomplishment was the person he was. In high school, a new player trying out for the team put on his gear wrong. The other players made fun of him, but Ernie instead introduced himself and showed the player how to put on his gear. If Ernie saw another player making a mistake in a play, Ernie quietly gave a few pointers on the side. He went out of his way to make friends with second-string players so they'd feel welcome. Ernie was known for his kindness and was the best kind of teammate anyone could ask for.

> ERNIE WAS THE FIRST OVERALL PICK OF THE 1962 NFL DRAFT. SADLY HE PASSED AWAY FROM LEUKEMIA AT TWENTY-THREE, BEFORE HE EVER GOT TO PLAY HIS FIRST NFL GAME.

God, help me to be a true team player like Ernie!

OCTOBER 4

CARL FRIEDRICH GAUSS

1777–1855 • GERMANY

KEEP YOUR LIGHT SHINING

"No one after lighting a lamp puts it under the bushel basket, but on the lampstand, and it gives light to all in the house."

MATTHEW 5:15

Ask a math teacher about the greatest mathematicians of all time, and Carl's name will probably come up! Carl's list of accomplishments is huge. Carl made discoveries in algebra and geometry, which also helped him make discoveries in astronomy and cartography (which is making maps)! But as smart as he was, Carl struggled with perfectionism. He didn't want to publish any work that might have a mistake. As a result, he often kept his findings to himself. Some of his greatest discoveries weren't shared until after Carl died. Would the world have had the telegraph sooner, since Carl was the first to create it but didn't tell anyone? Would we have inventions that used his geometry discoveries that he never shared? Who knows!

> CARL COULD DO COMPLICATED CALCULATIONS IN HIS HEAD. HE OFTEN GAVE GOD CREDIT FOR HIS ABILITY TO SOLVE MATHEMATICAL RIDDLES.

God, help me shine my light, even when I'm nervous!

OCTOBER 5

T. S. ELIOT

1888–1965 • UNITED STATES AND ENGLAND

REASON TO HOPE

Why are you cast down, O my soul . . . ? Hope in God.

PSALM 42:5

When Thomas looked at the state of the world, his stomach felt a bit queasy. In the 1920s, countries across the globe were hurting from World War I, and many people were sad and angry. He wrote about it in a poem called *The Waste Land*. Writing usually made Thomas feel better, but not this time. *What would make the world better?* he wondered. *The right people leading? New ways of doing business?* Thomas wasn't sure. But he knew that the only One who could give hope for a better tomorrow was . . . God. Maybe everything wrong wouldn't be fixed. But God's love could unite people so that doing good would triumph over anger and chaos. Instead of writing about what was wrong in the world, Thomas began to write about solutions, like sharing God's love.

THOMAS WON THE NOBEL PRIZE FOR LITERATURE IN 1948 FOR HIS POETRY.

*God, thank You for giving us hope
when the world seems dark.*

OCTOBER 6

ESTHER JOHN

1929–1960 • PAKISTAN

CHASING AFTER GOD

*Proclaim the message; be persistent whether
the time is favorable or unfavorable.*

2 TIMOTHY 4:2

When she was seventeen, Esther started attending a Christian school. She saw God's love in one of her teachers, and before long, Esther was a Christian too! But her parents didn't agree with her choice. So at night she would read the Bible under her covers with a flashlight.

When Esther's parents wanted her to marry someone who wasn't a Christian, she ran away from her home. She found work at an orphanage, then a hospital. Eventually

> ESTHER WAS CHOSEN TO REPRESENT SOUTH ASIAN CHRISTIANS AS A STATUE IN WESTMINSTER ABBEY.

she attended a Bible training center. After she graduated, she began to ride her bike into remote villages in Pakistan. She'd teach women and children how to read and help them in the cotton fields. She also taught them about God. Esther soon grew popular among the people she visited. Every time she pedaled into the village, she was thrilled to share about the God she loved so much.

*God, I love You so much! I want to help
others know more about You too.*

OCTOBER 7

JAMES VANDERZEE

1886–1983 • UNITED STATES

PICTURE-PERFECT MOMENTS

This is the day that the Lord has made; let us rejoice and be glad in it.

PSALM 118:24

When he was about fourteen years old, James won a small eight-dollar camera in a contest. He immediately began to photograph family and friends, capturing their unique personalities. He was so good that people started paying him to take their photos! James had thought he wanted to be a musician, but he decided to make photography his career. He set up a studio in Harlem to capture people in their everyday and spiritual lives. From schoolchildren and church groups to wedding couples and celebrities, James captured who his subjects were and what their lives were like in that moment. That way they could look back and remember the family, friends, and other blessings long after the photo had been taken.

> JAMES QUIT PHOTOGRAPHY AFTER A WHILE BUT PICKED IT UP AGAIN A FEW YEARS BEFORE HE DIED—WHEN HE WAS IN HIS NINETIES!

God, thank You for the gifts You've given me today.

OCTOBER 8

ALOPEN

C. 600–C. 650 • CHINA

CARRYING GOD'S MESSAGE

"You will stand before governors and kings because of me."

MARK 13:9

Historians don't know much about the man named Alopen. They don't know exactly when he was born or died. They don't know how or why he became a Christian in his homeland of Persia. But they do know one thing: His faith was so important to him that he traveled thousands of miles across deserts and mountains on a missionary journey to China. When he arrived, Alopen was welcomed by an emperor named T'ai-Tsung. This emperor enjoyed learning about new things. He was

> IN 635, ALOPEN BECAME THE FIRST RECORDED MISSIONARY TO REACH CHINA. WE KNOW THIS BECAUSE OF A MONUMENT BUILT IN 781.

also curious about the God who Alopen had come so far to tell him about. The emperor took Alopen to his royal library. He asked the missionary to translate the books Alopen had brought with him. A few years later, the emperor paid to build the first Christian church in China.

Lord, give me the courage to tell others about You, no matter how far away.

OCTOBER 9

PAPIAS OF HIERAPOLIS

C.101–C.150 • HIERAPOLIS (MODERN-DAY TÜRKIYE)

LEARNING MORE ABOUT JESUS

Grow in the grace and knowledge of our
Lord and Savior Jesus Christ.

2 PETER 3:18

"Tell me again how Jesus said it," Papias asked the apostle John. Papias had never met Jesus but wanted to tell others about Him. So he talked to as many people who had known Jesus as possible. He thought documenting their experiences with Jesus might help others better understand Him and His teachings. Papias spent time with the apostle John asking many questions about Jesus. Papias wrote everything he learned in a book called *Explanations of the Sayings of the Lord*. The New Testament hadn't been put together yet, so many people in the ancient world used Papias's writings to learn what being with Jesus was like. Papias's work exists only in fragments today, but it still shows us what it was like to be a Christian walking with Jesus in the first century AD.

> MANY PEOPLE READ PAPIAS'S WORK UNTIL THE FOURTH CENTURY AD.

*God, I want to spend my life learning
more and more about You!*

OCTOBER 10

NELSON MANDELA

1918–2013 • SOUTH AFRICA

MESSY FORGIVENESS

*If we confess our sins, he who is faithful
and just will forgive us our sins.*

1 JOHN 1:9

Nelson was president of South Africa at a difficult time. For decades, the country had been split apart by racial segregation and violence. People were beginning to come back together, but many who had been harmed by violence and discrimination felt wronged—and were scared that something bad might happen again. Nelson decided the best way to bring everyone together would be through something called a Truth and Reconciliation Commission. People who had been wronged could tell their stories and receive help. And if someone had harmed another person, they could come forward to seek forgiveness. The process wasn't perfect, but Nelson was brave. He tried his best to bring the hurting country together, even if what he did was imperfect.

FOR HIS WORK TO BRING SOUTH AFRICANS TOGETHER, NELSON WON A NOBEL PEACE PRIZE.

*God, help me choose to forgive, even
when it's hard and messy.*

OCTOBER 11

SAINT GUMMARUS

717–744 • BELGIUM

RIGHT THE WRONGS

Whoever walks with the wise becomes wise, but the companion of fools suffers harm.

PROVERBS 13:20

Gummarus was a nobleman who grew up in the court of King Pepin. Gummarus was a hard worker and was kind to those around him. King Pepin saw the good works Gummarus did and arranged for him to marry a beautiful woman named Guinimaria. But Guinimaria was cruel to other people, preferred only the richest things, and didn't keep her promises. After eight years away in military service, Gummarus returned home to find that Guinimaria had scared everyone working at their house and spent all of their money. Gummarus corrected the problems his wife had caused. Though his relationship was unhappy, Gummarus grew closer to God and made sure his people were cared for.

> GUMMARUS IS THE PATRON SAINT OF DIFFICULT RELATIONSHIPS AND IS KNOWN FOR HELPING THE WORKERS ON HIS PROPERTY.

*God, when I see something wrong,
please help me make it right.*

OCTOBER 12

CÉSAR FRANCK

1822–1890 • FRANCE

CHOOSE KINDNESS

Those who are kind reward themselves, but
the cruel do themselves harm.

PROVERBS 11:17

César wasn't sure what to do. He was a professor who taught students to play the organ at the Paris Conservatory, a prestigious music school. He loved working with his students on music that was a bit different from the style of the day. But César's fellow teachers didn't like César's kindness to his students or the music he composed, much of which reflected his deep faith. They tried to get him fired. César didn't like to make people upset. But building up his students mattered more to him than being liked by the other teachers. He kept creating his style of music with students in his openhearted way. Soon the National Society of Music, who set the standards for French music, said they liked César's style of music. In the end, kindness and creativity won.

> CÉSAR'S HANDS WERE SO LARGE THEY COULD SPAN TWELVE WHITE KEYS ON THE KEYBOARD!

God, thank You for putting kindness for others in my heart.

OCTOBER 13

WAYMAN TISDALE

1964–2009 • UNITED STATES

KEEPING GOD NUMBER ONE

There is nothing on earth that I desire other than you.

PSALM 73:25

Basketball star Wayman Tisdale wowed crowds with his ability to run down the court and hit hoops, all with an electric smile on his face. He set records in college, won an Olympic gold medal, and played in the NBA for twelve seasons. Basketball was important to Wayman, but other things were important to him too: God, family, and playing bass guitar. When Wayman was growing up, he played bass guitar at the church where his dad preached. This was so important to Wayman that, in college, he asked his coach if he could still go on Sundays. The coach moved their practice time so Wayman could drive two hours each way to his dad's church. Even with all his professional success, Wayman was dedicated to the things that really mattered.

> THE DAY WAYMAN RETIRED FROM THE NBA, HE RELEASED A JAZZ ALBUM CALLED *DECISIONS*. AND HIS CAREER AS A JAZZ MUSICIAN WAS BORN!

God, help me to remember what really matters in life.

OCTOBER 14

SIR WILLIAM ROWAN HAMILTON

1805–1865 • IRELAND

TAKE A WALK

Ask for the ancient paths, where the good way lies;
and walk in it, and find rest for your souls.

JEREMIAH 6:16

When you're struggling to solve a problem, sometimes taking a break and going for a walk helps. Your brain gets some space to quietly solve the problem. That's what happened to William! He was out one day for a walk with his wife. He'd been trying to figure out how to study three-dimensional geometry. He believed he could see God's stamp on nature as he observed the world around him. As William and his wife traveled over a bridge, William realized he'd been looking at the solution all wrong! He didn't want to forget his idea, so he whipped out his pocketknife and began to carve it into the bridge. William's tenacity was rewarded with a new way of solving mechanical problems. A plaque today marks the spot of his carvings.

> WILLIAM'S WORK CONTRIBUTED TO THE DEVELOPMENT OF QUANTUM MECHANICS, WHICH WAS USED TO DEVELOP GPS, LASERS, MRIS, QUANTUM COMPUTERS, AND MORE.

God, when I'm struggling with something hard,
remind me it's okay to take a break!

OCTOBER 15

JOHN CONSTABLE

1776–1837 • ENGLAND

WHAT LINES UP

"I have come down from heaven, not to do my
own will, but the will of him who sent me."

JOHN 6:38

From John's earliest days, people expected him to do one thing—take over the family business of farming and milling. But he had a habit of following his heart and doing whatever lined up with his beliefs. When John was in his teens, he met a painter named Sir George Beaumont—and John decided he was going to be a painter too! After a bit of arguing, John's dad agreed to send him to art school. At the time, art schools trained their students to paint historical figures or scenes of famous battles. But John wanted to paint the quiet pastures and babbling brooks he grew up with in rural England. He became the most famous landscape painter in England! His art shows what the countryside looked like before trains, highways, and factories came along.

> JOHN PAINTED WITH DIFFERENT MATERIALS, DEPENDING ON HIS MOOD. SOMETIMES HE USED OILS; OTHER TIMES HE CHOSE WATERCOLORS.

God, help me do whatever lines up with Your will for me.

OCTOBER 16

GEORGES BERNANOS

1888–1948 • FRANCE

HELP THE HURTING

Cast your burden on the LORD, and he will sustain you.

PSALM 55:22

Georges lived at a time when the world was changing quickly—and with those changes came wars. Whenever someone new took power and started a war, regular people like you and I suffered. Invading forces would remove people from their homes, ruin their fields, and destroy their villages. This upset Georges. He wrote books about war and other current topics for readers around the world. His most famous book was *The Diary of a Country Priest*. It was about a fictional young priest who tried to serve the people suffering in his parish. The priest used what he had to help as he went door to door helping parishioners. Although his abilities were small, the priest's actions show how God can work through even our smallest attempts to help others. The book inspired many readers to help people struggling through hard times—no matter their ability.

> GEORGES HAS BEEN QUOTED PUBLICLY BY MULTIPLE POPES AND IS A FAVORITE WRITER OF CATHOLIC LITERATURE.

God, thank You for the ways I can help others.

OCTOBER 17

BETTY GREENE

1920–1997 • UNITED STATES

DARE TO FLY

Those who wait for the LORD shall renew their strength,
they shall mount up with wings like eagles.

ISAIAH 40:31

Early in her life, Betty Greene had two great loves: God and planes. As a teen, Betty took flying lessons when it wasn't common for young women to do so. During World War II, she flew different military planes and experimented with high-altitude flights. After the war, she used her flying talents for mission work. Betty became one of the founders of the Christian Airmen's Ministry Fellowship. For the next thirty years, Betty flew to places many hadn't gone before. The trips were long and dangerous. But Betty's courage pushed her to keep going. She transported missionaries, medical supplies, people who needed medical care, and even government officials. Through every flight, she remained skilled, calm, and joyful to do God's work—wherever He needed her.

> IN 1946, THE PERUVIAN GOVERNMENT HONORED BETTY FOR BEING THE FIRST WOMAN TO FLY OVER THE ANDES MOUNTAINS.

*God, give me the courage to soar into new
places You've designed for me to go.*

OCTOBER 18

CHRISTOPHER WREN

1632–1723 • ENGLAND

KEEP ON BUILDING

"Take courage! . . . For your work shall be rewarded."

2 CHRONICLES 15:7

Designer. Astronomer. Geometrician. One of the greatest English architects ever to live. These are just a few descriptions of Christopher Wren! Christopher designed fifty-three churches in London. Perhaps the grandest was Saint Paul's. But by 1665, it had fallen into disrepair. Employed by the king, Christopher had begun redesigning Saint Paul's when, along with two-thirds of London, the church was destroyed by a large fire. Christopher was tasked with rebuilding several churches and buildings around the city. He submitted plans for Saint Paul's, but the king kept rejecting them. "This design is too modest," the king would say. "No, this one is too grand." After thirty-five long years of designing, raising funds, and building, Christopher's work on Saint Paul's was finally complete. Its beauty and grandeur still inspire worshippers who gather there every Sunday.

> CHRISTOPHER'S DESIGN OF THE GRAND, CLASSICAL DOME ON SAINT PAUL'S HAS INSPIRED THE DOMES ON SEVERAL BUILDINGS, INCLUDING THE US CAPITOL.

God, help me stay persistent in the work I do for You.

OCTOBER 19

GALE SAYERS

1943–2020 • UNITED STATES

TRUE FRIENDS

A friend loves at all times, and kinsfolk are born to share adversity.

PROVERBS 17:17

Gale was an explosive NFL running back for the Chicago Bears. But during one game, Gale injured his knee and had to have surgery. He grumbled about his time away, but he worked hard to recover. He was happy to be back in the locker room with his friend Brian Piccolo. Brian and Gale were the first two players of different races to be roommates at NFL training camp. They didn't think anything of it; they were just great friends. One day, Brian discovered he had lung cancer. When Gale received an award after recovering from his knee injury, he dedicated the trophy to Brian and asked the audience to pray for Brian. In the end, Brian lost his cancer battle. Gale wanted to share his friend with the world. Their friendship inspired a movie called *Brian's Song*.

> GALE'S MOTTO WAS "I AM THIRD," MEANING GOD WAS FIRST, OTHERS WERE SECOND, AND HE WAS THIRD.

God, thank You for my friends.

OCTOBER 20

MARIAN ANDERSON

1897–1993 • UNITED STATES

PRAY ABOUT IT

He hears us in whatever we ask.

1 JOHN 5:15

As Marian's rich, operatic voice rang out from the steps of the Lincoln Memorial on Easter Sunday 1939, the crowd sat silently, drinking in the sound. She was one of the finest singers of her time. People first noticed Marian's talent in the church choir. Sometimes she performed at small local places. One day she was booked to sing at an important concert hall in New York City! But Marian didn't sing her best that night. She was so discouraged that she stopped singing for a year. Her mother encouraged her to pray about it, but Marian didn't think that would help. Finally, Marian did pray—and her heart felt lighter. She realized that a humble heart mattered more than a perfect voice. Marian went on to be very successful and sing for many important people.

> MARIAN EXPERIENCED MANY FIRSTS, INCLUDING BEING THE FIRST BLACK WOMAN TO PERFORM ON THE MAIN STAGE AT THE METROPOLITAN OPERA.

*God, help me put away perfection. Instead,
help me stay humble as I honor You.*

OCTOBER 21

GEORGES-EUGÈNE HAUSSMANN

1809–1891 • FRANCE

FOLLOW THE VISION

The plans of the diligent lead surely to abundance.

PROVERBS 21:5

Georges-Eugène had a tall task in front of him! Emperor Napoleon III had asked him to improve the ways people and goods moved around the city of Paris—and to improve Parisians' lives. Georges-Eugène got to work. He widened streets and lined them with trees so goods could be transported more easily and people had a pleasant place to walk. He then connected those roads to train stations. He increased the number of sidewalks and streetlamps, which led to a rise in sidewalk cafés (which Paris is still known for today!). Georges-Eugène's vision and hard work helped transform Paris into a beautiful, efficient modern city. Many countries around the world were inspired by his ideas for making their cities more beautiful and modern too!

> GEORGES-EUGÈNE BEGAN WORK ON THE NEARLY 400-MILE-LONG SEWER SYSTEM IN PARIS, MUCH OF WHICH IS STILL IN PLACE 140 YEARS LATER.

God, thank You for giving us the ability to solve problems.

OCTOBER 22

EL GRECO

1541–1614 • SPAIN

GO YOUR OWN WAY

Do not give heed to everything that people say.

ECCLESIASTES 7:21

"Why are the colors so bright?" "Why do the people's arms and legs look so . . . *long*?" El Greco had heard these questions about his paintings many times, but he didn't care. He had studied in Italy, where many artists thought painting things realistically was the most important. Other artists, however, believed that painting subjects the way they saw them, even if they didn't look *quite* real, was more meaningful. El Greco agreed with the latter group. A devoutly spiritual man, he painted mostly Bible stories and characters and used bold colors or longer features to draw people's eyes to certain parts of the picture he wanted them to focus on. El Greco painted the way he was confident worked best.

> EL GRECO INSPIRED MODERN ARTISTS LIKE PICASSO, WHO PAINTED SUBJECTS IN THEIR OWN STYLE AND TASTE. PICASSO THOUGHT EL GRECO WAS THE MOST OUTSTANDING OLD MASTER PAINTER.

God, thank You for giving me a vision to see the world around me in unique ways.

OCTOBER 23

JAN HUS

C. 1370–1415 • BOHEMIA (NOW CZECHIA)

WHAT'S TRUE?

Jesus said to him, "I am the way, and the truth, and the life. No one comes to the Father except through me."

JOHN 14:6

Jan was a curious reader. He enjoyed learning about what was true. When Jan was alive, many people did not learn to read. They relied on what others—like leaders of the country, their city, and their church—said. Jan noticed that many things the leaders were telling people weren't actually true. For example, if a rich person did something wrong, they could give money for their sin to be "forgiven." But Jan knew that wasn't what God said. And he told others they were wrong! The people who made money from this weren't very happy. They arrested Jan and told him to take back what he said, but Jan refused. He would rather give his life for the truth than to watch others be misled by lies.

> A HUNDRED YEARS LATER, JAN'S ACTIONS INFLUENCED ANOTHER YOUNG LEADER PASSIONATE ABOUT TRUTH: MARTIN LUTHER.

God, thank You for leaders like Jan who are dedicated to what is true.

OCTOBER 24

LEW WALLACE

1827–1905 • UNITED STATES

GETTING TO KNOW YOU

For they shall all know me, from the least of them to the greatest.

JEREMIAH 31:34

While talking with a man on a train who didn't believe in Jesus, Lew realized he didn't know much about his Christian faith. He decided to research not only about Jesus' life but also about the world He lived in. Lew read about first-century Judea and studied the plants, birds, clothes, and buildings common during that time. Lew decided to write a book about what he discovered called *Ben-Hur*. In the book, a man named Judah Ben-Hur is waiting for a grand Jewish king to come and save his people. But when Jesus shows up and says *He's* the king, Ben-Hur is skeptical. Eventually he believes in Jesus. *Ben-Hur* became one of the most popular books in the 1800s and was made into many plays and movies, helping introduce more people to Jesus.

PRESIDENT ULYSSES S. GRANT SAID HE ENJOYED *BEN-HUR* SO MUCH THAT HE READ IT FOR THIRTY HOURS STRAIGHT!

God, help me learn more about You each day.

OCTOBER 25

LEE ROY SELMON

1954–2011 • UNITED STATES

HOUSEBUILDER

By wisdom a house is built, and by understanding it is established.

PROVERBS 24:3

In 1976, a brand-new NFL team, the Tampa Bay Buccaneers, selected their very first player in the draft: defensive tackle Lee Roy Selmon. He was a fierce player and helped the Buccaneers go from the worst team in their conference to the first team just four years later! While Lee Roy could level another player with a tackle, off the field he was more interested in building a strong foundation for his life. Growing up on a farm in Oklahoma, Lee Roy's parents taught him about God and took him to church. Lee Roy used to say that building faith was like building a house. Brick by brick, each good decision would build the house taller and stronger. All you have to do to make your faith grow stronger is choose the next right thing.

> IF YOU'RE EVER IN A CAR DRIVING THROUGH TAMPA, FLORIDA, LOOK UP! YOU JUST MIGHT BE CRUISING ON THE LEE ROY SELMON EXPRESSWAY.

God, help me build a strong house of faith, brick by brick.

OCTOBER 26

CORRIE TEN BOOM

1892–1983 • THE NETHERLANDS

THE HIDING PLACE

You are a hiding place for me; you preserve me from trouble.

PSALM 32:7

Corrie and her family believed that every person was equal before God. So they opposed how Nazis were treating Jews during World War II. Corrie, along with her father, Casper, and sister, Betsie, began to hide Jews in their home. By day, Corrie worked in Casper's shop as a watchmaker, secretly meeting with people to help build a hiding place for Jews in their home and get ration books to buy extra supplies. One day, Nazis raided their home. Everyone in hiding remained safe! But Corrie, Betsie,

> CORRIE WROTE A BOOK ABOUT HER LIFE CALLED *THE HIDING PLACE*, WHICH WAS ALSO MADE INTO A MOVIE.

and Casper were arrested and sent to a concentration camp. Corrie survived, but Betsie and Casper died. She was eventually released and reunited with the rest of her family. But Corrie didn't want revenge. She spent the rest of her life sharing about how God wants us to forgive.

God, I want to learn to forgive in the same way Corrie did.

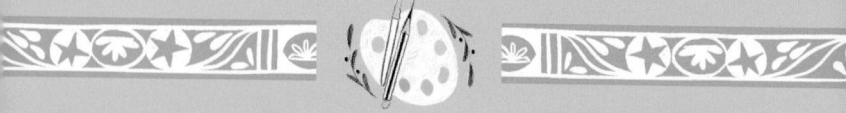

OCTOBER 27

CHRISTINE DE PISAN

1364–C. 1430 • FRANCE

TRAILBLAZER

> She girds herself with strength. . . . She opens her mouth with wisdom, and the teaching of kindness is on her tongue.
>
> **PROVERBS 31:17, 26**

Christine faced a dilemma. Her husband had just died, and she had three young children. At that time, there weren't many jobs for women. But Christine picked up her pen and got to work! Christine's father had worked at the royal court of the French king, so Christine had received an excellent education. She had read books and was a gifted writer. At first, she wrote love poems, which were quite popular! She also wrote a biography of France's king, Charles V, and a book about women known for their courage and bravery. She defended the value of women based on her study of Scripture and shared examples of honorable women in church history. Christine became one of the first women in Europe to earn a living by writing, and she blazed a trail for all women.

> CHRISTINE WAS THE ONLY PERSON TO WRITE ABOUT JOAN OF ARC DURING JOAN'S LIFETIME!

God, thank You for the strong and brave people in my life.

OCTOBER 28

ELLA FITZGERALD

1917–1996 • UNITED STATES

RIGHT AT HOME

"I have filled him with . . . knowledge in every kind of craft."

EXODUS 31:3

When she was growing up, Ella dreamed of being a dancer. At seventeen, after much practice, she felt ready. The Apollo Theater in New York City held an amateur night, where anyone could sign up to sing and dance. The winner would get to perform at the Apollo for a week—and jumpstart their career in show business! Ella watched the other performers backstage. The dancers were *really* good. Ella panicked. *They look like professionals! How can I compete?* She thought about another talent she had. As a child, she had spent lots of time singing in church and to jazz records with her mother. She decided to sing a jazz song that made her feel like she was back at home. Ella won her competition! And over the next five decades, she became one of the most beloved jazz singers in the world.

> ELLA WAS AN AVID BASEBALL FAN! SHE COLLECTED AUTOGRAPHED BALLS AND SPENT TIME WITH BASEBALL LEGENDS LIKE JACKIE ROBINSON AND WILLIE MAYS.

God, help me use the talents that make
me feel right at home with You.

OCTOBER 29

PERCY JULIAN

1899–1975 • UNITED STATES

PLANT POWER!

The earth brought forth vegetation: plants yielding seed of every kind..... And God saw that it was good.

GENESIS 1:12

Percy was fascinated by God's creation—especially plants. He was a brilliant chemist who had the patience to try an experiment again and again! Percy figured out how to create things from plants to help others. With a purple bean, Percy re-created a compound called *physostigmine* that doctors could use to open the pupil in someone's eye to more easily treat eye diseases. He made a foam from soybeans that, during World War II, extinguished fires on ships carrying airplanes. His soybean discoveries were also applied to house paint, paper coatings, and even foods! Percy believed his discoveries might help more people if he focused on making medicine. When the company he worked for said no, Percy opened his own lab! He not only made medicine but also hired more Black chemists, like himself, than any other lab in the US.

IN 1993, THE US POSTAL SERVICE CREATED A STAMP IN JULIAN'S HONOR.

God, the world You made is so cool! I want to keep learning more and more about it.

OCTOBER 30

REMBRANDT

1606–1669 • THE NETHERLANDS

KEEP ON LEARNING

An intelligent mind acquires knowledge, and
the ear of the wise seeks knowledge.

PROVERBS 18:15

Rembrandt loved to learn and to use the talents God had given him. He experimented with different instruments to create different works. Many people in the Netherlands knew him as a painter. But he also enjoyed etching, or scratching lines onto a piece of metal and applying ink to the surface to make a print. Rembrandt also liked to draw, using pencil or even chalk. He'd try different methods to make light and shadows. When he didn't have a model to paint, he'd often use his own face as inspiration! He created more than fifty self-portraits this way, in all different styles. Because Rembrandt remained a learner his whole life, he wasn't afraid to try new things, inspiring generations of artists after him.

> REMBRANDT WAS A REALIST—HE PAINTED THINGS JUST AS THEY ARE. REMBRANDT WAS SO DEDICATED TO REALISM THAT SOME SAY HE PREFERRED UGLINESS TO BEAUTY.

God, I want to keep learning, no matter how old I get!

OCTOBER 31

JIM PARKER

1934–2005 • UNITED STATES

RIGHT WHERE GOD WANTS YOU

For surely I know the plans I have for you, says the LORD, plans for your welfare and not for harm, to give you a future with hope.

JEREMIAH 29:11

At six foot three and 273 pounds, Jim was a player no defender wanted to encounter on the football field. Playing for the Baltimore Colts, he had the important job of protecting legendary quarterback Johnny Unitas. But despite his success, Jim didn't always feel like the best person for the job. He kept a suitcase packed during his entire NFL career, sure he would be let go for a better player. One day Jim called home and told his mom how he was feeling. "Don't worry about it," she said. "Have a little faith in God, and everything will be all right." Jim believed he was right where God had him. Despite feeling afraid, he kept going out on the field each week to do his best. And his best earned him a spot in the Pro Football Hall of Fame.

> JIM WAS SO TALENTED AT HIS JOB THAT HE PLAYED AS BOTH A LEFT TACKLE AND A LEFT GUARD—A RARE FEAT!

God, help me stay confident that I am right where You want me to be.

NOVEMBER 1

RUBY HIROSE

1904–1960 • UNITED STATES

SCIENCE SUPERHERO

[I] applied my mind to seek and to search out by
wisdom all that is done under heaven.

ECCLESIASTES 1:13

Ruby looked around the room. Out of the 300 scientists attending the 1940 American Chemical Society meeting, only ten—including her—were women. But Ruby wasn't intimidated. She had grown up as the daughter of Japanese immigrants. Not many families in Seattle looked like Ruby's. But Ruby worked hard to build a life for herself. She became a biochemist and biologist who studied how medicines affect different diseases. In the mid-twentieth century, one disease was especially scary: polio. Many children who got it became unable to grow or move the way they once had. Scientists, including Ruby, worked feverishly to create a vaccine. Her work on allergies (which she suffered from herself!) contributed greatly to the discovery of the polio vaccine. Because of Ruby's hard work, many children have never had to suffer from this terrible disease.

IN COLLEGE, RUBY STUDIED PLANTS THAT EXPLORERS LEWIS AND CLARK HAD WRITTEN ABOUT MORE THAN A HUNDRED YEARS EARLIER.

God, thank You for people who make our world safer.

NOVEMBER 2

JOSEPH HENRY

1797–1878 • UNITED STATES

SEE AND SHARE

Then God said, "Let us make humankind in our image, according to our likeness; and let them have dominion over the fish of the sea, and over the birds of the air."

GENESIS 1:26

Benjamin Franklin was the first great American scientist. But the second one? That was Joseph! He helped discover scientific principles like electromagnetism. He also worked closely with many others. He taught at Princeton and was beloved by his students. And he helped Samuel Morse develop the telegraph—one of the most important inventions in the history of communication! Joseph gave Samuel five miles of copper wire and also wrote his contacts in Washington, DC, asking them to support a test line. In 1846, Joseph was elected the first secretary of the Smithsonian Institution. While there, he encouraged a group of volunteers to study the weather, which became the US Weather Service and is still in operation today. John's gift for observation and relationships is still helping us!

> JOHN WAS ONE OF PRESIDENT ABRAHAM LINCOLN'S TECHNICAL ADVISERS DURING THE CIVIL WAR.

God, help me not only to see what You'd like me to see but also to share it with others.

NOVEMBER 3

HENRY OSSAWA TANNER

1859–1937 • UNITED STATES AND FRANCE

COLOR MY WORLD

Out of Zion, the perfection of beauty, God shines forth.

PSALM 50:2

Henry painted beautiful Bible stories drenched in color and light. He believed that religious pictures should be artistic and tell the Bible story faithfully. In 1891, Henry moved to Paris to enroll in an art school. There Henry entered a few Bible story paintings into an art show. His painting called *Daniel in the Lions' Den* was awarded an honorable mention—but *The Raising of Lazarus* won a medal! This was a big deal since artists who weren't French were rarely honored. The French government even purchased *The Raising of Lazarus*! Soon more people learned about Henry's beautiful Bible paintings. He eventually traveled to the Holy Land to see where Jesus had once walked. He spent the rest of his days sharing about Jesus through his art.

> IN 1969, THE SMITHSONIAN EXHIBITED HENRY'S WORK—THE FIRST MAJOR SOLO EXHIBITION OF A BLACK ARTIST IN THE UNITED STATES.

God, thank You for telling us who You are through Bible stories!

NOVEMBER 4

DANTE ALIGHIERI

1265–1321 • ITALY

HEAVENLY JOURNEY

The Lord has made everything for its purpose.

PROVERBS 16:4

Dante was upset. He had been banished from Florence, his hometown, for something he didn't do. Like many writers, he decided to process his feelings by writing—in his case, a poem. In this poem, Dante goes on a trip. But not a normal trip, like to the beach. On this trip, Dante goes to hell and then to heaven. Dante wondered what it would be like to travel to the afterlife he'd heard about since he was young. How would it feel to be in hell, far from God's presence? How would it feel to live in paradise with God forever? Being exiled was awful, but God used Dante in this situation. For centuries, this poem, *The Divine Comedy*, has helped countless readers picture the afterlife and discover how to grow closer to God.

DANTE CHOSE TO WRITE *THE DIVINE COMEDY* IN ITALIAN, NOT THE CUSTOMARY LATIN. THIS INSPIRED OTHERS TO WRITE LITERATURE IN THEIR OWN LANGUAGES TOO!

God, thank You for bringing good out of bad situations.

NOVEMBER 5

FRANZ JÄGERSTÄTTER

1907–1943 • AUSTRIA

LOYAL TO GOD

Let us hold fast to the confession of our hope without wavering, for he who has promised is faithful.

HEBREWS 10:23

Franz shook his head. How was he the *only* local citizen who had voted against Austria joining Germany? Adolf Hitler ruled Germany, and he seemed to be taking over Europe step by step. Franz was disgusted by the way Hitler's Nazis abused people. After Austria joined Germany, Franz was called into military service. He thought about who his loyalty belonged to—his country or God? He thought about Jesus giving His life to save others, and Franz made up his mind: He would choose God. After about six months, Franz was allowed to return to his farm. When he was called for service again, he refused to bow his head to Hitler—he would only bow to God. He was sentenced to death for following God.

> THE CATHOLIC CHURCH RECOGNIZED FRANZ'S LOYALTY TO GOD BY GIVING HIM THE TITLE OF "BLESSED."

God, I know exactly where I'm putting my loyalty: into Your loving hands.

NOVEMBER 6

GENE UPSHAW

1945–2008 • UNITED STATES

GOOD LOOKING OUT

A generous person will be enriched, and one who gives water will get water.

PROVERBS 11:25

When he was seven years old, Gene began to pick cotton in his small, segregated Texas town. His parents set out a few rules for Gene: Work hard, go to church, and do well in school. He took these lessons with him to his time as an offensive lineman for the Oakland Raiders and later as head of the NFL Players' Association (NFLPA). The NFLPA makes sure all NFL players can play safely and are paid fairly.

> AS A PLAYER, GENE WAS SELECTED TO THE PRO BOWL SEVEN TIMES.

Sometimes the changes Gene proposed meant team owners had to pay for new equipment or better salaries for players. Sometimes the owners didn't want to pay up. But Gene showed the owners that treating players well would help everyone in the long run. Gene's hard work and integrity earned everyone's trust.

God, help me work hard not only to do a good job, but to help others.

NOVEMBER 7

SOJOURNER TRUTH

C. 1797–1883 • UNITED STATES

BROTHERS AND SISTERS

There is no longer slave or free, there is no longer male and female; for all of you are one in Christ Jesus.

GALATIANS 3:28

"Did you hear? Sojourner is coming here to speak!" All around the eastern United States, people grew excited whenever they knew Sojourner was coming to town. Sojourner was born enslaved but had been set free as an adult. In the 1840s, she felt God calling her to tell other people about Him and that everyone was His child! That meant everyone in the country were brothers and sisters, and that God wanted them to live together as one. Sojourner drew large crowds wherever she went. She had a simple but powerful way of explaining that all people should be free and equal—men and women, no matter their race. She worked hard at this mission for the rest of her life.

> PRESIDENT ABRAHAM LINCOLN WAS SO IMPRESSED WITH SOJOURNER THAT HE INVITED HER TO THE WHITE HOUSE!

God, thank You for making me Your child. Help me treat all of Your children with love and respect.

NOVEMBER 8

ANGELA BURDETT-COUTTS

1814–1906 • ENGLAND

GIVE IT AWAY

Whoever is kind to the poor lends to the
Lord, and will be repaid in full.

PROVERBS 19:17

Angela was a young woman when she inherited her family's fortune. *What should I do with all this money?* she thought. She decided to help others! She funded schools for poor children. During the Crimean War, she sent money to soldiers' wives so they could feed and house their families. She also sent a state-of-the-art laundry drying machine to Florence Nightingale, the pioneering nurse working on the front lines to care for soldiers. Angela built churches, donated archaeological fossils, provided homes to young women in trouble, and even gave seed potatoes to Irish farmers to establish crops after the potato famine. Angela could have kept her money. But she decided that real wealth could be found in choosing to be generous with what she had.

> ANGELA GAVE MONEY TO HER FRIEND CHARLES BABBAGE, WHO INVENTED THE FIRST COMPUTER!

God, help me use what I have to help people around me.

NOVEMBER 9

SAM MILLS

1959–2005 • UNITED STATES

STRENGTH TO KEEP GOING

Let endurance have its full effect, so that you may be mature and complete, lacking in nothing.

JAMES 1:4

Lineman Sam Mills heard coaches say the same thing over and over: "You're too small to play here." Sam, five feet nine inches tall, would quietly put on his gear, run to the field, and perform so well that there was no doubt Sam could handle the job! He set records in high school and college—yet wasn't drafted into the NFL. So for the first three years after college, Sam played for another football league called the USFL and helped his team win three championships. Sam kept working hard and was known for his faith and integrity. When Sam's USFL coach left for a job in the NFL, he took Sam with him, where he played for twelve seasons! This Hall of Famer may not have been the biggest player on the field, but his determination and character shone through.

> SAM HELPED THE SAINTS GET TO THE PLAYOFFS FOR THE FIRST TIME IN TEAM HISTORY!

God, when other people doubt my abilities, remind me that hard work is just as important as talent.

NOVEMBER 10

SISTER GERTRUDE MORGAN

1900–1980 • UNITED STATES

ACCEPT HIS CALL

"Strive first for the kingdom of God and his righteousness, and all these things will be given to you as well."

MATTHEW 6:33

In 1934, Sister Gertrude felt called to do something she wasn't expecting—become a singing street preacher. In 1939, she moved to New Orleans to tell residents and visitors alike about God. In the 1940s, Sister Gertrude teamed up with two other street preachers to open a small chapel. They also operated a place where orphans and children who needed help could stay. But that's not all Sister Gertrude did for God! In the 1960s, she felt called to something new—painting. As she read the book of Revelation, she painted pictures of what the world to come would look like. To Sister Gertrude, she wasn't the one with talent—God was. She was just open to being His hands and doing good for Him.

> SISTER GERTRUDE OFTEN USED SIMPLE TOOLS LIKE PENS, PENCILS, AND CRAYONS TO CREATE HER ARTWORK.

God, help me stay open to new ways to share about You.

NOVEMBER 11

SIR GEORGE GILBERT SCOTT

1811–1878 • ENGLAND

RIGHT ON TIME

The Lord will fulfill his purpose for me.

PSALM 138:8

What would George do with his life? His parents didn't think he was smart enough to attend college like his older brothers. They didn't know what to do. So they let him wander the neighborhood, where George sketched the beautiful medieval churches around him. When George was fifteen, his parents sent him to live with a childless aunt and uncle. They gave George books on his favorite subject, architecture. George's enthusiasm for architecture grew, and soon he met a religious architect who took George in as an apprentice. Eventually, George became one of the most sought-after architects in England. His firm constructed or restored more than 500 beautiful churches and cathedrals, usually in the medieval style he loved as a boy.

> ONE OF GEORGE'S BEST-KNOWN DESIGNS IS THE ALBERT MEMORIAL IN LONDON, IN HONOR OF QUEEN VICTORIA'S HUSBAND, PRINCE ALBERT. SHE LIKED IT SO MUCH SHE MADE GEORGE A KNIGHT!

God, I trust that You'll show my purpose to me at the right time.

NOVEMBER 12

SAINT DIDACUS

C. 1400–1463 • SPAIN

QUIET SERVICE

God chose what is foolish in the world to shame the wise.

1 CORINTHIANS 1:27

Your life doesn't have to be filled with great big acts to matter. Didacus focused on small acts of devotion to God and service to others. When he was a boy, Didacus admired a nearby priest who lived a quiet life and asked to learn from him. Together they tended a garden and earned money making wooden spoons and bowls. When they weren't working, they were praying. Didacus ultimately joined a Franciscan order and dedicated his life to God. He was sent to the Canary Islands off Africa, where he taught people about Jesus and helped run a convent. Didacus joined his brothers at a celebration in Rome, but many got sick. Didacus tended them for months. He eventually returned to Spain, living in quiet service to God and helping his brothers.

SAN DIEGO, CALIFORNIA, IS NAMED AFTER DIDACUS.

God, help me remember that the little things I do matter to You.

NOVEMBER 13

THOMAS ANDREW DORSEY

1899–1993 • UNITED STATES

THE GOSPEL IN A WHOLE NEW WAY

Christ did not send me to baptize but to proclaim
the gospel, and not with eloquent wisdom.

1 CORINTHIANS 1:17

Thomas was a musician and composer living in Chicago. During the day, he worked and attended music school; at night, he played music at blues and jazz spots around the city. One night, while attending a church service, the music stirred Thomas's soul in a new way. Hearing that music alongside the gospel brought Thomas closer to Jesus than ever before. That week, he began writing songs to help others experience Jesus the same way. Thomas called the music "gospel music." And people loved it! He combined the style of his beloved blues and jazz with lyrics about God. Thomas wrote some of the most popular songs Christians still love today, such as "Precious Lord, Take My Hand" and "Peace in the Valley."

> "PRECIOUS LORD, TAKE MY HAND" WAS DR. MARTIN LUTHER KING JR.'S FAVORITE SONG.

God, help me use my talents to connect others to You.

NOVEMBER 14

PETRARCH

1304–1374 • ITALY

JUST ONE SPARK

As when fire kindles brushwood . . . make your name known.

ISAIAH 64:2

Sometimes it takes just a small spark to get a fire going. For the Renaissance, that spark was Petrarch! Petrarch loved to read, especially the classical literature of Greece and Rome. During Petrarch's life, there wasn't a central place where scholars could read manuscripts from the classical period. So Petrarch decided to hunt them down! He traveled around Europe collecting them. Over the next hundred years, others followed Petrarch's example and read classical writings about law, philosophy, science, and more subjects. They were inspired by these "new" ideas and expanded on them. That's how the Renaissance, or a period of "rebirth," came to be.

> PETRARCH WAS ALSO A RESPECTED POET. MANY OF HIS POEMS ARE ADDRESSED TO THE MYSTERIOUS LOVE OF HIS LIFE NAMED LAURA.

God, I want to be a spark for good! Please show me how.

NOVEMBER 15

JIM OTTO

1938–2024 • UNITED STATES

DREAM HELPERS

"Give to everyone who begs from you."

MATTHEW 5:42

Eleven-year-old Jim was listening to a football game on the radio and daydreaming. He saw himself wearing football pads and a helmet. He told his grandfather he was going to be a professional football player someday. But the road to the NFL wasn't easy. Jim had to overcome great financial difficulties. For a time, his family lived in a chicken coop because they couldn't afford anything else. But his parents encouraged him. And his pastor not only strengthened his faith but also paid for Jim's YMCA membership so Jim could exercise and get stronger. His high school football coach taught him the fundamentals of football. These people believed in Jim and did what they could to help him. Jim took their help, worked hard, and became a center for the Oakland Raiders. His dream came true!

> WHEN JIM WAS INDUCTED INTO THE PRO FOOTBALL HALL OF FAME, THE FIRST ONE HE THANKED WAS GOD. WITHOUT GOD, HIS DREAM NEVER WOULD HAVE BEEN POSSIBLE!

God, thank You for the people who help make my dreams come true!

NOVEMBER 16

G. K. CHESTERTON

1874–1936 • ENGLAND

BIG QUESTIONS

If any of you is lacking in wisdom, ask God . . . and it will be given you.

JAMES 1:5

G. K. loved to ask questions. What makes a person a hero or a villain? Can humor help us think about hard topics? How does faith change the way we look at the world? G. K. spent much of his life searching for these answers. He created fictional characters who asked these questions, such as Father Brown, a Catholic priest and amateur detective. He wrote books and newspaper articles exploring these questions. Readers appreciated how G. K. talked about these issues. Asking big questions helped G. K. strengthen his faith, and by sharing what he learned, he helped others strengthen their faith too. G. K. knew that God would help him find answers to life's biggest questions.

> PEOPLE STILL ENJOY FATHER BROWN STORIES TODAY. THERE'S ALSO A POPULAR TV SHOW BASED ON HIM!

God, sometimes I have big questions, and I don't always know the answers. Thank You for always listening.

NOVEMBER 17

BILL GLASS

1935–2021 • UNITED STATES

SHARING JESUS WITH EVERYONE

Remember those who are in prison.

HEBREWS 13:3

As a defensive end for the Cleveland Browns, Bill got folks to their feet with his dazzling plays on the football field. But that wasn't Bill's proudest accomplishment. He was more focused on telling people about Jesus, whether it was his fellow teammates or people in prison. Bill knew some Christians might scoff at him playing ball on Sundays. But he thought football opened doors so he could tell others about Jesus. He even enrolled in seminary to be better prepared! Bill started hosting Bible studies and prayer meetings at the team hotel before games. He'd pray with athletes, coaches, and even sportswriters. After Bill retired, he asked athletes from other sports like baseball, basketball, and the Olympics to join him to talk to people in prison. By 2019, Bill's ministry had visited more than 6 million people behind bars.

> A YOUNG MICHAEL JORDAN, THEN A COLLEGE STUDENT, ONCE JOINED BILL TO SHARE THE GOSPEL WITH FOLKS IN PRISON.

God, I want to tell others about You. Please show me how.

NOVEMBER 18

JAMES CLERK MAXWELL

1831–1879 • SCOTLAND

SEEING KINDNESS

The LORD is gracious and merciful.

PSALM 145:8

James was a brilliant physicist. Many compare his contributions to Sir Isaac Newton and Albert Einstein. His work expanding on Michael Faraday's theories of electromagnetism eventually led to the development of color photos and television, even computers and smartphones.

But James's brilliant observations didn't stop in the lab. He also concluded that God's fingerprints could be seen in creation and His love in kindness. In college, James was visiting a friend's family when he got sick. Instead of asking him to leave, the family nursed James back to health.

> JAMES WAS ALSO INTERESTED IN ASTRONOMY. HE CONCLUDED THAT SATURN'S RINGS WEREN'T COMPLETELY SOLID. THIS THEORY WAS CONFIRMED A HUNDRED YEARS LATER BY THE *VOYAGER* SPACE PROBE.

He wanted to show the same Christian love to others. For the next thirteen years, he taught a free science class for underprivileged men and also read a textbook aloud to a classmate who couldn't see well.

*God, no matter how much I have going on,
please help me remember to be kind.*

NOVEMBER 19

TOMÁS LUIS DE VICTORIA

C. 1548–1611 • SPAIN

ALL FOR HIM

I will sing and make melody.

PSALM 57:7

As young Tomás sang in the choir at Ávila Cathedral, little did he know his talent would be one day be used by an empress! Tomás loved the music of the church and wanted to spend his life creating it. When Tomás grew older, the king of Spain sent Tomás to Rome to study music. While there, Tomás became a singer, organist, teacher, and composer of church music. He even became a priest as well! Many composers in Tomás's time created music for people listening to music both in and out of church. But not Tomás! He didn't write as many pieces as other musicians, but what he did write was specifically for the church and was filled with emotion. He was determined to use his gifts to honor God.

> TOMÁS CREATED UNIQUE CHOIR PIECES IN A STYLE CALLED COUNTERPOINT, WHERE MORE THAN ONE MELODY IS SUNG AT THE SAME TIME.

God, I want to dedicate my life and work to honor You.

NOVEMBER 20

DAN REEVES

1944–2022 • UNITED STATES

THE NEXT STEP

Trust in the Lord with all your heart.

PROVERBS 3:5

Running back Dan Reeves was upset. He had just injured his knee so badly that his season—possibly even his career—might be over. *What am I going to do?* But Dan trusted God. "It turned out God knew what He was doing," Dan later said. After Dan's injury, his coach, the legendary Tom Landry, asked Dan to be a coach for the Cowboys. Dan turned out to be a better coach than he was a player! He became the youngest head coach in NFL history at that time. He took the Denver Broncos to three Super Bowls and the Atlanta Falcons to their only Super Bowl appearance. Through it all, Dan trusted God with wherever his path took him.

> DAN'S MOTTO WAS "I AM THIRD," MEANING "JESUS IS FIRST, OTHERS ARE SECOND, AND I AM THIRD."

God, help me trust Your plans—even if they surprise me.

NOVEMBER 21

HARRIET TUBMAN

C. 1820–1913 • UNITED STATES

COURAGEOUS CONDUCTOR

> "I have observed the misery of my people.... I will send you to Pharaoh to bring my people, the Israelites, out of Egypt."
>
> **EXODUS 3:7, 10**

On a cold night in December 1850, Harriet quietly led her niece Kessiah and Kessiah's children away from the family that had enslaved them. They traveled north from Baltimore, Maryland, toward freedom. Harriet had also been enslaved but ran away and found freedom. She decided to help as many people as possible find freedom too and believed that God would protect them. Over the next decade, Harriet returned to Maryland thirteen times to help dozens of enslaved people travel through a network called the Underground Railroad to freedom. She coordinated her escapes on Saturday nights so the news wouldn't break until Monday's newspaper came out, after they were safely out of distance. Harriet never lost a passenger and became the Underground Railroad's most famous conductor. Because of her courage and persistence, many called her "the Moses of her people."

> IN 2024, HARRIET WAS AWARDED THE RANK OF ONE-STAR BRIGADIER GENERAL BY THE MARYLAND NATIONAL GUARD FOR HER MILITARY SERVICE DURING THE CIVIL WAR. SHE SERVED AS A COOK, NURSE, SPY, AND SCOUT.

God, I'm in awe of courageous people like Harriet. Help me to be strong like her.

NOVEMBER 22

MAGDA TROCMÉ

1901–1996 • FRANCE

CARING WITH COMPASSION

Clothe yourselves with compassion, kindness,
humility, meekness, and patience.

COLOSSIANS 3:12

Growing up, Magda heard stories about her grandfather, who had escaped from Russia when it wasn't safe to stay there. She thought about how scared he must have been to leave his home, and wondered where he would have found his next meal if he ran out of money. One cold winter evening in 1940, a Jewish woman knocked on Magda's door. She was looking for food and shelter, and Magda knew what God would want her to say: "Come on in." Soon, more people knocked on Magda's door looking for help. Magda and her husband, André, knew they needed more helpers! Magda gathered the villagers in her town and asked them to help these refugees too. Together they helped thousands of Jews looking for safety.

> EVEN THOUGH MAGDA HELPED SAVE THOUSANDS OF LIVES, SHE DIDN'T BELIEVE SHE WAS A HERO. SHE WAS JUST HAPPY TO HELP.

*God, help me to open the door of my
heart to those who need help.*

NOVEMBER 23

J. WILLARD GIBBS

1839–1903 • UNITED STATES

KEEP YOUR HEAD DOWN

"Your Father who sees in secret will reward you."

MATTHEW 6:4

J. Willard Gibbs (who went by Willard) lived a quiet life. So how did he become someone Albert Einstein called "the greatest mind in American history"? Willard was a professor of mathematical physics at Yale. He enjoyed working in his lab and didn't care if his work impressed others or made waves. He was a pioneer in the field of thermodynamics. And his work helped to establish physical chemistry, which describes how atoms and molecules behave. Willard published his work in a small journal to try to make his work more popular. He never married. He was born and died in the same house. One biographer referred to him as an "unselfish, Christian gentleman." His brilliant work inspired other great scientists after him and helped change science forever.

> IN 1863, WILLARD RECEIVED THE FIRST DOCTORATE IN ENGINEERING GIVEN IN THE UNITED STATES.

*God, help me focus on doing good,
not on the praise I might get.*

NOVEMBER 24

HARPER LEE

1926–2016 • UNITED STATES

ANOTHER POINT OF VIEW

Have unity of spirit, sympathy, love for one another, a tender heart, and a humble mind.

1 PETER 3:8

Harper sat down at her typewriter, thinking about her father. He was a lawyer. He worked to get justice for people who had been wronged or wrongly accused. She thought of something he might say and began to type. "You never really understand a person until you consider things from his point of view, until you climb into his skin and walk around in it." This became the central idea for *To Kill a Mockingbird*. Harper grew up in Alabama at a time when Black people were unfairly separated from others. They couldn't share public spaces or even the same job opportunities. Harper knew this was wrong. So she wrote a book showing what it was like to walk in someone else's "skin." This book became a huge bestseller and continues to change minds about how we treat others.

> HARPER WAS A HUGE FAN OF THE WRITER C. S. LEWIS. HER FAVORITE OF HIS BOOKS WAS *MERE CHRISTIANITY*.

God, when I have a problem with someone, help me remember to look at things from their point of view.

NOVEMBER 25

WILLIAM EDMONSON

1874–1951 • UNITED STATES

CARVING A LEGACY

Even to old age and gray hairs, O God, do not forsake me, until I proclaim your might to all the generations to come.

PSALM 71:18

William wasn't quite sure where his next job would come from. He'd spent much of his life as a janitor at Nashville Woman's Hospital, but the hospital had closed. He began doing odd jobs. One was as an assistant to a stonemason. William learned to carve limestone rock and had a knack for it. William said it felt like a voice from heaven guided him to sculpt. Soon his backyard began to fill up with sculptures, or what he called his "miracles." Many of his miracles were related to the Bible. Sometimes William created Bible characters like Jesus or small lambs and doves. Sometimes he even carved real-life people, like preachers or First Lady Eleanor Roosevelt! Though he carved only the last seventeen years of his life, William's art made a lasting impact.

> IN 1937, THE MUSEUM OF MODERN ART (MOMA) IN NEW YORK CITY SHOWED WILLIAM'S SCULPTURES. HE BECAME THE FIRST BLACK PERSON TO HAVE AN EXHIBIT AT MOMA.

God, I'm glad I can do great things for You, no matter what my age is!

NOVEMBER 26

BARON WILLIAM THOMSON KELVIN

1824–1907 • SCOTLAND

TRY AGAIN

Though we stumble, we shall not fall headlong,
for the Lord holds us by the hand.

PSALM 37:24

News of President Lincoln's death in 1865 took two weeks to reach Great Britain. In 1881, when President Garfield died, Great Britain learned the news in just a few hours. How? Because in 1866, North America and Europe were connected by a telegraph wire that ran under the ocean! And William helped make that happen. William was a brilliant scientist and engineer and took charge of the project to connect the two continents by telegraph wire. He invented new machines to transmit better signals. He boarded a ship from Ireland to Newfoundland, Canada, a 1,600-mile trip where the wire would be laid in the ocean. They almost succeeded the first time—until the cable snapped off close to Canada! By 1866, they completed their mission! They could send messages across the ocean almost instantly.

LORD KELVIN WAS ALSO A PIONEER IN THERMODYNAMICS. A DEVOUT CHRISTIAN, HE BELIEVED THAT SCIENCE AND RELIGION COULD BENEFIT FROM EACH OTHER.

God, help me remember that even if I don't succeed at first, I can still try again.

NOVEMBER 27

CARTER G. WOODSON

1875–1950 • UNITED STATES

REMEMBER, REMEMBER

Remember the days of old, consider the years long past; ask . . . your elders, and they will tell you.

DEUTERONOMY 32:7

Carter was a brilliant scholar and historian. He earned a PhD from Harvard University—the second Black person to do so. Carter studied the way African Americans had contributed new ideas in science, art, music, and life in the United States. And he wanted more people to know about them! In February 1926, he asked his college fraternity brothers to help with an idea. He wanted to start something called Negro History Week to highlight the accomplishments of important Black artists, inventors, and other people in history. Some places around the country expanded their celebrations from a week to a whole month. In 1976, President Gerald Ford asked Americans to officially recognize Black History Month. Thanks to Carter, we still celebrate it each February.

> CARTER CHOSE FEBRUARY FOR BLACK HISTORY MONTH BECAUSE OF TWO IMPORTANT BIRTHDAYS THAT MONTH: FREDERICK DOUGLASS AND ABRAHAM LINCOLN.

God, thank You for the examples of smart, courageous people who came before me.

NOVEMBER 28

MARIA GAETANA AGNESI

1718–1799 • MILAN (MODERN-DAY ITALY)

PAVING THE WAY

*Whether you eat or drink, or whatever you do,
do everything for the glory of God.*

1 CORINTHIANS 10:31

Maria was a marvel. By age nine, along with her native Italian, she knew Latin, Greek, and Hebrew. She loved to study math and to go to church but detested dressing up in fancy gowns and attending parties. Maria thought she'd rather enter a convent and serve others. But since her mother had died, Maria agreed to stay home to help around the house. Maria continued her math studies and even wrote a book on differential calculus, where she talked about a new type of curve she discovered, which scholars still call "the Agnesi curve." Maria became the first renowned female mathematician. As she grew older, she dedicated more of her time to serving others and studying the Bible. She built hospices for people who couldn't afford medical care.

> MARIA WAS SO GOOD AT MATH THAT POPE BENEDICT XIV APPOINTED HER A PROFESSOR OF MATHEMATICS AT THE UNIVERSITY OF BOLOGNA.

God, help me use my gifts to bring You glory.

NOVEMBER 29

NICOLAUS COPERNICUS

1473–1543 • POLAND

TRUTH TELLER

Truthful lips endure.

PROVERBS 12:19

Nicolaus was an astronomer who made many important discoveries. He discovered that the planets move around the sun. He noticed that earth tilts on an axis, which gives us the different seasons. He even discovered that after Earth in the solar system come Mars, Jupiter, and Saturn—in that order! But Nicolaus was afraid to tell anyone about these discoveries. At the time, people believed that the sun and other planets moved around Earth. They thought anyone who believed differently deserved to be punished! So Nicolaus didn't publish his ideas until the year he died. But doing so was still a brave act. Many later scientists were inspired by his work, from Galileo and Johannes Kepler to Sir Isaac Newton.

> MANY SCHOLARS SAY THAT NICOLAUS WAS NOT ONLY THE FATHER OF MODERN ASTRONOMY—HIS WORK SPARKED THE ENTIRE SCIENTIFIC REVOLUTION.

God, even when I'm afraid, please help me speak the truth.

NOVEMBER 30

JOHN BLOW

1649–1708 • ENGLAND

GO WHERE YOU'RE NEEDED

Then I heard the voice of the Lord saying, "Whom shall I send, and who will go for us?" And I said, "Here am I; send me!"

ISAIAH 6:8

From the time he was eleven years old, John made beautiful music. He was a chorister for the Chapel Royal, singing in the church choir for the king's family. After that he became the organist for Westminster Abbey, one of the largest churches in England. He later taught the choir where he used to sing. In that role, he influenced many young artists—including his brightest pupil, Henry Purcell. Young Henry went on to become the next organist of Westminster Abbey while John went to another church to lead the choir. But then Henry died suddenly. Westminster Abbey asked John to come back to his old job. Some people might not do that, but John didn't mind. He went where he was needed to create beautiful music for God.

> JOHN WROTE THE FIRST OPERA IN THE ENGLISH LANGUAGE, CALLED *VENUS AND ADONIS*.

God, wherever You need me, please lead me there.

DECEMBER 1

SAINT CHARLES DE FOUCAULD

1858–1916 • FRANCE AND ALGERIA

ARROWS POINTING TO GOD

"You are the light of the world. A city built on a hill cannot be hid."

MATTHEW 5:14

By the time he was six, Charles was an orphan. Though he was raised by a grandfather with a strong faith, Charles decided he didn't believe in God. He joined the army, which took him to Algeria and Morocco. As a soldier, he partied. But Charles was influenced by the deep faith of the people he met. "My God," he prayed, "if You exist, let me come to know You." He traveled back to France, where he studied the Bible and decided to follow God again! Charles spent seven years as a Trappist monk and prayed alone in Nazareth and Jerusalem. Then he went to the Sahara Desert, where he lived among the Taureg people. He wanted them to see his life and say, "If this is what God's servant is like, what must God Himself be like?"

> CHARLES BECAME SO FLUENT IN THE TAUREG LANGUAGE THAT HE TRANSLATED THE GOSPELS INTO TAUREG.

God, help me live in a way that points others to You.

DECEMBER 2

BLESSED RAFAL CHYLINSKI

1694–1741 • POLAND

LISTEN TO YOUR HEART

"Whoever serves me must follow me, and where
I am, there will my servant be also."

JOHN 12:26

When Rafal was a boy, he was known by another name: Melchior. And Melchior loved God so much that he talked about Him all the time. This earned Melchior a nickname: "the little monk." After college, Melchior joined the army. He was such a good leader that he rose to the rank of captain. But something about his job didn't feel right. Melchior felt he could serve God in a better way. He shared these feelings with his fellow soldiers. "But you're so good at this!" they said. "You should stay here." But Melchior decided to listen to his heart, and he left the army. He became a priest and took a new name: Rafal. He traveled to cities across Poland sharing about God. People loved his simple sermons, his listening ear, and his kind heart.

> RAFAL WAS A GIFTED MUSICIAN! HE SOMETIMES PLAYED HARP, LUTE, AND MANDOLIN TO ACCOMPANY HYMNS.

God, please show me how to serve Your people.

DECEMBER 3

EVANGELINE CORY BOOTH

1865–1950 • ENGLAND AND UNITED STATES

MY POINT OF VIEW

We have gifts that differ according to the grace
given to us . . . ministry, in ministering.

ROMANS 12:6–7

Evangeline looked at the organization her father had founded, the Salvation Army, and thought, *Who else could we help?* She moved from England to Canada, then later to the United States. Evangeline launched a chain of homes for working women. She also founded hospitals for unwed mothers. In 1906, Evangeline began The Army's first disaster relief efforts after a devastating earthquake rocked San Francisco. When World War I broke out, she started the Donut Lassies. They were a group of 250 women who volunteered to serve supplies and baked goods to US soldiers to lift their spirits. Evangeline became the first woman to lead the Salvation Army in 1934. She used her special point of view as a woman to help even more people.

> THE FIRST FRIDAY EACH JUNE IS DONUT DAY. SOME DONUT SHOPS GIVE A PORTION OF THEIR PROCEEDS TO THE SALVATION ARMY IN HONOR OF THE DONUT LASSIES.

God, help me use the unique way I look at the world to do good works in Your name.

DECEMBER 4

DEFORD BAILEY

1899–1982 • UNITED STATES

GOD'S TIMING

*Be strong, and let your heart take courage; wait for the L*ORD*!*

PSALM 27:14

Some say success is when talent meets opportunity. For DeFord, that meant success happened when he least expected it! He lived on a farm with his aunt and uncle near Nashville, Tennessee. He contracted polio at age three, which bent his back for the rest of his life, but DeFord didn't let this stand in his way. At eighteen, he moved to Nashville and worked all kinds of jobs. Six years later, while in a store for bike parts, DeFord's amazing talent—playing the harmonica—surprised the store owner. The store owner had recently launched a radio station and invited DeFord to play. Shortly after, DeFord played for a new radio show called *The Grand Ole Opry* and found thousands of fans across the country—along with becoming country music's first Black star.

> DEFORD COULD PLAY TUNES THAT MIMICKED SOUNDS HE HEARD ON THE FARM GROWING UP, LIKE AN EXCITING FOX CHASE OR EVEN A TRAIN PASSING THROUGH.

God, thank You for surprising me with
opportunities when I least expect them.

DECEMBER 5

LAURA INGALLS WILDER

1867–1957 • UNITED STATES

YOUR NORTH STAR

He has said, "I will never leave you."

HEBREWS 13:5

Once again, Laura found herself in the back of her family's covered wagon, off to find somewhere new to live. Life in the American West during the 1800s was difficult. Sometimes crops didn't grow or harsh weather destroyed them. Farmwork was hard, and people got sick, injured, or even died. When this happened, people didn't have money for food, clothes, and shelter. Many families like Laura's experienced these hardships and had to move to find new farms or work.

> LAURA'S BOOKS ABOUT HER LIFE, THE LITTLE HOUSE SERIES, HAVE SOLD MORE THAN 60 MILLION COPIES!

But no matter where Laura went, she knew God was with her. She could wander from the big woods of Wisconsin to the banks of a creek in Minnesota, from the plains of South Dakota down to sunny Florida, and still find God. Even when she was scared, Laura found hope and comfort in God's presence.

Lord, thank You for staying close to me wherever I go.

DECEMBER 6

BLESSED ADOLPH KOLPING

1813–1865 • GERMANY

GOD'S FAMILY

We, who are many, are one body in Christ, and individually we are members one of another.

ROMANS 12:5

Thirteen-year-old Adolph loved God, and he loved going to school. But his family needed money, so Adolph became an apprentice to a shoemaker. While working, Adolph saw many factory workers. These people couldn't make a living as farmers anymore, so they moved to the city for work. Many felt sad and alone away from their families. Adolph decided to go back to school and become a priest. One day, a group of young workers created a club and asked Adolph to lead it. Each week, the young men would talk about God and sing hymns. The club members became close, like the family they missed back home. Adolph worked to expand the club so more people could have a loving family, either back home or at the club.

> TODAY THE KOLPING ASSOCIATION HAS MORE THAN 450,000 MEMBERS IN FIFTY-FOUR COUNTRIES!

God, thank You for my family—and for friends who feel like family.

DECEMBER 7

GEORGE HALAS

1895–1983 • UNITED STATES

CLOSED DOOR, OPEN WINDOW

> "Look! I have set before you an open door,
> which no one is able to shut."
>
> **REVELATION 3:8**

George was a talented athlete who played football, basketball, *and* baseball when he was at the University of Illinois. But he had a hard time avoiding injuries. After he returned home from World War I, he was drafted by the Yankees. But after only twelve games, George injured his hip and couldn't play anymore. He took a job for a company that also had a football team who played for fun. George asked some talented friends to play for the team too. He decided to buy the team and joined with other team owners to form a brand-new football league called the National Football League. And George's team? They became the Chicago Bears, one of the oldest teams in the NFL.

> IN THE EARLY YEARS, GEORGE PLAYED. HE COACHED. HE OVERSAW TICKETS, THE GROUNDS CREW, AND GETTING THE WORD OUT ABOUT GAMES!

*God, if my dream gets sidelined, help me
see the new one You have for me.*

DECEMBER 8

JOHN MICHELL

1724–1793 • ENGLAND

WHAT'S IMPORTANT?

For everything created by God is good, and nothing is to be rejected, provided it is received with thanksgiving.

1 TIMOTHY 4:4

As a Cambridge professor, John wowed people with his original ideas. After Lisbon, Portugal, was nearly destroyed by an earthquake in 1755, John couldn't stop thinking about *why* it had happened. He studied the quake and concluded that the earth is made of layers and plates, and when those plates move, they create waves—which causes the surface to shake! John was the first person to write about this. He was also the first person to make several correct observations about magnets.

> JOHN WAS ALSO THE FIRST PERSON TO HYPOTHESIZE THAT BLACK HOLES EXIST.

John's job at Cambridge was important, but one day he decided something was more important: love! John's job required him to remain unmarried, but John fell in love with a woman named Sarah and wanted to marry her. So John became a pastor, and he kept researching on the side.

God, help me remember what's most important in life: loving others!

DECEMBER 9

ALEXANDER POPE

1688–1744 · ENGLAND

GO AHEAD, LAUGH!

A cheerful heart is a good medicine.

PROVERBS 17:22

Have you ever heard the phrase "You catch more flies with honey than with vinegar"? That's a fancy way of saying, "If you want someone to listen to you, don't be mean—be nice!" Or, in the case of Alexander Pope, be funny! Alexander was brimming with ideas, especially about the way people lived during his time, in 1700s England. To get people to think about what he was saying—that rich people ought to think about real problems like helping people get enough food instead of on little things like buying more ribbons for their clothes—Alexander wrote about these rich people in a silly way. And it worked! People read Alexander's words and thought about what he said.

> ALEXANDER WAS THE FIRST FULL-TIME PROFESSIONAL WRITER IN THE ENGLISH LANGUAGE.

God, thank You for the gift of laughter! Help me see when it can open up doors for You.

DECEMBER 10

GARY CARTER

1954–2012 • UNITED STATES

MAN OF HONOR

> I am not ashamed of the gospel; it is the power of
> God for salvation to everyone who has faith.
>
> **ROMANS 1:16**

At six foot two and more than 200 pounds, Gary was like a boulder when he blocked home plate. He was a Major League Baseball catcher, and he made throwing runners out look easy. He could also smack the baseball into the outfield to drive in a teammate on base. So why did Gary's teammates tease him? Because off the field he didn't do what they did. While his teammates went out partying, Gary went home to his family. He didn't smoke or drink. He didn't curse, and he didn't brag. He gave interviews to most reporters who asked. And he shared about his faith in Christ. Gary didn't care about being a "cool" pro athlete. He had three loves in his life: his family, baseball, and God. And that's what Gary worked hard to honor every single day.

GARY HELPED THE NEW YORK METS WIN THE 1986 WORLD SERIES!

God, no matter what people say, help me honor You each day.

DECEMBER 11

GEORGE MACDONALD

1824–1905 • SCOTLAND

WRITING FOR GOD

> I love you, O Lord, my strength.
>
> **PSALM 18:1**

George's main goal was to love God with all his heart. His second was to help others to see, feel, and know God's love too! George preached many sermons about this. He told his college students about God. But he reached the most people through his writing. George wrote more than fifty books, and many of them were fictional stories. It didn't matter what kind of book he wrote; George showed his readers that living with God's love would help them grow and fulfill their life's purpose. And because of his efforts, George influenced many fantasy writers who came after him, including J. R. R. Tolkien, Madeleine L'Engle, and C. S. Lewis. George never could have known how much his passion for God would spark the same feeling in others—who would then pass it on!

> GEORGE'S BEST-KNOWN STORY WAS *THE PRINCESS AND THE GOBLIN*, A CHILDREN'S BOOK.

God, I want my passion for You to spread far and wide!

DECEMBER 12

FRANCES PERKINS

1880–1965 • UNITED STATES

LABOR OF LOVE

Six days you shall labor and do all your work. But the seventh day is a sabbath to the LORD your God; you shall not do any work.

DEUTERONOMY 5:13–14

When you're older and get a job, you'll work probably forty hours a week. Your workplace will be safe. If you're unable to work, you'll be able to get some money so your family has food and shelter. This is all true because of one person—Frances Perkins! During college, Frances toured factories. Back then, they were not safe! Machinery was dangerous. Buildings had hardly any light or even bathrooms for workers. People had to work too many hours with no breaks or days off—or they would lose their jobs. Frances's strong faith motivated her to speak out against injustice. When President Franklin D. Roosevelt appointed her as the secretary of labor, she passed laws to help workers across the country be treated fairly!

> FRANCES WAS THE FIRST WOMAN TO SERVE IN A US PRESIDENTIAL CABINET.

God, whatever I do when I grow up, help me to work at it with all my heart.

DECEMBER 13

GRAND DUCHESS ELIZABETH

1864–1918 • ENGLAND AND RUSSIA

A ROYAL SERVANT

"For the Son of Man came not to be served but to
serve, and to give his life a ransom for many."

MARK 10:45

Elizabeth was from a royal family; her grandmother was England's Queen Victoria. As a young woman, Elizabeth married Sergei, son of Russia's ruler Tsar Alexander II. For twenty years Elizabeth wore beautiful gowns, danced at royal balls, and met important people. But then Sergei was killed. Suddenly her royal life seemed empty and pointless. Elizabeth decided that instead of remarrying, she'd go into what she called "a greater world—the world of the poor and suffering." She sold her jewelry and possessions to open the Mary and Martha Home, a place where women could pray and serve others. Soon they opened a hospital where anyone could receive care for free. The women also gave away more than 300 meals a day. Instead of being served, Elizabeth chose instead to be a servant-leader.

> ELIZABETH SLEPT ON A WOODEN BED WITHOUT A MATTRESS WHEN SHE LIVED AT THE MARY AND MARTHA HOME.

God, please create a servant's heart in me.

DECEMBER 14

JAN KARSKI

1914-2000 • POLAND

SPEAK UP

Take no part in the unfruitful works of
darkness, but instead expose them.

EPHESIANS 5:11

Jan was a Polish government official who couldn't believe what he was seeing. Invading Nazis were rounding up Jewish families and forcing them to live in a small part of the city of Warsaw. He learned that the Jews had hardly any food, and sick people had no medicine. Many Jews were being taken to concentration camps, and most never returned. Jan was horrified. His faith inspired him to speak out to tell the world what was happening to the Jewish people so it could be stopped. Jan met with world leaders and told them what he saw. He wrote a book about it. Jan felt like he didn't do enough. But he tried his hardest to give the Jewish people a voice to the outside world.

> BECAUSE OF JAN'S HARD WORK, IN 1994 HE WAS AWARDED HONORARY CITIZENSHIP TO ISRAEL. HE CALLED IT "THE PROUDEST AND MOST MEANINGFUL DAY OF MY LIFE."

*God, please give me the courage to find
help for those who need it.*

DECEMBER 15

BLESSED MARY FRANCES SCHERVIER

1819–1876 • PRUSSIA (MODERN-DAY GERMANY) AND UNITED STATES

GIVE IT AWAY

Some pretend to be rich, yet have nothing; others pretend to be poor, yet have great wealth.

PROVERBS 13:7

Born into a wealthy family, Frances had everything she needed. But at thirteen, Frances lost her mother, and her world came crashing down. She cared for the family in her mother's absence. Soon everyone noticed that Frances cared for the poor in addition to serving her family. She gave away her family's possessions to those in need and joined other young women to run a soup kitchen. Soon Frances and the young women began to live together to more easily help people. They called themselves the Sisters of the Poor of Saint Francis. In 1858, the sisters founded a congregation in the United States. In 1863, Mother Frances made her first US visit, helping wounded soldiers in the Civil War. On her next visit, she helped the poor, sick, and needy.

> AT MOTHER FRANCES'S DEATH, THERE WERE MORE THAN 2,500 MEMBERS OF THE SISTERS OF THE POOR OF SAINT FRANCIS WORLDWIDE. THEY STILL HELP IN HOSPITALS AND RUN HOMES FOR THE AGED.

God, help me use my blessings to help others and honor You.

DECEMBER 16

GEORGE WHITEFIELD

1714–1770 • ENGLAND AND AMERICA

WAKE UP!

Proclaim the message . . . and encourage, with the utmost patience in teaching.

2 TIMOTHY 4:2

George was the most well-known preacher in the 1700s. He began his career in England, where he became known as "the greatest preacher England ever produced," then traveled to America. From steamy Georgia all the way up to chilly Massachusetts, George preached to massive crowds. He often preached in fields because church buildings wouldn't fit the crowds! He told the people they could have a "new birth" in Jesus. No matter what they had done before, Jesus would take away their sins and give them a brand-new life. He told them that God freely gives grace to those who believe in Him and that they didn't have to earn it. People were excited to hear this message, and George helped many people "awaken" to a new life of faith.

IN HIS LIFETIME, GEORGE PREACHED AT LEAST 18,000 TIMES.

God, thank You for giving me a faith that makes me feel excited to know You!

DECEMBER 17

ANN LOWE

1898–1981 • UNITED STATES

KEEP GOING

Consider him who endured such hostility against himself from sinners, so that you may not grow weary or lose heart.

HEBREWS 12:3

Sewing brought Ann so much joy. And no matter what, Ann used her fierce perseverance to finish her work. When Ann was sixteen, her mother died. Ann stepped up and took over the business. At design school in New York, teachers kept Ann separate because she was Black. But her work was so good that teachers began using her dresses as examples. Soon word spread about Ann's talent. She sewed the finest dresses for important clients. In 1953, Ann designed and sewed one of the most talked-about dresses for a famous wedding—between future president John F. Kennedy and First Lady Jacqueline "Jackie" Bouvier. The original dress, which had taken eight weeks to create, was destroyed in a flood! Ann worked night and day to remake the dress in less than eight days, and it was admired worldwide.

> ANN HAD A GIFT FOR CREATING FLOWERS OUT OF FABRIC. AS A GIRL SHE TOOK SCRAPS OF CLOTH AND CREATED GARDENS OUT OF THEM.

God, help me keep going through challenges, no matter how hard they are.

DECEMBER 18

DON SHULA

1930–2020 • UNITED STATES

GOOD START TO THE DAY

O LORD, in the morning you hear my voice; in the
morning I plead my case to you, and watch.

PSALM 5:3

It didn't matter where he was—at home or on the road—NFL coach Don Shula was going to be in the pew for 7 a.m. Mass. For twenty-five years, Don coached the Miami Dolphins and became one of the winningest coaches in NFL history. While his players looked to him for answers, every morning Don made sure to look to God for his. Don faced all kinds of problems in his coaching career: players who left for other teams, disagreements with other coaches, seasons that saw more losses than wins. But whenever Don started out the day thanking God and asking for His guidance, his day was different. His problems may not have gone away, but instead of dread, he felt hope.

> AT 347 WINS, DON SHULA HAS COACHED MORE WINNING GAMES THAN ANY OTHER COACH IN NFL HISTORY.

God, help me start each day by looking to You.

DECEMBER 19

BLESSED URBAN V

C. 1310–1370 • FRANCE

OTHERS FIRST

Do nothing from selfish ambition or conceit, but in humility regard others as better than yourselves.

PHILIPPIANS 2:3

In 1362, cardinals in the Catholic Church elected a new pope, but he turned down the job. Flustered, they voted again and named their second choice, a man known for having a good heart. Urban V had been called "Guillaume" by friends and family. Guillaume was a lawyer and monk who lived a simple, quiet life and loved God. And now that he was pope, he didn't expect people to serve him. This was different from some church leaders, who enjoyed others thinking they were important and deserved nice things. Instead of thinking about how his new job could help him get ahead, Urban V looked at what he could do to help others. For him, that meant restoring churches and monasteries to serve people in their towns.

> URBAN V WAS A CHAMPION OF LEARNING. HE ESTABLISHED SOME OF THE FIRST EUROPEAN UNIVERSITIES IN CITIES LIKE VIENNA AND KRAKÓW.

God, help me think of serving others before I think of serving myself.

DECEMBER 20

BENJAMIN BANNEKER

1731–1806 • UNITED STATES

APPRECIATING GOD'S AMAZING WORLD

When I look at your heavens, the work of your fingers.... O LORD,
our Sovereign, how majestic is your name in all the earth!

PSALM 8:3, 9

Benjamin was always curious about how things worked. The son of a freed slave, Benjamin didn't have formal schooling but loved books and learning. In his twenties, he made a clock that kept perfect time—something unheard of in rural Maryland in the 1700s! As a farmer, Benjamin tracked how much sun and rain the fields got and how weather affected his crops. A new family moved to the farm down the road and built a gristmill. Benjamin and his neighbors, the Ellicotts, became fast friends. They enjoyed the same books, and George Ellicott introduced Benjamin to astronomy. Benjamin learned everything he could about it, and at fifty-eight years old, Benjamin predicted an eclipse! He began writing about his findings in a series of almanacs, in addition to writing against slavery and war.

> BECAUSE OF HIS ACCOMPLISHMENTS AS AN ASTRONOMER AND MATHEMATICIAN, BENJAMIN WAS INVITED TO MAP THE PLACE WHERE THE NEW CAPITAL OF THE UNITED STATES WOULD BE: WASHINGTON, DC!

God, I love sharing about the world You made with others.

DECEMBER 21

JENNY LIND

1820–1887 • UNITED STATES

BEYOND THE LIKES

If we live, we live to the Lord . . . we are the Lord's.

ROMANS 14:8

More than 40,000 people waited eagerly at New York Harbor for the ship carrying Swedish opera star Jenny Lind. Jenny had never meant to become a celebrity. One day as a child, she was singing to her cat with the window open. People outside heard, and soon Jenny was enrolled in opera school! By age eighteen, she was wowing audiences all over Europe. Jenny loved performing, but she didn't sing for fame. She sang because she loved it. She also gave a large portion of her earnings to charity. By age twenty-nine, Jenny was ready to retire from opera. Her tour through America, organized by showman PT Barnum, was her last. She married her piano accompanist and spent her days growing their family and singing in charity concerts. She loved her small, quiet life.

> FOR HER SWEET SINGING VOICE, JENNY'S NICKNAME WAS "THE SWEDISH NIGHTINGALE."

God, I don't want to live my life for "likes." I want to live it for You.

DECEMBER 22

BLESSED JACOPONE DA TODI

C. 1230–1306 • UMBRIA (MODERN-DAY ITALY)

CHANGE OF HEART

> The Lord is . . . patient with you, not wanting any
> to perish, but all to come to repentance.
>
> **2 PETER 3:9**

Jacopone was sitting in the stands at his town's celebration, happy with his life. He had a beautiful wife, Vanna. As a lawyer, he was respected and had nice things. Life was going well. But in an instant, everything changed. The stands collapsed, and Vanna tragically died. Jacopone saw that Vanna was wearing an item of clothing he'd never noticed. It was a belt made of rough fiber so Vanna would think of God when she felt the fiber rub against her skin. At that moment, Jacopone decided to change his life. He gave away all his things. Instead of fine robes, he dressed in rags. Instead of writing legal documents, he wrote songs and poems for God. Jacopone's life shows that it's never too late to change to honor God.

> JACOPONE IS A NICKNAME MEANING "JAMES THE CRAZY." THAT'S WHAT PEOPLE CALLED JACOPONE AFTER HE CHANGED. AND HE EMBRACED THE NICKNAME!

God, thank You for being patient with us always.

DECEMBER 23

JOHN HARPER

1872–1912 • ATLANTIC OCEAN

UNSINKABLE FAITH

Those who trust in the LORD are like Mount Zion,
which cannot be moved but abides forever.

PSALM 125:1

The *Titanic* was filled with chaos—people screamed as the ship began to sink. But pastor John Harper was calm. He'd placed his daughter Annie and sister Jessie on a lifeboat headed for safety while he stayed to minister to others still on the ship. He'd been given a life jacket to wear if the ship went down. He met a panicked man and asked, "Are you saved? Do you believe in Jesus?" When the man said no, John took off his life jacket and said, "I think you'll need this more than I will." Soon, the *Titanic* slipped under the water. Annie, Jessie, and the man with the life jacket were rescued, but John was never seen again. His great faith and selflessness are still remembered more than a century later.

> THE CHURCH JOHN FOUNDED IN SCOTLAND NOW BEARS HIS NAME: HARPER MEMORIAL BAPTIST CHURCH.

God, show me how I can tell others about You.

DECEMBER 24

ROMARE BEARDEN

1911–1988 • UNITED STATES

NEW WAYS OF SEEING

> With the eyes of your heart enlightened, you may know what is the hope to which he has called you.
>
> **EPHESIANS 1:18**

What would a Bible story look like if it happened today? What if the characters looked like our friends and neighbors? How would that change the way we understand the story? Romare was an artist whose pieces often showed Bible stories in ways people hadn't seen before—especially the story of Jesus. In an abstract piece, he showed the angel Gabriel telling Mary that she would give birth to baby Jesus. He imagined what Mary and her cousin Elizabeth might have looked like if they spent time together in the 1940s.

> LATER IN HIS LIFE, ROMARE BEGAN TO CREATE COLLAGES—WHAT HE IS MOST KNOWN FOR.

Through *cubism*, an art style using geometric lines and shapes, Romare created a series that showed Jesus dying and raising from the dead. Depicting these stories in new ways helped people think about a story in a fresh way.

God, open my eyes to see You in new ways!

DECEMBER 25

IDA B. WELLS

1862–1931 • UNITED STATES

LIGHT OF TRUTH

"Those who do what is true come to the light, so that it may be clearly seen that their deeds have been done in God."

JOHN 3:21

Ida believed that every person should have the same rights—the chance to go to school, live in a safe place, and vote. Born enslaved in Mississippi, Ida was freed by the Emancipation Proclamation. But freedom didn't result in equal rights. As a young woman, she bought a first-class train ticket but was removed from her seat because she was Black. While teaching, she noticed that schools serving Black students didn't receive new books and supplies like schools serving white students did. Crimes against Black people often went unpunished. Ida believed that the way to change these things was to "turn the light of truth on them." If people would open their eyes to the problems, something could be done. As Ida traveled throughout the US and the world speaking about this, she prayed that God would give her courage to help her people.

> IDA MET WITH TWO PRESIDENTS, WILLIAM MCKINLEY AND WOODROW WILSON, TO ASK FOR THEIR HELP.

God, please give me the courage to help others in Your name.

DECEMBER 26

GERARD MANLEY HOPKINS

1844–1889 • ENGLAND

GOD OF THE SMALL THINGS

God chose what is low and despised in the world, things that are not, to reduce to nothing things that are, so that no one might boast in the presence of God.

1 CORINTHIANS 1:28–29

"The world is charged with the grandeur of God," wrote Gerard, a Jesuit priest who was also a poet. Gerard attended an Anglican church growing up, and he wrote poems from the time he was a young man. But after college, Gerard decided to attend the Catholic Church and become a priest. He stopped writing poetry to focus on his priestly work. But after a while, Gerard couldn't help himself and started writing again! He saw God's beauty in the soft morning light. He saw God's love when folks comforted others who were grieving. So Gerard decided to share poems about these observations with a few friends. But he didn't share them publicly. After Gerard died, a friend published his poems. And the world was touched by Gerard's words about God.

> GERARD'S WORK INFLUENCED MANY TALENTED POETS AFTER HIM, LIKE T. S. ELIOT AND W. H. AUDEN.

God, help me remember what I do can show Your love.

DECEMBER 27

SAINT FABIOLA

UNKNOWN–C. 400 • ROME

HELP OTHERS WHO ARE HURTING

Bear one another's burdens.

GALATIANS 6:2

Fabiola seemed to have everything going for her. She was born into a wealthy family, had plenty of money, and eventually married a nobleman. But behind closed doors, Fabiola's husband was cruel to her. She eventually divorced him and remarried. When Fabiola's second husband died, she decided to devote her life to the church. With her significant wealth, she built the first Christian public hospital in the Western world, where she personally helped care for patients. Fabiola donated large sums of money to churches and religious communities around Rome. She even journeyed to Bethlehem, where she lived in a convent to serve dying people and study Scripture. Fabiola used the hard events of her past and her resources to help others.

> FABIOLA WAS FRIENDS WITH SAINT JEROME, THE HISTORIAN.

God, no matter what happens to me, please keep my heart soft toward others.

DECEMBER 28

CHICO MENDES

1944–1988 • BRAZIL

TAKE CARE OF GOD'S WORLD

The LORD God took the man and put him in the garden of Eden to till it and keep it.

GENESIS 2:15

As a boy, Chico watched as his dad cut through the bark of the *Hevea* tree and a milky-white sap poured out. Chico joined his dad on trips into the Amazon rainforest so they could make rubber from the tree sap. But wealthy ranchers had begun cutting down the trees to raise cattle. This took jobs from families like Chico's, but cutting down the rainforest also affected the animals, plants, and people who lived there. Chico believed in caring for God's creation, so when he got older, he talked to government officials about ideas for creating products from the trees without hurting them. This would generate income for workers *and* be good for the environment. In 1988, Brazil agreed with Chico and created an "extractive reserve," just like Chico had envisioned.

> BECAUSE OF HIS ENVIRONMENTAL WORK, CHICO WAS INVITED TO SPEAK IN FRONT OF THE US CONGRESS.

God, I want to be a good steward of the world You made. Please show me how.

DECEMBER 29

SOPHIE G. LUTTERLOUGH

1910–2009 • UNITED STATES

CURATION CURIOSITY

God made the wild animals of the earth of every
kind . . . and everything that creeps upon the ground
of every kind. And God saw that it was good.

GENESIS 1:25

At the National Museum of Natural History in Washington, DC, visitors noticed they could ask the elevator operator seemingly any question—and she knew the answer! In 1943, when Sophie began to work there, the museum had no information desk. So Sophie began studying the displays on her lunch break. If she didn't understand something, she would ask the curator. After a while, she asked the insect curator if he had any open jobs. He hired Sophie! She sorted and identified the thousands of insects the museum had received to study. Sophie didn't know much about insects, but she read books and took college courses. Her work was so good that she was promoted to research assistant, where she helped discover forty new specimens. Her curiosity and determination opened new doors!

> IN 1979, SCIENTISTS NAMED A MITE AFTER SOPHIE! IT WAS CALLED *PYGMEPHORUS LUTTERLOUGHAE*.

God, I love the big world You made, down to the tiniest detail!

DECEMBER 30

FLORENCE NIGHTINGALE

1820–1910 · ENGLAND

GOOD CARE

[God] . . . binds up their wounds.

PSALM 147:3

Florence walked from bed to bed late at night, lamp in hand, caring for injured British soldiers. Florence was leading a group of nurses at a military hospital in Türkiye. The soldiers needed wounds treated and bandaged. They needed baths to stay clean and food to help them gain strength. To lift their spirits, they needed help writing letters home. Florence was gifted at organizing people and believed caring for others was a way she could serve God. So she trained the nurses on how to properly care for the soldiers. Florence also knew important people working in the British government and wrote to ask for supplies. Under the care of Florence's nurses, soldiers recovered more quickly! Back home, Florence started a school for nurses. Her efforts made nursing a valued career and changed the way nurses cared for patients forever.

> FLORENCE WAS ALSO GOOD WITH NUMBERS AND INVENTED A NEW KIND OF PIE CHART!

God, help me care for others the way You care for me.

DECEMBER 31

SADAO WATANABE

1913–1996 • JAPAN

MEETING PLACE

*I have become all things to all people, that
I might by all means save some.*

1 CORINTHIANS 9:22

Sadao became a Christian when he was seventeen. And he wanted to tell other people in Japan about Jesus. Sadao was a creative person, so he decided to share his faith through a traditional Japanese folk art technique called *katazome*. In katazome, an artist uses stencils to dye pieces of cloth, usually for kimonos that people wear. But instead of creating beautiful clothes, Sadao decided to show Bible stories on his katazome. Sadao knew that Japanese people would open their hearts to Jesus more easily if they learned about Him in a way that was familiar—like seeing a Bible story depicted in a way that looked familiar to them. Sadao used his artistic gift to help people meet Jesus exactly where they were.

> SADAO MEANT FOR HIS ART TO HANG IN COMMON PLACES. BUT TODAY HIS PIECES ARE IN MUSEUMS ALL OVER THE WORLD!

*God, help me to share about You in ways
people can easily understand.*

A NOTE ON SOURCES

The author used a wide range of sources to write this book.
If you would like a complete source list, please contact the publisher at
customercare@harpercollins.com.

Heroes, Dreamers, and Saints

© 2026 Thomas Nelson

Tommy Nelson, PO Box 141000, Nashville, TN 37214

All rights reserved. No portion of this book may be reproduced, stored in a retrieval system, or transmitted in any form or by any means—electronic, mechanical, photocopy, recording, scanning, or other—except for brief quotations in critical reviews or articles, without the prior written permission of the publisher.

Published by Tommy Nelson, 501 Nelson Place, Nashville, TN 37214, USA. Tommy Nelson is an imprint of Thomas Nelson. Thomas Nelson is a registered trademark of HarperCollins Christian Publishing, Inc.

Tommy Nelson titles may be purchased in bulk for educational, business, fundraising, or sales promotional use. For information, please email SpecialMarkets@ThomasNelson.com.

Scripture quotations are taken from the New Revised Standard Version Bible. Copyright © 1989 National Council of the Churches of Christ in the United States of America. Used by permission. All rights reserved worldwide.

ISBN 978-1-4002-5501-6 (audiobook)
ISBN 978-1-4002-5500-9 (eBook)
ISBN 978-1-4002-5509-2 (HC)

Without limiting the exclusive rights of any author, contributor or the publisher of this publication, any unauthorized use of this publication to train generative artificial intelligence (AI) technologies is expressly prohibited. HarperCollins also exercise their rights under Article 4(3) of the Digital Single Market Directive 2019/790 and expressly reserve this publication from the text and data mining exception.

HarperCollins Publishers, Macken House, 39/40 Mayor Street Upper, Dublin 1, D01 C9W8, Ireland (https://www.harpercollins.com)

Library of Congress Cataloging-in-Publication Data

Names: Kerr, Amy author | Muñoz, Isabel illustrator
Title: Heroes, dreamers, and saints : 365 true stories of faith and courage / written by Amy Kerr ; illustrated by Isabel Muñoz.
Description: Nashville, TN : Thomas Nelson, [2026] | Includes bibliographical references. | Audience: Ages 8-12 | Summary: "Deepen your faith, grow in wisdom, and put your faith into action with this 365-day devotional for kids. Heroes, Dreamers, and Saints is a fascinating journey through history, highlighting 365 notable Christian and Catholic figures who have made a difference in the world"— Provided by publisher.
Identifiers: LCCN 2025030612 (print) | LCCN 2025030613 (ebook) | ISBN 9781400255092 hardcover | ISBN 9781400255009 epub
Subjects: LCSH: Christian biography—Juvenile literature | LCGFT: Biographies
Classification: LCC BR1704 .K47 2026 (print) | LCC BR1704 (ebook) | DDC 270.092/2 [B]—dc23/eng/20250821
LC record available at https://lccn.loc.gov/2025030612
LC ebook record available at https://lccn.loc.gov/2025030613

Written by Amy Kerr
Illustrated by Isabel Muñoz
Art Direction: Tiffany Forrester
Cover Design: Tiffany Forrester
Interior Design: Denise Froehlich

Printed in India

26 27 28 29 30 NT 10 9 8 7 6 5 4 3 2 1

Mfr: NT / Faridabad, India / February 2026 / PO# 12319673